In this volume in the *New Cambridge History of India*, Dr Stewart Gordon presents the first recent comprehensive history of one of the most colorful and least understood kingdoms of India: the Maratha polity. The kingdom was founded by Shivaji in the mid-seventeenth century and spread across much of India during the following century. It was subsequently conquered by the British in the nineteenth century, but none the less provided the basis for the formation of many princely states.

Since independence a huge mass of administrative documents of the Maratha polity and many important family papers have become available to scholars. Stewart Gordon draws on this material to explore the origin of the Marathas in the Muslim kingdoms of the Deccan, their emergence as elite families, patterns of loyalty, and strategies for maintaining legitimacy. He traces how the Maratha armies developed from bands of lightly armed cavalry to European-style infantry and artillery and assesses the economics that funded the polity, especially taxation and credit. Finally, the author considers the legacy of the Maratha polity: the profound effects it had upon revenue administration, law, education, trade patterns, migration, and the economic and social make-up of Central India, Gujarat, and Maharashtra.

In this book, Stewart Gordon presents a picture of everyday life in the Maratha polity as well as an important example of the dynamics of kingdoms during this period. *The Marathas 1600–1818* will be widely read by students and specialists of Indian, military, and colonial history as well as by anthropologists.

THE NEW CAMBRIDGE HISTORY
OF INDIA

The Marathas 1600–1818

THE NEW CAMBRIDGE HISTORY OF INDIA

General editor GORDON JOHNSON

Director, Centre of South Asian Studies, University of
Cambridge, and Fellow of Selwyn College

Associate editors C. A. BAYLY

Professor of Modern Indian History, University of
Cambridge, and Fellow of St Catharine's College

and JOHN F. RICHARDS

Professor of History, Duke University

Although the original *Cambridge History of India*, published between 1922 and 1937, did much to formulate a chronology for Indian history and describe the administrative structures of government in India, it has inevitably been overtaken by the mass of new research published over the last fifty years.

Designed to take full account of recent scholarship and changing conceptions of South Asia's historical development, *The New Cambridge History of India* will be published as a series of short, self-contained volumes, each dealing with a separate theme and written by a single person, within an overall four-part structure. As before, each will conclude with a substantial bibliographical essay designed to lead non-specialists further into the literature.

The four parts are as follows:

I The Mughals and their Contemporaries.

II Indian States and the Transition to Colonialism.

III The Indian Empire and the Beginnings of Modern Society.

IV The Evolution of Contemporary South Asia.

A list of individual titles already published and in preparation will be found at the end of the volume.

THE NEW CAMBRIDGE HISTORY OF INDIA

II · 4

The Marathas
1600–1818

STEWART GORDON

CAMBRIDGE
UNIVERSITY PRESS

CAMBRIDGE UNIVERSITY PRESS
Cambridge, New York, Melbourne, Madrid, Cape Town, Singapore, São Paulo

Cambridge University Press
The Edinburgh Building, Cambridge CB2 2RU, UK

Published in the United States of America by Cambridge University Press, New York

www.cambridge.org
Information on this title: www.cambridge.org/9780521268837

First published 1993
This digitally printed first paperback version 2006

A catalogue record for this publication is available from the British Library

Library of Congress Cataloguing in Publication data
Gordon, Stewart, 1945–
The Marathas 1600–1818/Stewart Gordon.
p. cm. – (The New Cambridge History of India; II.4)
Includes index.
ISBN 0 521 26883 4 (hc)
1. Maratha (Indic people) – History. 2. India – History – 1500–1765.
3. India – History – 18th century. 4. India – History – 19th century.
I. Title. II. Series.
DS485.M349G67 1993
954′.7025 – dc20 92–16525 CIP

ISBN-13 978-0-521-26883-7 hardback
ISBN-10 0-521-26883-4 hardback

ISBN-13 978-0-521-03316-9 paperback
ISBN-10 0-521-03316-0 paperback

CONTENTS

MAPS

GENERAL EDITOR'S PREFACE

The New Cambridge History of India covers the period from the beginning of the sixteenth century. In some respects it marks a radical change in the style of Cambridge Histories, but in others the editors feel that they are working firmly within an established academic tradition.

During the summer of 1896, F. W. Maitland and Lord Acton between them evolved the idea of a comprehensive modern history. By the end of the year the Syndics of the University Press had committed themselves to the *Cambridge Modern History*, and Lord Acton had been put in charge of it. It was hoped that publication would begin in 1899 and be completed by 1904, but the first volume in fact came out in 1902 and the last in 1910, with additional volumes of tables and maps in 1911 and 1912.

The *History* was a great success, and it was followed by a whole series of distinctive Cambridge Histories covering English Literature, the Ancient World, India, British Foreign Policy, Economic History, Medieval History, the British Empire, Africa, China and Latin America; and even now other new series are being prepared. Indeed, the various Histories have given the Press notable strength in the publication of general reference books in the arts and social sciences.

What has made the Cambridge Histories so distinctive is that they have never been simply dictionaries or encyclopedias. The Histories have, in H. A. L. Fisher's words, always been 'written by an army of specialists concentrating the latest results of special study'. Yet as Acton agreed with the Syndics in 1896, they have not been mere compilations of existing material but original works. Undoubtedly many of the Histories are uneven in quality, some have become out of date very rapidly, but their virtue has been that they have consistently done more than simply record an existing state of knowledge: they have tended to focus interest on research and they have provided a massive stimulus to further work. This has made their publication doubly worthwhile and has distinguished them intellectually from other sorts of reference book. The editors of the *New Cambridge History of India* have acknowledged this in their work.

The original *Cambridge History of India* was published between 1922 and 1937. It was planned in six volumes, but of these, volume 2 dealing with the period between the first century AD and the Muslim invasion of India never appeared. Some of the material is still of value, but in many respects it is now out of date. The last fifty years have seen a great deal of new research on India, and a striking feature of recent work has been to cast doubt on the validity of the quite arbitrary chronological and categorical way in which Indian history has been conventionally divided.

The editors decided that it would not be academically desirable to prepare a new *History of India* using the traditional format. The selective nature of research on Indian history over the past half-century would doom such a project from the start and the whole of Indian history would not be covered in an even or comprehensive manner. They concluded that the best scheme would be to have a *History* divided into four overlapping chronological volumes, each containing about eight short books on individual themes or subjects. Although in extent the work will therefore be equivalent to a dozen massive tomes of the traditional sort, in form the *New Cambridge History of India* will appear as a shelf full of separate but complementary parts. Accordingly, the main divisions are between I. *The Mughals and their Contemporaries*, II. *Indian States and the Transition to Colonialism*, III. *The Indian Empire and the Beginnings of Modern Society*, and IV. *The Evolution of Contemporary South Asia*.

Just as the books within these volumes are complementary so too do they intersect with each other, both thematically and chronologically. As the books appear they are intended to give a view of the subject as it now stands and to act as a stimulus to further research. We do not expect the *New Cambridge History of India* to be the last word on the subject but an essential voice in the continuing discussion about it.

ACKNOWLEDGEMENTS

I wish to thank the following scholars who read, discussed, and critiqued early drafts of this manuscript: Donald Attwood, John Richards, Richard Tucker, Richard Barnett, Eleanor Zelliot, and A. R. Kulkarni. In Pune, I wish to thank the "Court 12 group" for vigorous discussions of Maratha history, the sponsors of various seminars at which I was allowed to present papers, and the director and staff of the Pune Daftar. Finally, I gratefully acknowledge the American Institute of Indian Studies for support for my studies of Maratha history over the past two decades.

GLOSSARY

Afagis	first generation immigrants from Arabia or Central Asia
Ahir	armed lineages, located in north-eastern Malwa
babti	from the Persian, a portion or share of the government revenue from a district; the actual fraction varied from 16 percent to 22 percent
bakhar	an indigenous history or memoir
bargir	cavalryman riding a horse belonging to his leader; later, refers to light cavalry generally
bargir-giri	a style of warfare based on light cavalry which emphasized mobility rather than frontal attack in a plains battle
bhakti	fervent popular Hindu faith expressed in vernacular songs, often associated with Krishna
Bhandari	a Maharashtrian caste, which originally prepared liquor from coconut trees
Bhil	'tribal' hunters and gatherers located across a broad band of Rajasthan, Madya Pradesh, and Maharashtra
bigar	a tax payable in local labor
bigha	unit of land measure, typically 400 square rods, but the size of the rod varied from district to district
chaudhri	in areas north of Maharashtra, the head of an elite family controlling village and pargana rights in a local area
chauth	the claim to one-quarter of the government's share of the revenue
C.K.P.	Chandraseniya Kayastha Prabhu, a non-Brahmin writer caste
daftar	a compilation of documents, often from one family or one official
Dakhni	a language which evolved mainly in the Muslim courts of the Deccan with elements of Arabic, Persian, North Indian Urdu, and the indigenous Deccan languages; also refers to Muslims born in India
dakshina	the distribution of presents to Brahmins
darbar	a formal audience
Deccan	'South', generally refers to the area south of the border of a kingdom based in North India
dehezada	detailed register of the villages and landholdings in a pargana
Desh	the plateau area of Maharashtra which is located east of the Ghats

Deshasta	a group or person indigenous to the Desh of Maharashtra
deshmukh	head of an armed elite family in control of a pargana
Deshpande	records keeper for a pargana
Dhangar	shepherd
diwan	the head of the king's administration, usually the highest civilian office in the kingdom
faraskhana	a police office
Ghats	the western mountains which parallel the coast 30–50 miles inland; term used for steps leading down to a river or tank, often constructed as an act of religious merit
havildar	in Bijapuri usage, a government-appointed civilian/military administrator over several parganas; more generally, a leader of a troop of cavalry
hon	a gold coin
hundi	a check, payable at sight or in a specified time in a distant city
inam	hereditary grant for special services or merit
istawa	a stepwise increasing revenue settlement commonly used in recovery from natural disaster or devastation
jagir	a grant for the maintenance of troops
Jat	largest cultivating caste in much of North India, formed into lineages which competed for control of the Delhi–Agra–Gwalior area
kamavisdar	Maratha local administrator; his area was usually several parganas
Konkan	coastal plain, below the Western Ghats
Kshatriya	one of the four large Vedic categories of peoples; responsible for fighting in wartime and ruling in peacetime
Kulkarni	village records keeper
kumkum	ground color, especially used for the forehead mark
Kunbi	cultivator
Lohar	ironworker
mahal	from a simple term for 'house', the administrative use came to mean a revenue district as small as a single village or as large as a pargana
mansab	Mughal grant of revenue for maintenance of a specified number of troops
Marathi	Sanskrit-based language of the current state of Maharashtra
mirasdar	an owner of village agricultural land
mokasa	an assigned portion of the government's share of the revenue
muqqadam	village headman
muzumdar	general term for records keeper
nayak	armed elite families in South India; usually their original service had been with Vijaynagar
nazar	formal gift to a superior, often in return for the grant of rights to revenue

palki	a sedan-chair for travelling
pargana	a long-standing geographically compact unit of 20–100 villages
patil	village headman
peshwa	the head of the central government records keepers; later the head of the Maratha polity
peth	a sector or district of a city usually centered on a market
pindaris	irregular troops attached to the Maratha armies used mainly for plunder
pir	a Muslim saint
Prabhu	a non-Brahmin writer caste
pundit	a Brahmin scholar
qazi	Muslim judge, whose decisions were based on Sharia law
Rajput	a broad spectrum of men in military service in North India which slowly evolved into a caste
rasad	the advance paid by a kamavisdar to the Maratha government which was recovered from the revenues of his area; typically, one-third to one-half of yearly estimated revenue
Rohilla	immigrant Afghans who had settled mainly in an area east of Delhi and formed one of the main competing groups in the second half of the eighteenth century
sanad	a contract, specifying rights and responsibilities
sannyasi	Hindu holy man who has renounced the world
saranjam	non-hereditary grant for maintenance of troops
sardar	broad term for noble or noble family
sardeshmukh	a high position of authority over a group of deshmukhs
sardeshmukhi	the claim to one-tenth of the government's share of the revenue, based on a position as sardeshmukh or head of the deshmukhs, generally a royal right
sarkar	a Mughal administrative division, smaller than a subah, and usually composed of several parganas; also, a general term meaning government
sarnobat	a Persian term meaning the leader of a band
silahdar	a Persian term meaning a cavalryman who enlisted with his own horse and equipment
subah	A large Mughal administrative unit, typically dozens of parganas
subahdar	the administrative and military head of a province
Sutar	carpenter
swaraj	independent rule, that is, not dependent for legitimacy on a sanad from any other power
tacavi	government loans at low rates for building or rebuilding local infrastructure
Thakar	a caste centered in Northern Konkan, also a title of respect given to a leader
upari	a landless laborer, often seeking refuge from some disturbance in his home village

GLOSSARY

vazier	in Muslim sultanates of the Deccan, the highest official after the sultan
vritti	a long-standing grant for religious service or merit
watan	the home, core rights forming the basis of a family's status and wealth
zamindar	a broad Mughal term covering a wide variety of local armed landed elites

INTRODUCTION: HISTORIOGRAPHY
AND BIBLIOGRAPHY

The writing of the history of Maharashtra and the Marathas is almost as old as the polity itself. The first histories, termed bakhars, and written in Marathi by Brahmin eulogists, were the product of the late seventeenth century to the mid-eighteenth century. The current consensus is that much of the genre was hagiographical and often confused in dating and placing events. Nevertheless, the best of this literature – the Shabasad Bakhar and the 91-Kalami Bakhar – is important both for the facts and the tone of the heroic and tragic events which form the basis of the popular history of Maharashtra.[1]

Unfortunately, many of the statements of even these two most reliable bakhars have found their way into scholarly writing without careful use of corroborating evidence. Considered critically, however, the bakhar literature does raise several important issues for our understanding of the Maratha polity. First, this literature treats Shivaji – founder of the polity – as a near divine figure, regularly inspired by the goddess Bhavani to great deeds, which were primarily important as a Hindu resistance to Muslim domination and as leading to the establishment of a Hindu state. This theme of some decisive difference between Shivaji's Maharashtrian kingdom and earlier Muslim Maharashtrian kingdoms is an important one which runs regularly through the later historiography on Maharashtra. Just what those differences were and how they came about are critical to any discussion of the Maratha polity.

The second theme raised by these early histories is Shivaji as the ideal Hindu leader. A great part of the continuing interest in Shivaji is as a historical role model of perfect behavior. Any discussion of Shivaji, then, must deal with the events that any school-child in Maharashtra can relate, events that show courage and high moral character and charismatic leadership. With this background, it is understandable why acts of realpolitik, of dubious moral justification, get short shrift in much of the later writing. Recent research and published documents

---

[1] Both of these bakhars have recent editions in Marathi edited by V. S. Vakaskar: *91-Kalami Bakhar* (Poona, 1962) and *Sabhasadaci Bakhar* (Poona, 1973).

now allow a more balanced discussion of Shivaji and the early Maratha polity.[2]

Within a decade of the British conquest of Maharashtra (1818), two developments spurred the indigenous interest in Maratha history. The first was a series of reports by early British administrators of the conquered territories. These usually were based on both a search for documents of the previous Maratha government and questioning of clerks and others (mainly Brahmins) who had served the Marathas. Much of what became "Maratha" history was created out of the questions of the British, the answers of their informants, and misunderstandings on both sides.[3]

At the same time, an intense dialogue began between Christian missionaries and Brahmin pundits; it covered the nature of Indian society, Hinduism, and the role of Brahmins. By the 1840s and 1850s, this debate led to the vigorous development of a locally sponsored, Marathi-language press, mostly concerned with philosophical and social questions. Simultaneously, there was increasing pressure from the British colonial government (both through the census and the courts) to define and close castes and subcastes.[4] This pressure led both Brahmin and Maratha individuals and groups to rethink their history and the history of Maharashtra. Some of the general journals began including ballads and family histories, and a strictly historical journal, *Bodhsagar*, appeared in Bombay in 1849–50.

In 1863, the second and much more widely circulated edition of Grant Duff's English-language history of the Marathas sharpened the debate. The author, an early administrator in the new Bombay government, produced three volumes that covered the rise of Shivaji in the mid-seventeenth century up to the British conquest in 1818.[5] This

---

[2] The best discussion of the bakhar literature is the study in Marathi by R. V. Hervadkar, *Marathi Bakhar* (Pune, 1975). The consensus is that the Shabasad and the 91-Kalami are the most reliable bakhars for the Shivaji period. A flavor of this literature can be found in the translations of P. P. Patwardhan and H. G. Rawlinson, *A Sourcebook of Maratha History* (reprinted by the Indian Council of Historical Research, Calcutta, 1978).

[3] Some of the more famous of these reports are as follows: M. Elphinstone, *Report on the Territories Conquered from the Peshwa* (1809), T. Jenkins, *Report on the Territories of the Raja of Nagpur* (1827), T. B. Jervis, *Geographical and Statistical Memoir of the Konkan* (1840), W. H. Sykes, "On the land tenures of the Dekkan," *Journal of the Royal Asiatic Society*, 2 (1835), and J. Malcolm, *A Memoir of Central India* (London, third edition, 1832).

[4] The terms of the debate and generational differences are covered in Richard Tucker, "The early setting of the non-Brahmin movement in Maharashtra," *Indian Historical Review*, 7, 1–2 (July, 1980–January, 1981), 134–58.

[5] James Grant Duff, *History of the Marathas* (London, 1818, reprinted Jaipur, 1986).

study, in several ways, set the terms for all subsequent debate about what the Maratha polity "was," the central principles of governing, and even the "character" of the Marathas and Brahmins involved. Let me suggest some of Grant Duff's viewpoints here; others will be suggested further into the text. First, Grant Duff gave only a cursory review of the period of the rise of Shivaji and, thus, downplayed continuities with prior kingdoms in Maharashtra. Second, for Grant Duff, history was mainly political history. He was interested in the wars and battles, the factions at court, and who won and lost. Other aspects, particularly economic and social, form only small parts of the narrative. Third, Grant Duff focused only on the head of the polity and occasionally on a few of the most powerful men who were his commanders. We get no picture of life outside court or sectors of the polity not immediately involved with the court. Fourth, the narrative is strictly chronological; it never steps back to consider long-term trends or changes. Finally, there is no question but that Grant Duff was proud of the British conquest and celebrated the brave acts of the British military involved. He emphasized great failures, especially the character of crucial leaders of the Maratha polity, which allowed for British conquest.

Much of the subsequent historiography on the Maratha polity should be read as a gloss on Grant Duff. Each generation of historians of Maharashtra needed to "prove" Grant Duff was wrong, and that the Maratha polity represented something important to the political needs of the day. In the 1890s, for example, the early "moderates," especially M. G. Ranade, tried to establish that in the seventeenth century the Marathas as a people emerged from a political, social, and religious renaissance. They represented an incipient "nationalism" and Shivaji's resistance to the Mughal Empire should be seen as the resistance of the emerging "nation" to foreign domination. The parallels to the emerging resistance to the British in Ranade's own time placed Shivaji in the position of a leader of a principally secular, "national" movement of the seventeenth century.[6]

Another theme added to the study of Shivaji and the Maratha polity in the nineteenth century was that of Shivaji as a military strategist.

[6] M. G. Ranade, *The Rise of Maratha Power* (Bombay, 1900). It should be noted, however, that it was Mountstuart Elphinstone, the well-known Bombay administrator of the early nineteenth century who, in his *History of India*, first referred to the Marathas as a "nation" and to Shivaji's activities as a "war of independence."

British writers wanted to see Shivaji primarily as a glorious rebel, capable of sustained resistance against a superior Mughal force. His use of mobility and terrain spoke to British military concerns in India.[7]

One very positive effect of these attempts to critique Grant Duff was the search for documents of the Maratha polity. The main source, the huge quantity of Maratha central government documents captured by the British in 1818, was, by colonial policy, closed to historical research. (The British perceived these documents as a dangerous source of national pride and probable sedition, and the archive remained closed until independence.) The first alternative source was the archives of the princely states and the larger Maratha families. Thus there appeared before 1900 histories of important Maharashtrian families, for example Shinde, Holkar, the Satara Rajas, the Pratnidhi family, the Angres, and the Dabhades.[8] The decades after 1900 saw a series of dedicated collectors combing the countryside in search of the documents of the Marathas which had not found their way to the central archives. What were located were mainly the family collections of administrative families, plus the land grants and records of smaller Maratha families. The collecting and printing of these documents was seen as important national work, leading to a new and more accurate history of the Marathas. The most famous of these collectors was V. K. Rajwade, who published thousands of documents along with extensive introductions.[9]

Largely in response to these private publications, the Bombay government permitted a series of volumes of selections from the vast

---

[7] C.f. Dennis Kincaid, *The Grand Rebel: An Impression of Shivaji, Founder of the Maratha Empire* (London, 1937).

[8] Most of these early family histories were never printed in large editions and most are long out of print. Some examples would include M. M. Atre, *Thorle Malhar Rao Holkar yanchen Charitra* (Life of Malhar Rao Holkar) (Poona, 1893), G. N. Deva, *Srimanta Ahilyabai yanchen Charitra* (Life of Ahilyabai) (Bombay, 1892), and J. P. Saranjame, *Sinde hyanche gharanyacha itihasa* (History of the Shindes) (Poona, 1872).

[9] Important associations for historical research were founded at this time in Pune and several regional towns of Maharashtra. Their lectures and publications gave a dynamism and excitement to the movement to recover the history of the Marathas. Examples of family and other documents collected in the 1900–30 period include D. V. Apte, *Candracud Daftar* (Poona, 1920), the early volumes of *Sivacaritra Sahitya*, published by the Bharat Itihas Samshodak Mandal, V. V. Khare (ed.), *Aitihasik Lekh Samgraha* (Miraj, 1918–26), and V. K. Rajwade (ed.) *Marathyanchya Itihasacin Sadhanen* (published Poona, Bombay, etc., 1898–1918), and K. V. Purandare (ed.) *Purandare Daftar* (Poona, 1929). Many important volumes from this period are now available only at the Bharat Itihas Samshodak Mandal, Pune.

central government archive. The first printing was thirteen volumes between 1917 and 1925, selected and glossed by Rao Bahadur Wad.[10] Subsequent selections were begun by G. S. Sardesai in 1928. The series now runs to forty-five volumes and continues today. Because they are readily available and in Devangari script (rather than the difficult Modi of the originals), these are the selections which form the basis of much of the historical scholarship on Maharashtra.[11] They, however, have two drawbacks. First, the majority of the volumes were published in the British period and were explicitly intended to be of a "non-controversial" nature; thus, crucial and important documents and subjects were often simply left out. Second, in spite of the volume of printed material (perhaps 50,000 documents by now), the selection process has hampered many kinds of research. In areas such as economic history, the selections tended toward those which the historians found typical of the Maratha "system," rather than long runs of documents of a particular area or family, which might have showed conflict or trends and changes.[12]

In the 1930s and 1940s, the process of publication of documents, if anything, accelerated.[13] The writing of Maratha history also changed in this period. In response to deteriorating relations between Hindus and Muslims, Shivaji and the Maratha polity took on a new significance for a new generation of historians. The importance of the Maratha polity, for this group, was as a Hindu resistance to the overbearing and oppressive Muslim government, the Mughal Empire. Shivaji, thus, was turned into an ideal Hindu ruler, struggling against the foreign Muslim

[10] Two typical volumes which came out of the joint editorship of Rao Bahadur G. C. Wad and D. B. Parasnis were *Kaifiyats, Yadis, etc.* (Bombay, 1908), and *Selections from the Satara Rajas and the Peishwas' Diaries* (Bombay, 1907).

[11] The princely states were also an important source of printed documents. See, for example, A. N. Bhagwat (ed.) *Holkar Shahitchya Itihasachi Sadhne* (Indore, 1924–25). Unfortunately, both the documents selected and the histories of the families written from them were sometimes attempts to glorify the family or settle old scores, such as rivalries and conflicts with other families.

[12] This type of history, because of the fragmented nature of the documentation, tends to use material from all areas and all periods of Maratha history in search of a "Maratha" system. Some of the best, seminal work is plagued by this problem. See, for example, the two important studies by S. N. Sen, *Administrative System of the Marathas* (Calcutta, 1925) and *Military System of the Marathas* (Calcutta, 1928), and V. T. Gune, *The Judicial System of the Marathas* (Poona, 1953).

[13] For example, see D. B. Diskalkar, *Historical Papers of the Sindhias of Gwalior: 1777–1793* (Satara, 1940), *Historical Selections from Baroda State Records*, 5 vols. (Baroda, 1934–39), G. H. Khare (ed.), *Hingane Daftar*, 2 vols. (Poona, 1945–47), V. V. Thakur (ed.), *Holkarsahica Itihasacin Sadhanen* (Indore, 1944–45).

rule.[14] The parallels to the situation of the 1940s were apparent to all sides. Muslims were "foreigners" and the proper government for India should be a Hindu government. The best that Muslims could expect was what they got under Shivaji, the "tolerance" and general morality expected of a benign Hindu ruler.[15]

In the decades after independence, there have been several significant trends in the study of Maratha history. The first is the publication and use of documents from the surrounding rivals of the Marathas – English, French, Portuguese, and Mughals.[16] Within Maharashtra, scholars have produced a very useful series of regional studies and biographies.[17] Overall, Shivaji and the Maratha polity have retreated to regional, rather than national symbols. This is perhaps understandable. Historically, though the Marathas ruled much of northern and central India in the eighteenth century, they were known as just another government, certainly neither the most efficient nor the most benevolent that the area had known.

In the last ten years, Shivaji and the Maratha polity have assumed importance in yet another political struggle. Within Maharashtra, the struggles among Brahmins, non-Brahmins, and Untouchables have focused attention on the social reform aspects of Shivaji's reign. In his person, as a Maratha, he has become a symbol of non-Brahmin power. More interestingly, Marxist and Untouchable writers have seized on his attempts to decrease the power of the independent landed elites as both consciousness of the need to end caste discrimination and a commitment to the task.

[14] The best known of this group is G. S. Sardesai, *Marathi Riyasat* (Bombay, 1935) and *New History of the Marathas* (Bombay, 1946).

[15] Two complementary bibliographies form the starting point for the history of Maharashtra and the Marathas: first, V. V. Divekar, *Survey of Material in Marathi on the Economic and Social History of India* (Pune, 1981); second, D. S. Kharbas, *Maharashtra and the Marathas, Their History and Culture: A Bibliographic Guide to Western Language Materials* (Boston, 1975).

[16] See, for example, the volumes edited and translated by V. G. Hatalkar, *French Records Relating to the History of the Marathas* (Bombay, 1983–), P. S. Pissurlencar, *Portuguese Maratha Relations* (Bombay, 1983), J. N. Sarkar, *The Military Dispatches of a Seventeenth Century General* (Calcutta, 1969), the reprinting of H. M. Elliot and J. Dowson, *The History of India as Told by Its Own Historians*, 7 vols. (Allahabad, 1964), and J. Sarkar, *House of Shivaji* (New Delhi, 1978).

[17] See, for example, M. Malgonkar, *Puars of Dewas Senior* (Bombay, 1963), S. G. Vaidya, *Peshwa Bajirao II and the Downfall of the Maratha Power* (Nagpur, 1976), A. R. Kulkarni, *Maharashtra in the Age of Shivaji* (Poona, 1967), G. T. Kulkarni, *The Mughal–Maratha Relations: Twenty Five Fateful Years (1682–1707)* (Poona, 1983). A compilation of recent writing is R. C. Majumdar and V. G. Dighe's *The Maratha Supremacy*, Volume Eight of the *History and Culture of the Indian People* (Bombay, 1977).

Within Maharashtra, current writing on Shivaji and the Maratha polity explicitly or implicitly goes round and round the following three themes: (1) the Maratha polity as a "rising" of the regional consciousness of Maharashtra (2) the Maratha polity as Hindu response to oppressive Muslim rule, or (3) the Maratha polity as brave attempt to change the nature of Hindu society and better the lot of its poorest members. The more specific questions addressed by current historians arise from one or more of these three general concerns: Was Shivaji an ideal Hindu ruler? Was he a social reformer? How secular was he? Was the Maratha polity a Hindu state? Was the resistance to the Mughal Empire based on the perception of Mughals as "foreign"? How much of the success of the Maratha polity can be attributed to a developing regional consciousness in Maharashtra? What failures or problems led to British conquest?

It is now almost fifty years since independence and perhaps time to stop writing Maratha history as a gloss on Grant Duff, as only the failure of a resistance to colonial rule. It is time to stop combing the records for some historical figure to blame for the British conquest. It is less glamorous and less heroic to see the Maratha polity as one among many in the seventeenth and eighteenth centuries, not as a proto-nationalist resistance against the foreigner, nor as a Hindu crusade against Islam. Now, however, the only way an historian can reach these invalid conclusions is by ignoring or doing violence to the more than adequate historical records that have become available in the decades since independence.

In the last fifteen years, a small group of foreign historians of pre-colonial Maharashtra has explored quite different themes. Throughout, this scholarship is characterized by the use of primary Marathi sources (often from the Pune Daftar or the Bharat Itihas Samshodak Mandal) and active collaboration with scholars and scribes in Maharashtra. Overall, the focus has been away from the political events of court and campaign and towards the countryside, especially the relation of economic and political processes. Some of these studies have, for example, examined the dynamics of state and caste, and rural labor relations.[18] My own work has been on the nature of conquest, the

[18] See these examples of the work of Hiroshi Fukazawa: "State and caste system (jati) in the eighteenth century Maratha kingdom," *Hitotsubashi Journal of Economics* (June, 1968); "Rural servants in the 18th century Maharashtrian village – demiurgic or jajmani system," *Hitotsubashi Journal of Economics* (February, 1972); several sections in *The Cambridge Economic History of India Vol. I, c. 1200–c. 1750* (Cambridge, 1982).

relation of state and local areas, and on changes in military practice.[19] Others have focused attention on the great families which dominated Maratha history and the related processes of money use and credit.[20] A third group of studies has examined patterns of conflict in the Maratha polity and the whole nature of "rights" within it.[21] Finally, a fourth group of scholars has studied the religious and literary history of the Maratha polity.[22]

This volume will respectfully draw on this body of history, both older and modern, produced both inside and outside Maharashtra. The overall perspective is to allow the Maratha polity to stand on its own as a significant part of India's history. The discussion focuses mainly on economic and military questions and long-term trends and cycles; it will downplay the political narration in favor of many themes not covered in Grant Duff or subsequent histories. First, we will use the Maratha polity as a main example of the dynamics of kingdoms of the period – how they came together and decentralized. The perspective will be not only from the court, but from the families who gave or withdrew loyalty. The historical sweep is necessarily longer than usually considered; we will consider the experience of Marathas and Brahmins in service under the Deccan sultanates and see the Maratha polity as the natural successor state to these kingdoms. Second, we will look at the Maratha polity in terms of social mobility for selected groups and individual families. Naturally, this will include patterns of downward mobility, for those who, for example, lost out in succession disputes. Third, we will consider the economics that funded the polity, especially taxation and credit. Throughout we will be seeking long-

[19] Typical are "The slow conquest: administrative integration of Malwa into the Maratha Empire," *Modern Asian Studies*, 11, 1 (1977); "Forts and social control in the Maratha state," *Modern Asian Studies*, 22, 1 (1979); "Recovery from adversity in eighteenth century India: rethinking villages, peasants and politics in pre-modern kingdoms," *Journal of Peasant Studies*, 8, 4 (Fall, 1979).

[20] See these examples of Frank Perlin's work, "Of 'white whale' and countrymen in the eighteenth-century Maratha Deccan: extended class relations, rights and the problem of rural autonomy under the old regime," *Journal of Peasant Studies*, 5 (1978); "Proto-industrialization and pre-colonial South Asia," *Past and Present*, 98 (1983); "Money use in late pre-colonial India," in John F. Richards (ed.), *The Imperial Monetary System of Mughal India* (New Delhi, 1978).

[21] See especially Andre Wink, *Land and Sovereignty in India: Agrarian Society and Politics under the Eighteenth-century Maratha Svarajya* (Cambridge, 1986).

[22] See, for example, the work of the following scholars: Anne Feldhaus, *The Deeds of God in Rddipur* (Oxford, 1984); Eleanor Zelliot and Maxine Bernstein, *The Experience of Hinduism: Essays on Maharashtra* (Albany, 1989); G. A. Deleury, *The Cult of Vithoba* (Poona, 1960); M. S. Mate, *Temples and Legends of Maharashtra* (Bombay, 1962); S. B. Tulpule, *Classical Marathi Literature* (Wiesbaden, 1979).

term changes, such as the shift from tribute to regular tax collection. Fourth, we will examine the nature of loyalty and legitimacy, as continuing and insoluble problems. Fifth, the Maratha polity presents a fascinating case study of military and technological change and its social and economic effects – both at court and at the local level. Finally, we must consider the legacy of the Maratha polity – what, within India, did it change forever. As we shall see, it had profound effects on revenue administration, law, education, trade patterns, migration, and the economic and social make-up of Central India, Gujarat, and Maharashtra.

CHAPTER 1

THE GEOPOLITICS OF MAHARASHTRA

For an understanding of the spatial framework of the Maratha polity there are several crucial terms which appear throughout this study. The two most important are the Deccan and Maharashtra. The Deccan, which translates as "south," is an old term appearing in the Vedic literature and the Mahabharata as Dakshinapatha. It meant the area below the Tapti River, and suggested an area suitable for conquest. Throughout history, "Deccan" has retained these overtones, the perspective of a northern conqueror considering possible domains. What constituted the Deccan, at any particular moment, depended on where the kingdom's southern border lay and what lay beyond. Over the whole historical period, the area from the Tapti to the Godavari was frequently integrated into northern empires, and the area south of it, between the Godavari and the Krishna, became the Deccan.[1] In this sense, I will use the term Deccan not as a fixed place, but only as a relational term, the area beyond the southern border of a northern-based kingdom.

The term "Maharashtra" is much easier to define. It is simply the area where Marathi is the dominant language. As a place, Maharashtra was mentioned from the first century AD onwards, but not until inscriptional evidence of the seventh century is it possible roughly to map the region. *Ma ho leska* (Maharashtra) figures prominently in the narrative of the Chinese Buddhist pilgrim, Hsuan Tsang, in this period. With the further development of Marathi, between 800 AD and 1300 AD, we can trace a definite linguistic region. For example, the saint-reformer Chakradhara travelled all over the Marathi-speaking region, preaching and plying his trade as a barber. He was proud never to set foot in Kanada or Telegu areas. The minute record of his journeys gives the limits of the Marathi language.[2] It agrees to a remarkable extent with the map of find-spots for Marathi inscriptions. This Marathi-language region is represented on Map 1. We should not think of this

---

[1] S. M. Alam, "The historic Deccan: a geographical appraisal," in V. K. Bawa (ed.) *Aspects of Deccan History: Report of a Seminar* (Hyderabad, 1975), 16–29.

[2] M. G. Panse, "Regional individuality of Maharashtra," in Bawa (ed.), *Aspects of Deccan History*, 139–40.

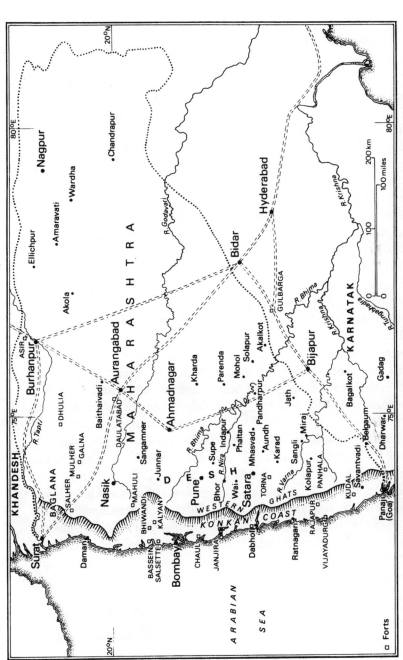

Map 1. Maharashtra of the seventeenth century showing the main roads and towns (adapted from André Wink, *Land and Sovereignty in India: Agrarian Society and Politics under the Eighteenth-century Maratha Svarajya* [Cambridge, 1986], 87. The roads are from Irfan Habib, *An Atlas of the Mughal Empire* [Oxford, 1982], map 14-B. The linguistic boundary is taken from O. H. K. Spate and A. T. A. Learmonth, *India and Pakistan: A General and Regional Geography* [Bungay, Suffolk, 3rd edn, 1969], Figure 23.4.

line as a sharp boundary, however. Recent research suggests that it is more like a broad strip, perhaps fifty miles wide, inside which considerable bilingual areas would be found, with much less on either side.[3] Many other patterns would tend to support this boundary. For example, Maharashtra grows mainly wheat, cotton, and pulses and very little rice, while Andhra grows rice, sugar, and millet.[4] Pilgrimage routes, trading patterns, and marriage networks would also support this Marathi-language boundary.

There is also a long tradition of political boundaries matching linguistic ones. When the western Chalukya kingdom broke into two successor states in the opening of the twelfth century, it fissured into two core areas, the Marathi-speaking areas of Maharashtra and the Kanada-speaking areas of Karnataka. In Maharashtra, the new Yadava dynasty immediately began to use vernacular Marathi as their official language and patronized the important pilgrimage sites of Maharashtra.

What of the overall geographic features of this region? First, the northern and southern boundaries have no defensible features; they are readily open to invasion. Second, the region itself is sharply divided into three subregions – the Konkan, the Ghats, and the Desh. The Konkan is the narrow coastal strip, about thirty miles wide, which lies below the mountains. Rainfall in the Konkan is over eighty inches a year. Its other feature is the presence of important coastal ports. The Ghats rise sharply from the Konkan coast and are characterized by steep separated peaks and few passes. These mountains are wooded (and were much more so in previous centuries); most of the rainfall runs back into the Konkan. Fodder and food are scarce, and the only items of trade are forest products – medicinal herbs, timber, honey, and the like. The Ghats were important for their hill forts. In this strip, perhaps thirty miles wide and running north–south the whole length of Maharashtra, more than two hundred hilltops have been fortified over time, many of them over and over again by successive local or regional powers. Until the introduction of European cannon in the late eighteenth century, those in the fort possessed a strong strategic advantage over those outside. The third region, the Desh, is a broad

[3] See Charles J. Bennett, "The morphology of language boundaries: Indo-Aryan and Dravidian in peninsular India," in David E. Sopher (ed.), *An Exploration of India: Geographical Perspectives in Society and Culture* (Ithaca, 1980), 234–51.

[4] Jayshree Gokhale-Turner, "Images of Maharashtra," in N. G. Wagle, *Region and Regionalism in Indian Politics* (London, 1980).

plateau widest at the Ghats and narrowing to the east. The portion closest to the Ghats is in the rain shadow of the mountains and not very productive. Further east, however, the plain has typically been fertile and well populated.[5] It has three main rivers, the Purna-Tapti at the north, the Godavari, and the Krishna-Bhima, the most important river of the Desh, which has important ancient settlement sites as well as the Maharashtrian pilgrimage site of Pandharpur. We must emphasize that the Desh and the Konkan were (and are) utterly different ecologically, and formed what Braudel has termed "natural" trading regions. We shall explore each region's agriculture and specialities shortly.

This threefold division of Maharashtra has created certain geopolitical realities for any kingdom and would-be conquerors or rebels. The Ghats thoroughly divide the two productive areas of the region. Any kingdom based in the Desh must control the Ghats to control, first, the trade routes to the coast and, second, the productive agriculture of the Konkan. Thus, a Desh-based kingdom's "drive to the west" is a given. The Ghats' strength made it the natural retreat area for rebels, from which they could raid either of the productive areas, the Konkan or the Desh. (This they had to do as the Ghats could not agriculturally support even a small army.) Both states and rebels also had to deal with the monsoon, which tended to isolate the Konkan (because of swollen, unfordable rivers) and made the passes through the Ghats even more difficult. The monsoon divided the year into a campaigning season, from October to May, and an agricultural season, from May to September, and armies were arranged accordingly, with most troops returning home to plant in May.

In this geographic context, the story of the "Marathas" properly begins about the time of the Muslim invasions of Maharashtra, that is about 1300 AD. The initial raid into the Deccan was by Ala-ud-Din-Khilji, rebel nephew of the sultan in Delhi. The early looting expeditions, which covered much of Maharashtra and Karnataka, were followed by conquest, annexation, and the extinction of the Yadava dynasty. Thus, the period from 1300 to 1320 was one of intense conflict in Maharashtra, with many dominant lineages killed and many more migrating south to escape the Muslim conquest. For example, the stories of the Sufi saints of the period regularly extoll their

---

[5] Shown and mapped in D. G. Kulkarni, *The River Basins of Maharashtra* (New Delhi, 1970), 58.

slaughter of the "infidels."[6] As the warrior-lineages tried to regroup, they were pushed farther to the south. (Later, as is well known, remnants of warrior-lineages from Andhra founded the state of Vijaynagar south of the Tungabhadra river.) This phase of intense conflict ended by about 1350 with the establishment of the Bahmani dynasty, more Muslim settlers arriving from the north, and the cutting of political ties with Delhi. The new dynasty got down to the business of establishing forts and collecting taxes. Following the conquest, there were few, if any, forced conversions, no attempt to translate the Muslim canon into Marathi to facilitate conversion, and a general policy of continuing the existing grants to Hindu temples.

The Muslim dynasties that stayed and ruled Maharashtra for the next 350 years were profoundly important in defining paths of social mobility, areas of government involvement and patronage, military and civilian bureaucracy, and styles of resistance. As we shall see, those who prospered in these centuries were the families which came to be termed "Maratha" and Brahmins from the Desh. Let us begin with the Marathas.

The term Maratha has several suggested etymologies, none of which are satisfactory. They do not explain how the term arose, the dynamics of how it was used, by whom, in reference to whom. None of the suggested origins tell us why such a term would arise at a particular period or in response to a particular series of events. On the face of it, "Maratha" is different from the terms "Bengali" or "Tamil." Everyone of long residence in a Bengali-speaking areas and speaking Bengali is a Bengali. Similarly, there might be Tamil Brahmins or Tamil Christians, but they would all be Tamils. Not all Marathi-speaking residents of Maharashtra are Marathas, not by any means. The case, as we shall see, is similar to Rajasthan – where all Rajasthani-speaking residents are not Rajputs.

The term Maratha may be an old one, but the inscriptional evidence is scarce and vague. There is, for example, an inscription in the Bedsa cave (dating from the first century AD) that uses the term Maharathini to refer to a queen, just as there is a fifth-century Singhalese chronicle that calls a region Maharattha.

There is nothing, however, in this early evidence to indicate that the use of the term Maratha meant anything other than a resident of Maharashtra. This is also the sense of the early Muslim chroniclers. Al

[6] Richard Eaton, *Sufis of Bijapur: 1300–1700* (Princeton, 1978), 19–44.

Baruni (1020 AD) mentions Marhat Des as the area south of the Narmada river and Ibn Batuta (1340 AD) notes that the people around Daulatabad were Marathas.

Over the next two hundred years, the term came to mean a new elite, the Maratha chiefs who brought bands of followers to serve the Bahmani kingdom or those rebelling against it.[7] The new meaning is well established by the time of Ferishta's history of the Deccan in 1600. The process seems to fit a well-established pattern for the creation of new caste categories that arise in response to new possibilities for upward economic mobility.

Looking backward from ample material on the eighteenth and nineteenth centuries, we know that "Maratha" as a category or a caste represents the amalgamation of families from several castes – Kunbi, Lohar, Sutar, Bhandari, Thakar, and even Dhangars (shepherds) – which existed in the seventeenth century and, indeed, exist as castes in Maharashtra today. What differentiated, for example, "Maratha" from "Kunbi"? It was precisely the martial tradition, of which they were proud, and the rights (watans and inams) they gained from military service. It was these rights which differentiated them from ordinary cultivators, ironworkers, or tailors, especially at the local level.

How then did the term arise in what seems to be the critical period between 1400 and 1600? The most likely origin would be in the places of military service, the Bahmani armies and especially the armies of the five successor states. It would have arisen as a descriptive term for units speaking Marathi, as opposed to Dakhani units (units composed of Moslems born in India) or 'Afagis (units composed of recent Moslem immigrants from Arabia or Central Asia).[8] Ibrahim Adil Shah of Bijapur (1535–57) showed preference for troops from Maharashtra, especially as a counterbalance to the power of Dakhani and 'Afagi troops. Marathi came to be the language of government in the Muslim kingdom of Ahmadnagar during this period. Probably, the term Maratha gained credence slowly; the early references to these troops were as "bargirs," a generic term for cavalry who did not furnish their

[7] I am indebted to Dr. Anne Feldhaus for a reference to the use of the term marhatem in Smritisthal, a Mahanubhav text attributed to the fourteenth or fifteenth century. In the text, Bhatobas assures his listeners that in spite of the Muslim invasions and political upheaval, "Maratha rule" (likely referring to the Yadava kingdom) would last as long as he did (with implications of his own immortality). See U. N. Despande, Smritisthal (Pune, 1939, reprinted 1960).

[8] I. A. Ghauri, "Organization of the army under the sultanates of the Deccan," Journal of the Pakistan Historical Society, 14, 3 (July 1966), 147–71.

own horse and equipment. This is how the Mirat-i-Ahmadi referred to all such troops in the seventeenth century, i.e. the Bargirs from Ahmadnagar. Later they became Maratha units, with their own horses and equipment, operating under Maratha chiefs and leaders.

This origin would account for the varied and impossible to reconcile lists of the "true" Maratha families compiled in the nineteenth century.[9] It fits perfectly with the origin and development of the term Rajput, whose martial ideology developed through service to the Mughal Empire. Eventually, kinship and marriage restrictions defined this Rajput group as different from other elements in the society of Rajasthan. The hypergamous marriage pattern typical of Rajputs tacitly acknowledged that it was a somewhat open caste category; by successful service in a state army and translating this service into grants and power at the local level, a family might become Rajput. The process required changes in dress, eating patterns, the patronage of local shrines closer to the "great tradition," and an end to widow-remarriage.[10] A hypergamous marriage with an acknowledged (but possibly impoverished) Rajput family would follow and with continued success in service the family would, indeed, become Rajput. All this is well documented in relations between Rajputs and tribals, such as Bhils, in Central India.[11]

I see no reason why the term Maratha did not develop in the same way. First came service that differentiated certain families from the ordinary cultivator; grants made these families involved in revenue collection and further differentiated them at the local level. Simultaneously, a new ethic developed that included martial training and hunting, different patterns in dress (such as the more complicated turban), changed patterns of diet, the employment of genealogists, and

[9] Three such lists are considered in R. E. Enthoven, *The Tribes and Castes of Bombay*, III (Bombay, 1922), 21–25.

[10] Norman Ziegler, "Some notes on Rajput loyalties during the Mughal period," in J. F. Richards (ed.) *Kingship and Authority in South Asia* (Madison, Wis., 1978). The process is analyzed in much more detail in D. H. A. Kolff, *Naukar, Rajput, and Sepoy: The Ethnohistory of the Military Labour Market in Hindustan, 1450–1850* (Cambridge, 1990). Kolff suggests, quite rightly, that several of the terms commonly thought of as "castes" – Sikh, Pathan, Rajput, Afghan – were, in fact, terms dependent on military employment and intimately linked to the perquisites and linkages of soldiering, ibid., 57–58.

[11] Surajit Sinha, "State formation and Rajput myth in tribal Central India," *Man in India*, 42, 1 (January-March 1962), 35–80. This perspective, that "caste" is, and always has been, embedded in the politics of kingship and service, I share with Nicholas Dirks, see *The Hollow Crown: Ethnohistory of an Indian Kingdom* (Cambridge, 1987). I wish to thank Nick for many conversations around these themes.

restrictions on widow-remarriage. Eventually, these changes came to be solidified in a kinship network that conformed to the "correct" behavior, financed mainly by the solid wealth of grants for military service. Thus, the term "Maratha" was a relational and interactional term that described a newly emerging service elite.

As we shall see, the nature of the development of the category Maratha goes a long way towards describing the continuing factional politics which dominated the Maratha polity's history. Many of the great families arose simultaneously, in service to the five Deccan Muslim kingdoms, not in service to a single conqueror. (As we shall see, many families were of at least equivalent age, legitimacy, and power to Shivaji – the founder of the Maratha polity – and resisted his attempts to establish authority.) Families, thus, held service grants which solidly established them in a certain territory. The famous Maratha trait of clinging, at all costs, to local rights to land revenue can be understood as the refusal of a new landed elite to return to the status of a purely service elite, able to be moved at the beck and call of the polity, paid by whatever lands were assigned to them.

The defining of Maratha as a new caste category continued throughout the period of the Maratha polity and into the nineteenth century, along the lines of the Rajput model already described. There were attempts to list and define the "pure" Maratha families and to close the caste by observing practices not possible to poorer farmers, such as secluding women. There was strong emphasis on soldiering as the only proper vocation for a true Maratha.

Let us return from this brief digression to the Maharashtra of the fourteenth and fifteenth centuries. For certain groups, Maharashtra would seem to have been a very different place after the Muslim conquest. The warrior-lineages were either gone or making accommo- dation with the new rulers. What of the effect on Brahmins, especially Brahmins associated with courtly patronage? Let us suggest one example: under the earlier Hindu dynasties of Maharashtra, there would have been a whole round of kingly rituals to be performed at various times each and every year to ensure not just fertility but the continued proper ordering of the entire cosmos. What happened when these rituals were simply no longer performed by the Muslim rulers? Another example: in Hindu thought, such as the Arthashastra, it was the king's moral obligation to be the ultimate arbiter of caste relations, acting on the precepts of his Brahmin advisers. His moral authority, in large part, came from this role. What were Brahmins to make of new rulers who did not belong to the correct caste to be king and were not keen to enter the unknown territory of caste disputes? The fact is that the changes were not as profound as we might expect. Because the number of Muslims in the Deccan was always very small, they were never more than the core administration, based in towns and forts, and were heavily dependent on local talent for administration and tax collecting.[12] From early on, various groups of Brahmins served the Muslim states of the Deccan, and were crucial to their functioning. They filled all the middle and lower levels of the tax-collecting administration. After the break-up of the Bahmani kingdom, it was the successor Muslim state of Ahmadnagar which controlled much of Maharashtra (in the fifteenth and sixteenth centuries). Deshasta Brahmins ran virtually the whole administration; they had suffered little under Muslim rule, and probably gained a degree of social mobility. They were thus familiar with revenue terms and practices throughout the region and were well positioned to form the administration of the new Maratha polity of the mid-seventeenth century.

Throughout the fifteenth and sixteenth centuries in Maharashtra, much was happening in Hinduism outside courts and Brahmin-controlled temples. Itinerant and local preachers were developing a popular form of Hindu faith, which came to be known as bhakti. It is too easy to identify the rise of these fervent religious practices as a reaction to the Muslim conquest. It is important to note that bhakti did not begin in Maharashtra, and its origin long predated Muslim conquest. It arose in Tamil country as early as the mid-tenth century as a reaction to the overly formal, ritualistic Vedic practices of the time. As an overall movement, bhakti stressed fervent devotion in the vernacular language of the follower to the deity, usually Krishna.[13]

In Maharashtra, it is also important to remember that early bhakti predated the Muslim invasions. The fervent devotion and preaching and writing in the local vernacular language paralleled developments in Tamilnadu of the preceding two centuries. The writings of Namadev, a

[12] Hiroshi Fukazawa, "A study of the local administration of Adilshahi Sultanate (AD 1489–1686)," *Hitotsubashi Journal of Economics* (June 1963), 37–65. See also I. A. Ghauri, "Local government under the sultanates of Bijapur and Golconda," *Journal of the Research Society of Pakistan*, 3, 102 (Jan.-April 1966), 43–62.

[13] A good cross-regional survey of the bhakti movement can be found in Eleanor Zelliot, "The medieval bhakti movement in history: an essay on the literature in English," in Bardwell L. Smith (ed.), *Hinduism: New Essays in the History of Religion* (Leiden, 1976).

saint of the Pandharpur school, illustrate trends of this early period. It is important and typical that Namadev (preaching around 1310–50) was not a Brahmin, but rather a tailor. The movement centered on an all-embracing love of God; it rejected caste restrictions in external ritual (such as prohibitions on low-caste persons entering temples) and, likewise rejected caste as any indication of spiritual development. It promoted the all-embracing experience of the pilgrimage (especially to Pandharpur). This was a radical message and it became more so. It threatened the role and authority of Brahmins in temple ritual and in life cycle ceremonies. After all, if it was the love of God that mattered, what did it matter if the rituals surrounding the images were performed correctly according to the arcane knowledge that only Brahmins possessed?

Bhakti was thus well positioned to respond to the core moral crisis which Muslim invasion and conquest represented. Such responses to crises "in the order of things" are typical across many cultures and time periods. The first response is often a call to faith and only faith as the answer. This suggests a fundamental questioning of the institutions charged with keeping things morally "in order." Emotional, direct appeals to God are common in such a crisis. As the years pass, and the moral order is still not right, it is typical to question feature after feature of the culture. Again, it is no surprise that bhakti selected caste as what was wrong with the culture, making it vulnerable to this sort of conquest. The enforcing of caste rules and prohibitions was associated with the very Brahminical structure which had failed. Later, in such a movement, self-criticism gives way to trying to find a new moral order. One typical response is to adopt what can be tolerated from the incorrect rulers; these adoptions can range all the way from aspects of the dress of the rulers, through eating habits, through revenue and judicial terminology to fluency in the ruler's language and on to full-scale conversion. Another response, also found in bhakti, was development of millenarian movements, which view the present as the last and dark age.

While individual adoptions of Muslim culture varied, the bhakti movement, as a whole, found the idea of faith common to both bhakti and Islam. Many poet–saints, of both Hindu and Muslim origin, tried to find common bases for prayer and worship. Among the Marathi poet–saints, a few were Muslim, such as Shah Muntoji Bahmani (of the royal family of Bidar) and Husain Ambarkhan, a Muslim poet who wrote a commentary on the Bhagvatgita and was an ardent follower of Ganesh.[14] On the local level, there is considerable evidence of, for example, Hindus worshipping at the tombs of Muslim saints (pirs). Some Hindus found the idea of brotherhood, so central to Islam, enormously attractive because of its implicit critique of caste. These ideas were preached across Maharashtra and soon spread to North India.

As with any movement of this size and duration, there were many and complex threads in bhakti – quietist, fervent and emotional, anti-caste, anti-Brahmin, syncretist and interested in Islam. We must always see bhakti as first and foremost in conflict and dialogue with the mainstream of Maharashtrian Hinduism, which was conservative in practice, temple-oriented and Brahmin-dominated, used Sanskrit in ceremonies, and supported caste as a social form. It is in this context that we should understand that very few strands of bhakti dealt with the secular/political/military world. None preached resistance to Islamic rule as a fundamental precept.

The most one can say of bhakti's programmatic was that it proposed several new definitions of personal moral behavior between persons and groups in society. We must expect that different aspects appealed to different constituencies, and that the focus shifted over time. Thus, the anti-caste aspects appealed to lower caste members. The emerging Maratha elite found local shrines to patronize.[15]

Now we must turn from the intellectual and religious ferment of Maharashtra to look more intensively at the rights these new service elites gained. Put most simply, what was worth competing for in seventeenth-century Maharashtra? It certainly was not land. There was an abundance of land and relatively few people. It was also not cash generated by trade. Maharashtra, especially the Desh region, had a generally low level of monetization. Let us review the evidence. First, major trade routes, such as Burhanpur to Surat or Burhanpur to Bijapur, skirted the region, and there were few mart cities (see

[14] A. R. Kulkarni, "Social relations in the Maratha country in the medieval period," *Indian History Congress Proceedings*, Thirty Second Session (Jabalpur, 1970), 238–39. There were, of course, other well-known Muslim poet–saints, such as Shekh Mohammad, preaching and writing on themes common to bhakti.

[15] It is interesting that there seem to be no bhakti poet–saints who refer to themselves as "Maratha," though almost all preachers and writers refer to themselves by family name and caste – tailor, potter, gardener. I am indebted to Eleanor Zelliot for this observation and find it further evidence for the emergence of "Maratha" as a relational category during this period.

Map 1).[16] Second, if we examine local grants, they were almost always expressed in the produce of villages, plus services, rather than cash.[17] Third, all the revenue settlement evidence from the first half of the sixteenth century suggests a low level of monetization. For example, a field near the town of Shirwal received a settlement in this period which was intended to bring it back into cultivation after a time of disruption. It was a stepwise increasing demand, spread over five years. What was to be paid, however, was not money, but grain, grass, and, later, cotton. A document of the same period details the "Bahamani" settlement of the village of Khed (near Pune); it specified the dues to the government as one third of the produce, with no attempt at measuring fields or altering the demand year by year. More generally, Malik Amber's third settlement of Maharashtra in the 1620s conceded that it was difficult to collect the revenue in money, and reverted to grain and fodder per field cultivated.[18] Still, to say that there was generally a low level of monetization and no large-scale trading cities is not to imply that villages were somehow self-sufficient or that trade did not exist. Quite to the contrary, in the seventeenth century, northern Maharashtra and Khandesh participated in the vigorous cotton trade which centered on Surat and Burhanpur. Of the more than 150 varieties of manufactured cotton cloth mentioned in Surat records, several were loomed in the Khandesh valley and exported.[19] Further south, there was also a regional trade between the Desh and the Konkan, also a well-developed coastal trade. The Desh and the Konkan were ecologically complementary regions. Consider the products that grow in the Konkan, but not on the Desh: coconuts (raw and dried, the husk processed into coir mats and rope, coconut oil for hair and cooking), mangoes, jackfruit, betel nuts, dried fish, salt (from sea-water), herbs and honey (from the forested regions), rice, sea shells

[16] The only Maharashtrian city with a product named in the local trade records was Paithan with its still produced Paithani silk saris. Junnar (north of Pune) was a paper-making center and Chaul (on the coast) was a weaving and ship-building center. Neither was, however, a mart city. See section on non-agricultural products of the Deccan and Maharashtra by H. Fukazawa, *The Cambridge Economic History of India Vol. I: c 1200–c.1750* (Cambridge, 1982).

[17] Many of these are found in G. H. Khare (ed.) *Persian Sources of Indian History (Aitihasik Farsi Sahitya)*, I–v (Pune, Bharat Itihas Samshodak Mandal, 1934–61). See also A. R. Kulkarni, *Maharashtra in the Age of Shivaji* (Pune, 1967), 91.

[18] Ghauri, "Local government," 44–45.

[19] S. P. Sangar, "Indian fabrics (seventeenth century)," in A. G. Pawar (convener), *Maratha History Seminar* (Kolhapur, 1971), 39–53. See also S. P. Sangar, "The Khandesh textiles in the seventeenth century," *Journal of Historical Research*, 16, 2, 59–62.

(as ornaments), timber and bamboo. All these products appear in the market documents of the Desh towns of the seventeenth century. Next, consider what the Desh produced which did (and does) not grow in the Konkan: sugarcane (for jaggery, the main sweetener), cotton, onions and garlic, tobacco, turmeric (crucial for fish curing). Perhaps the most important of all were the pulses grown on the Desh. The heavy rains of the Konkan made vegetables available only in limited seasons, and pulses from the Desh were (and are) the basic complement to the rice diet of the Konkan. Except in the heaviest monsoon periods, bullock caravans regularly carried these items of trade (plus items of copper, iron, and brass which came from outside Maharashtra) up and down the Ghats to weekly markets in both areas.[20]

The coastal trade also connected natural areas of supply to areas of demand. Spices and coconuts, timber and roofing tiles moved north to the regions of Sind and Kathiawad; horses and dried fruits came on the return voyages.

All of this is in answer to the question of what, in the Maharashtra of the mid-seventeenth century, was worth competing for. The only thing was various rights to shares of produce of the land, beyond subsistence. Consistently, throughout the region and the period, 40–50 percent of the produce of the land went to various right-holders and the king. At the village level, there was the headman (patil) and the records keeper (kulkarni). At the pargana level, a long-standing unit of 20–100 villages, there was the deshmukh (the "mouth of the land," representative of this group of villages) and the deshpande (pargana-level records keeper). These various local elite families received about 15 percent of the government collection. The remainder the king usually granted in one of two ways, as saranjam (non-hereditary grant for maintenance of troops) or as inam (hereditary grant for special service or merit).

Though the history of this system is fragmentary, it is worth noting that the most important of these rights – patil and deshmukh – arose through colonization. Maharashtra was so thinly populated in the sixteenth and seventeenth centuries that even prime riverine land was available. A man who brought his relatives and others and opened land

[20] I am indebted to Mr G. T. Mantri for much of this information. His work has taken him to villages, small towns, and markets throughout the Konkan and the Desh for almost a half-century. His observations are corroborated in O. H. K. Spate and A. T. A. Learmonth, *India and Pakistan: A General and Regional Geography* (Bungay, Suffolk, 3rd edn, 1967), 694–96.

THE GEOPOLITICS OF MAHARASHTRA

became village headman or patil. He, in essence, owned the village land and granted it to newcomers. (Thus, we find that a patil family typically still owned 30–40 percent of the village cultivated land in records of the eighteenth century.) A higher level of entrepreneurship and colonization meant, in a compact area, starting up several new villages or bringing in men who would. Such a man would have become a deshmukh, as well as the village headman (patil), of the villages that he directly started. Every deshmukh was, therefore, first a patil.[21] Let us emphasize that in the rain-shadow areas of Maharashtra there was a regular cycle of depopulation and recolonization. For example, the well-documented Mahadurga famine of 1630 produced widespread depopulation and subsequent opportunities for recolonization.

Even in the best of times, Maharashtra had limited communications and transportation and any king needed the deshmukhs and the patils for local control and revenue collection. Thus, we must not think of these crucial rights as simply a sum of money given to an individual for services or merit. Rather, they were complex rights which involved the holder and his family in the fabric of rural society – in revenue settlement and collection, adjudication and appeals, maintaining a body of troops recruited from the area, and ritual leadership at various festivals throughout the year.

By the seventeenth century, rights and responsibilities were routinely laid out in a sanad, the contract between the right-holder and the government, which formalized the financial, military, judicial, and ritual rights and obligations. It is important to understand these formal relations before turning to the additional implicit roles, found only in the correspondence between right-holders and the king. Let us begin with the contract of a deshmukh with the central government. (Dozens of these contracts exist at the Pune Archives.) The deshmukh was to remain loyal to the sultan (of Bijapur or Ahmadnagar), pay the fixed annual tribute to the royal treasury or to a designated person, co-operate with any royal representatives in his area, and provide a person who paid a surety bond for his good conduct. His local duties included, first and foremost, the development of cultivation and prosperity in his area (including finding and bringing back runaway cultivators). The deshmukh maintained a body of troops to keep the

---

[21] The vast majority of these entrepreneurs were Maratha, but some deshmukhs came from other groups – Brahmin, Prabu, Muslim, and Jain.

peace in his area, making these troops available for campaign against the kingdom's enemies, recalcitrant nearby deshmukhs, or even disloyal high officials. The deshmukh convened local judicial assemblies, as necessary, and recorded the results for the central government. The deshmukh was also responsible for raising local free labor (bigar) for the maintenance of roads, the building of forts, and gathering fodder for passing armies.

And what of the deshmukh's rights? He was granted hereditary tax-free lands and villages.[22] From these he had the right to collect all customary taxes and dues. In addition, he had the right to keep a small percentage of the taxes collected from his villages. These local taxes included both those collected in money and those collected in kind. For example, the money taxes included transit duties, bazaar taxes, fines, and a well-irrigation tax. In kind, the deshmukh collected shoes from the shoemaker, repair of agricultural implements from the carpenter, timber from the wood-gatherers, service from the mahar, coconuts and mangoes from the growers, and free labor from the village. In addition, the deshmukh had rights of precedence at local festivals and to deference in his local villages and capital. Finally, his rights included the keeping of armed retainers.[23]

Existing mid-sixteenth-century documents give us the formal characteristics of the revenue system. Probably, most settlements consisted of a simple division, based on the year's harvest. One such example is from the area around the village of Rohidkhore, subah Maval. Such a settlement gave half of the produce to the government and half to the village. There was no attempt to measure, no attempt to evaluate the quality of land or to consider the cash value of the crop.[24] From these

[22] We must differentiate here between four types of land tenure which received preferentially lower tax rates in Maharashtra in this and later periods. The first, termed "watan," was a hereditary tenure which depended on satisfactory service of some sort. This included all sorts of local "officials," such as deshmukhs, village headmen, local and regional record-keepers. The second sort of tenure was termed "inam" and was a hereditary reward for previous service or merit. It was not necessarily completely tax-free, though generally taxed at a lower rate. The third type was "saranjam" or "mokasa" which was land specifically granted for the maintainance of military troops. It often paid the same rates as other agricultural land; the government's share was merely alloted to the grantee. The fourth type of grant was known as "vrittis" which were generally long-standing religious or merit donations. All of these distinctions are laid out in Ramchandra Nilkanth's seventeenth-century treatise on statecraft, the *Ajnapatra*, see, "The Ajnapatra or royal edict" (trans. S. V. Puntambeker), *Journal of Indian History*, 8, 2 (August 1929), 214–19.

[23] Fukazawa, "Local administration of Adilshahi Sultanate," 47–55.

[24] B. G. Tamaskar, *Life and Work of Malik Amber* (Delhi, 1987), 261–62. In this case, the villagers were dissatisfied with a division settlement, and wanted the more sophisticated

scattered formal grants, we get the general picture of a deshmukh as a hard-working, local bureaucrat, involved in tax collection and expansion of agriculture.

Other, less common documents, show this to be a limited and quite distorted view of the role of the deshmukh in Maharashtra of the seventeenth century.[25] Let us now, for example, look at the full terms of deshmukhi rights of the middle of the seventeenth century. Our example comes from the Satara district of southern Maharashtra and consists of the details of a mid-century grant to the famous Ghorpade family, as continued in 1696.[26] The deshmukh requested and received a personal audience with the Maratha king. As a result of the audience, the king issued a sanad (grant contract). In it the king acknowledged the deshmukh as the holder of Vandan fort, in the vicinity of Satara, and that the family had been the holders of the deshmukhi rights under the previous Adil Shah government. The rights to be continued were as follows:

(1) One-quarter rupee from each chavar of cultivated land (a unit of approximately 60 acres)
(2) ¼ percent of the produce of each weaver, per year
(3) From the oilpresser of each village, ⅛ seer daily (about 3 oz.)
(4) From each mango grove, 5 out of every 100 picked
(5) Each year, at the bullock festival, jaggery (unrefined sugar) and oil (amount not specified)
(6) From each village, per bigha (about 2.5 acres) ¹/₂ seer (less than 1 oz.) of clarified butter per year
(7) From each village, per chavar, 17½ percent of the yield of the jiriyat (unirrigated farming)

settlement developed by Malik Amber in the first decades of the seventeenth century. The document appointed an assessor to undertake the work. He was to bring together the deshmukh, the deshkulkarni, the muqqadam, and other leading people and tour the area, village by village. They were to classify each field, whether grade one, two, three, or four. They were then to estimate the produce of the fields, based on the testimony of several farmers. The final figures were to be checked by the examination of fields in each category selected by a separate assessor.

[25] Throughout this discussion of the intrinsic tensions between the king and his "co-sharers," the deshmukhs, and other officials, let me acknowledge both the writings of and discussions with Andre Wink, who has focused attention on the centrality of these tensions to the state-building process. Specific references will be cited below.

[26] The full text of this grant (in Marathi) is in V. G. Khobrekar (ed.), *Records of Shivaji Period* (Bombay, 1974), 92–94. I wish to thank G. T. Mantri for collaboration in all the translations from this source.

In addition to these rights in all villages, this deshmukh, Hammant Rao Krishnaji Ghorpade, held the patilki (village headman rights) for several villages within the area of his deshmukh. The basic entitlement in these villages was 5 from every 100 kandys (a measure) of produce, as he had received under the previous Adil Shahi government. He received from Raja Ram two additional villages.

Further, in two nearby villages, the deshmukh received a new inam grant of one chavar (sixty acres) of unirrigated land and a 12.5 acre mango grove in recognition of meritorious service to the king for trying to reconcile a dispute between two generals.

This grant includes lands, the standing trees, and the leaves fallen on the earth [and belongs] to you and your son and your grandsons, and all the heirs hereafter, exclusive of hali pati and pestar pati [two small cesses]; you should take possession and enjoy it henceforth. If any Hindu obstructs this grant, he will be treated as committing the sin of killing a cow in Benares. If any Muhammadan obstructs this grant, it will be treated as committing the sin of killing a pig in Mecca.[27]

Even this single grant of deshmukh rights alerts us to several important features of the system. First, note that what was granted here was not just the deshmukh right, but a series of rights, all in the same area. Let us term these "nested" rights. Thus, the same man held not only a strong fort in the area, but was headman of three of the villages in his deshmukhi jurisdiction, as well as holding hereditary inam rights to acreage and a grove of mangoes in one village. This pattern was absolutely typical of the position of landed, armed elite families of seventeenth-century Maharashtra. Second, the deshmukh must not be construed as an ancient hereditary right, somehow insulated from larger politics. Quite to the contrary; note how the right was granted in personal audience of the king and in response to meritorious service to the king. Deshmukhs were, as we shall shortly explore, powerful, active negotiators in the politics of the day. Third, note that the village headman's rights and obligations were not specified in the document. These, more than deshmukh rights, were subject to local custom and practice and rarely involved intervention of the king. Though the mix would vary, it is perhaps worth suggesting the parameters of this patil right. He received a small share of whatever the government collected in cash. More substantial would be the payments in kind – typically a handful of grain and pulses from each cultivator, plus fowl and meat

---

[27] Ibid. See also Kulkarni, *Maharashtra*, 39–43.

from those who raised them. The patil was also entitled to free services from all of the village artisans, such as a pair of shoes, cloth, messenger services, and drummers. Finally, the patil led all village festivals and ceremonies, such as Dasara, Diwali, and Holi, and received oil, cakes, and images during each.[28] This patil right also required the approval of the villagers before it could be transferred to a new family. Often, the villagers resisted such change. For example, one village replied to Shivaji, who wanted to shift the patil right, as follows: "We are poor cultivators but we would never surrender our village under pressure to someone else; but you are the master of the region; if you so desire we are helpless."[29] Fourth, note that no kulkarni or deshpandiya rights (village and pargana record-keeper rights, respectively) were included in this grant. This is typical and expected. The Ghorpade family was Maratha and almost certainly illiterate. Record keepers were Brahmin, literate families. Conversely at this period, we find few Brahmin families holding deshmukh positions.

And what was the deshmukh to do to fulfill the responsibilities of the contract? Much depended on the level of social control in the larger polity. In a time of peace and adequate rains, the deshmukh seemed more like a revenue official; this is how he is portrayed in most of the histories of Maharashtra (based on the spotty published documents). We see him, in these documents, accompanying the revenue officer of the kingdom, committing himself, as responsible party, for the payment of the revenue. We see him in these documents trying minor civil cases, encouraging peasants to enlarge the area of cultivation, and making sure that new areas were duly recorded in the records kept by the kulkarni. In cases where the deshmukh family could not decide on succession, or was in active conflict, the state intervened and divided the right.

More interesting, and more common, was the deshmukh's role in remission in times of adversity. An early document, dated 1600, from the Pune area illustrates this process. The letter says that the Nizamshahi government (at Ahmadnagar) was approached by the cultivators, traders, and muqqadam and deshmukh of the area. They stated that the mokasa holder (the grantee of the government's share of

---

[28] For a full description of patil rights, see S. N. Sen, *Administrative System of the Marathas* (Calcutta, 1976), 131–34. For adjudication of boundary disputes, see V. T. Gune, *The Judicial System of the Marathas* (Pune, 1953), 203.

[29] A. R. Kulkarni, "Social mobility in Maharashtra," in A. G. Pawar (convener), *Maratha History Seminar* (Kolhapur, 1971), 109–10.

the revenue) had completely devastated the region, including "the irrigated land, the unirrigated land, the houses in the towns, and the orchards. The people have fled." Therefore the deshmukh was ordered by the government to set up a very low land revenue settlement for the next year, and gradually increase it over the next seven years, in order to bring the area back into cultivation.[30] This role hints at the larger than local importance of the deshmukh. In this case, he had to deal with the cause of the people fleeing, find them or replacements, negotiate the repopulation of the villages, and stand responsible for the gradual increase in revenue, based on a formula of expected performance.

It is not possible, however, to understand the dynamics of the deshmukh position from this or any other single document. For that, we must follow the actual letters of a family over a long period of the seventeenth century. Fortunately, the recent publication of the documents of the Mane family of Mhasvad (in southern Maharashtra, about sixty miles east of Satara, see Map 1) allows this long-term view. First, a cluster of these documents from 1666–67 shows the dependence of the Adil Shah government on the deshmukhs for local military forces and the use of these forces in larger campaigns.

April, 1666

Sayyad Ilias Saya Khan, commander, pleased with the valor of Rataji Narsingrao Mane in repulsing the attack of Mirza Raja Jai Singh on Bijapur, recommended to Ali Adil Shah II [sultan of Bijapur] that the deshmukhi watan of Kasbe Kaladhon be granted to Rataji Mane. So a watan sanad is issued.[31]

The accompanying papers refer to Rataji Mane as deshmukh and sardeshmukh (head of any and all deshmukhs) of both pargana Man and the newly granted town of Kaladhon, entitled to the share of the government revenue given to the sardeshmukh. He was further honored with the grant of the sardeshmukhi of the pargana Mangalavede for his services in the war against the Mughals, and one gold hon from each of ten villages. If we plot these new grants, once again the "nested" pattern emerges. Kaladhon is about twenty miles south west of Mhasvad, while Mangalavede is about forty-five miles east. Both were probably adjacent to the Mane family's core area of Man pargana. Of the villages giving Rataji one hon each year, seven of the ten were within twenty to thirty miles of Mhasvad.

[30] Khobrekar, *Records of Shivaji*, 11–12.
[31] Ibid., 124.

Other papers of the same months illustrate the use of Rataji's troops closer to home.

Ali Adil Shah II writes to Rataji that you have Kasegaon as mokassa [grant] for people working in the faraskhana [police] and the palki-bearers. These villages are troubled by Naiji Pandre, who has claimed that he has the mokassa grant and began collecting the revenue, by force. So, proceed immediately on receipt of the firman [order], with the necessary force and give stern warning to Punjaji Jamadar, who represents said Naiji Pandre. Expel him, and warn him not to come again ... Inform us accordingly.[32]

Two months later, in recognition of expelling Naiji Pandre from his district, Rataji Mane was rewarded with robes of honor from the Bijapur court. "Wear it and be honored; you have done good service."[33] Within three weeks, Rataji was ordered on another mission:

Ali Adil Shah II writes that Narsoji and Yeshwant Rao Mankoji have troubled the people of Malgaon, pargana Kagal [near Santwadi] and have taken shelter with the headman of Benur; recruiting infantry and cavalry, they have plundered Malgaon, collecting 209 cattle and bulls, also some goods. So, immediately on receipt of this letter, proceed to Malgaon. Give stern warning to both these men. Ask them to produce the cattle, bulls, and goods [and] bring them back to Malgaon; deliver them to the people, with the assistance of the muqqadam. Advise the people of Malgaon that they will be given protection, and that there will be no further trouble ... Also capture Narsoji and Yeshwant Rao. Send them here, with necessary guard. See that there will be no further complaints in this regard.

Note that Malgaon is in the Konkan, more than 220 miles from the Mane family base in Mhasvad. In late June, during the monsoon, this would have meant a difficult journey down the Ghats of more than seven days. Whatever convoy took the prisoners to Bijapur would have been gone for several weeks.

In the next year, Rataji undertook two more tasks, using his troops to enforce the authority of Bijapur. At the request of Ali Adil Shah II, he drove out one Kandoji, from a village that had been granted to Kandoji and was now resumed. He was also instructed to warn two Nimbalkar brothers that they should leave the territory as it belonged to Ali Adil Shah II, not Shivaji. Presumably, Rataji completed both tasks, because he was later rewarded with robes of honor.

These tasks and responsibilities highlight the complexity of the deshmukh role. They were the most important source of troops in the

---

[32] Ibid., 129.
[33] Ibid., 130.

countryside, probably more important than troops housed in the forts of the area. We have seen them used to repel invaders, disarm rebels, and join other troops as main-force fighting units of the kingdom. It is important to note the close ties between this loyal family and the Bijapur king, which included personal audiences, many letters, and robes of honor.

In even more troubled times, which characterized much of the seventeenth century, the office of deshmukh became more like high-risk, high-return investment than some imagined stable rural elite position. To illustrate this process, let us briefly consider the history of the Yadavs, another deshmukh family of southern Maharashtra, located at Karad, about half way between Sangli and Satara.[34] The testimony the family gave in 1716 says that they had been deshmukhs of Karad for generations, when the story begins in the first decades of the seventeenth century.[35] (In fact, the Yadav family bought at least some of their earliest rights – perhaps around 1500 – from the Jagdale family which had to raise money for a large gift to the Bahmani king to recover certain estates in the area which had been sequestered. Other rights, especially the deshmukh of Karad, had been added in the seventeenth century.) Perhaps around 1620, one Mudoji Nimbalkar was involved in an unexplained armed dispute with the family, which involved the taking of the fort of Karad; the Bijapur government sided with Nimbalkar, and the whole Yadav family was removed from the deshmukh right.[36] The results were catastrophic. "From that day, our revenue stopped." The family moved to a small village in the same area and threw themselves on the mercy of a relative (perhaps a cousin) who still enjoyed a grant. There is little information on the family for the next two decades. The deshmukh rights of Karad had, meanwhile, been held by several high officials of the Bijapur court and passed to Shahji, Shivaji's father. The Yadavs throughout the middle decades of the

[34] An extensive collection of the Yadav family documents has recently been published by Shivaji University. The broad history of service under the Adil Shahi government is covered in the oral testimony of the division of the family grant, document #332, dated 1716. D. A. Pawar (ed.) *Tarabaikalin Kagadpatre* (Kolhapur, 1969). I am indebted to Shiresh Chitge for collaboration in the translation of these documents.

[35] A fascinating look at the further complexity of the issues comes from Andre Wink's work on the Jagdales, the opposition claimants for the deshmukh rights in the Karad area. He has pieced together the story from a variety of published and unpublished Marathi documents. See *Land and Sovereignty in India: Agrarian Society and Politics under the Eighteenth-century Maratha Svarajya* (Cambridge, 1986), 162–65.

[36] Ibid. The Jagdale documents assert that the Yadavs joined with Nimbalkar in raiding Bijapuri territory and were, therefore, removed from their estates. The results were the same.

seventeenth century appealed to both Shahji and the Bijapur court for the return of the deshmukh rights of Karad.[37] Through patronage of the cousin with whom the family had originally taken refuge, one Yadav son, then the other, was introduced into service in Shivaji's army.[38] For the next forty years, the sons tried to get the deshmukh rights back, appealing to Shivaji (who had inherited the deshmukh right to Karad) and his successors every time that they performed especially important service. The grant was just as regularly delayed and denied. Tens of thousands of gold hons changed hands in this process; the brothers used every patronage network they could develop. It was not until the Maratha state was under mortal attack in 1789 that the negotiations got serious; two villages were granted, but not the deshmukhi of Karad. Finally, the family took service with the Mughals in the early eighteenth century, and it was Aurangzeb who confirmed them as deshmukhs of Karad. Let us draw out several points from this story of the Yadav family. First, it emphasizes that deshmukh rights were intimately intertwined with the politics of the courts; the Yadavs offended the Adil Shah court and were removed. Second, in this case, they had no recourse or income once they were removed. There were no "ancestral" lands to retire to. The family took shelter with a relative and started the long process of service, as ordinary soldiers. This was as serious a loss as we find in the whole political system. In general, we might visualize a continuum of possible family losses for the "wrong" choice in a critical faction dispute at court or an invasion of their area. At the "mild" end would be a fine and prompt reinstatement. More serious would be loss of peripheral rights outside the home area. More serious yet would be loss of some key deshmukh rights, village headmanships, and forts in the home area (constituting what the family felt to be its "watan," the patrimony of rent-free lands and other perquisites). The most serious loss, of course, would be the loss of the entire "watan," as happened to the Yadavs. Third, there was no problem in transferring the deshmukh rights to Muslim members of court or to a Maratha not resident in the area (Shahji and his son

[37] Ibid. The Jagdale documents assert that a gota was assembled in Masur (near Karad) – composed of cultivators, artisans, and Bijapur officials – which established by means of old sanads the rights of the Jagdale family to the deshmukhi of Masur. The Jagdale documents say that Shahji ignored the Bijapur government order to surrender the rights. Understandably, the Yadav documents are silent on this point.

[38] Ibid. Meanwhile, the Jagdale family made the wrong choice of supporting Afzal Khan and the Bijapur army which had come to "control" Shivaji in 1659. After Afzal Khan's defeat, Shivaji's troops took the Jagdale fort and killed the head of the family.

Shivaji). This is typical of the period; many deshmukhi rights were sold or divided during family disputes or the periodic famines – 1630–36, 1650–55, 1690–93, 1710–12.[39] Equally common and more destructive were the invasions and wars of the same period. If we track any region of Maharashtra, it was invaded on the average about every ten years throughout the century. On the other hand, recall that the ratio of cultivators to available land was very low; this means that if a deshmukh was actually able to provide protection, by negotiation or armed strength, the family was likely to be able to recruit and keep peasants from less secure areas.[40]

The recently published Mane family documents allow us to watch this negotiation process at work. (It is perhaps worth emphasizing, once again, the importance of private family documents for the understanding of Maharashtrian history, and the crucial continuing search for and publication of these documents.) In the late 1670s, the Bijapur government was fighting for its life against the Mughal forces of Aurangzeb. Histories most often focus on the battles and sieges, but negotiations with deshmukhs were equally important. Aurangzeb first wrote to Nagoji Mane (son of Rataji) in October 1678 with a vague offer of sardeshmukhi (which he already held from Bijapur) and jamadari (military service grant, but of unspecified size), if Nagoji would come personally to his camp. There the matter sat for seven years; in the interim, Bijapur had fallen to the Mughals. Aurangzeb, the Mughal Emperor, wrote to Nagoji Mane that, as the pargana Man had been recently added to the empire, Nagoji was granted a jagir (grant for military service) of 1,350,000 dams (33,750 rupees). A postscript, added to the bottom of the document, noted that the city of Mhasvad which had been taken from the enemy, "is now under the administration of Nagoji Mane."[41]

If only these documents had been printed, we would assume that the

[39] Khobrekar, *Records of Shivaji*, 95–97. Also, Pawar, *Tarabaikalin*, 488–89, for the voluntary division of the Yadav deshmukh rights. For the sale of rights during famine, see Kulkarni, *Maharashtra*, 96–97.

[40] Many of the terms associated with rural revenue relationships suggest this cycle of depopulation and repopulation much more than stable, secure agriculture. For example, the term "uprari" denotes a non-resident or refugee cultivator in a village. There were, for example, regular methods for them to become landowning peasants if the original land-holders absconded. To cite just one more example, there were regular methods of negotiation and terms offered to try to bring back groups of cultivators who had absconded. A sample of this process is found in the original Modi documents in the Pune Daftar, Peshwa Khandesh Azmas Rumals, no. 187, "account of sardeshmukhi," and no. 198, "warning letter."

[41] Khobrekar, *Records of Shivaji*, 134–37.

Mughal Empire could simply dictate terms to a local deshmukh family like the Manes. Fortunately, the record picks up again ten years later. We find Nagoji and Aurangzeb still haggling about what level of military service and pay he was entitled to, and which other members of the family would be taken into service. Nagoji was holding out for a mansab of 7,000, seven forts in his area, the grant of seven parganas in the area of Mhasvad with rights to try criminal cases, plus a ceremonial drum, elephant, a horse with gold harness, 70,000 Rs. in immediate cash, only one-fourth of his horses to be branded (implicitly acknowledging that he would keep fewer troops than required), and no requirements to provide fodder when the army was in his area. Aurangzeb was offering a mansab of 5,000, payable from the revenues of Berar (far from Nagoji's home area of Mhasvad), and no other relatives in service. A year later, this offer decreased to a mansab of only 3,000. Nagoji finally entered service at 4,000 in 1700. The jagir required both a nazar (gift) on taking it up and surety for good conduct. A year later the surety bond was released, but Nagoji got little of what he wanted – only two of the forts, none of the cash, no gold trappings, and no drum. In another two years, as we shall later discuss, he had shifted sides to the Marathas under Shivaji's grandson Rajaram.[42]

What, then, have we learned from this discussion of the position of deshmukh in seventeenth-century Maharashtra? First, it was a "hinge" position which involved the holder (and his family) in face-to-face contact with both the king and court and the cultivating villagers in his area. Second, the granting of these rights was the principal way any government built and maintained loyalty in what was not an urban-based "high" culture, but rather a fort-based, rural, relatively poor agricultural area. Third, the role of the deshmukh shifted dramatically in times of disputed authority. In the best of times, with stability and prosperity, the deshmukh was much like a government official. His powers and perquisites were spelled out in detail in a written contract (sanad) with the government he served.[43] He assisted government revenue officers in making the settlement in

[42] The full complement of "nested" rights of the Mane family is laid out in a document printed in *Shiva Charittra Sahitya* (Pune, Bharat Itihas Sanshodhak Mandal, 1926–65), v, 845. There is considerable overlap with the list of inam villages presented to Aurangzeb in 1689. See Khobrekar, *Records of Shivaji*, 138.
[43] "Regular" settlements, which measured, classified, and documented land in the deshmukh's area were the time-tested means a central government used to gain information

his area and was responsible for the revenue collection. He tried local civil cases and used his troops to arrest local marauders, or to join main force armies on campaign. His pay was specified and circumscribed by the contract with the state. It is all too easy to see these as the only roles of the deshmukh, because government documents tended to be produced largely in periods of stability, and – as we have discussed – selective publication has overemphasized order, stability, and continuity.

The seventeenth century was far from the best of times, and much of Maharashtra consisted of disputed border areas. These conditions made the deshmukhs much more like high-risk rural entrepreneurs and negotiators than paid bureaucrats in the revenue administration. Many areas were periodically devastated by famine or war; this made the deshmukh right available to a family bold enough or strong enough to defend and repopulate it. Every deshmukh family occupied a strong local fortified house, often several, and trained its youth in warfare. Brave military service also could bring rights, and – as we have seen – long-distance service in fighting a state's enemies could bring considerable enhancement of rights. When the state itself was in doubt through factional conflict or invasion, the position of the deshmukhs was even more powerful, critical, and risky. They were forced to take sides in factional disputes and successions. With troops and support, at a critical moment, they could be king-makers or lose everything. They risked this involvement because they needed the court as much as any faction needed them. It was only the over-arching polity which legitimized their own position of rights to revenue in their area. Even more important, it was the sanad from the court which gave an individual authority over his own kinsmen and the state's backing if they opposed him, as they often did. The history of Maharashtra and the Maratha polity is, thus, the history of these deshmukh families. There is no better summary of the position of these families than by Ramchandra Nilkanth, high official of the Maratha polity and an astute seventeenth-century observer of politics and statecraft. In the *Ajnapatra*, he wrote as follows:

They are no doubt small but independent chiefs of territories. The weak manage to exist by rigidly maintaining the tradition of power though decreasing from the

and a modicum of control. The technique was common to both the Mughals and the Deccan sultanates. See R.F. Alavi, "Murshid Quli Khan's revenue reforms in the Deccan," in *Studies in the Medieval Deccan* (Delhi, 1977), 61–72.

Emperor downwards. But they are not to be considered as ordinary persons. These people are really sharers in the kingdom. They are not inclined to live on whatever watan (rights) they possess, or to act loyally towards the king who is the lord of the whole country and to abstain from committing wrong against any one. All the time they want to acquire new possessions bit by bit, and to become strong; and after becoming strong their ambition is to seize forcibly from some, and to create enmities and depradations against others. Knowing that royal punishment will fall on them, they first take refuge with others, fortify their places with their help, rob the travellers, loot the territories and fight desperately, not even caring for their lives. When a foreign invasion comes they make peace with the invader with a desire for gaining or protecting a watan, meet personally with the enemy, allow the enemy to enter the kingdom by divulging secrets of both sides, and then becoming harmful to the kingdom get difficult to control. For this reason the control of these people has to be cleverly devised.[44]

Taking this perspective, we explicitly reject kingdom "boundaries" as a useful or functional way of understanding the complex political entities of the seventeenth- and eighteenth-century Deccan. Rather, we must see families with clusters of "nested" rights, which are often highly interpenetrated with other families' rights. When a family sought service with a competing faction or another polity, it withdrew a whole cluster of rights – ritual, economic, judicial, military – from one polity and gave it to another. Families shifted loyalty much more on the basis of factional politics than they did on the basis of proximity to something later historians would call a "frontier" with a neighboring polity.

What of villages in this period? We must similarly reject any general description (such as that in dependency theory or world systems theory) of Maharashtra's villages as stable, producing only subsistence agriculture, low in stratification, and participating in little trade. First, subregions within Maharashtra varied considerably in their participation in trade and orientation towards cash-cropping. In the northern areas of Khandesh and Aurangabad, there was, for example, a very old tradition of cotton cultivation and manufacture, which grew considerably under Mughal rule in the sixteenth century. Second, we have seen that Marathas regularly served in the armies of the Muslim Deccan kingdoms. This meant that men of even small villages went on campaign, were often paid in cash, and returned to their village with experience of the outside world. Third, the system of survival in these

---

[44] "Ajnapatra" (trans. Puntambeker), 214. I wish to thank Frank Perlin for several discussions on the importance of deshmukh families for the history of Maharashtra.

troubled times did not stop at the village boundary. Migration was a common response to adversity – war, famine, or drought. These patterns of migration were common until the beginning of this century. Since brothers generally lived in the same village, refuge was, as we have seen, with a more distant male relative. In addition, there was a structured system by which those fleeing personal or local adversity found shelter in any village. They became "uparis," that is, landless laborers welcomed for their addition to village productivity. In time, if they stayed, they might become landholders (mirasdars). Occasionally, refuge or service might also be sought with the wife's family; this is the pattern we find, for example, in the Shinde family late in the seventeenth century. The considerable variation in the actual cultivation found in villages year by year and the explicit records of depopulation and repopulation suggest considerable migration and entrepreneurial activity, rather than a stable, static village. Fourth, we must recall the considerable stratification in Maharashtra's villages in this period. The village headman and the Brahmin records keeper had substantially more land than average, plus rights in kind and service. Also, the grantee of the government's share (a saranjamdar or jagirdar) lived in the village of his rights, and was of a much wealthier family than the surrounding peasants. Like deshmukhs, these village elites were negotiators with considerable power in the fluid system of the time. Finally, we must not forget that ordinary cultivators were not passive victims of larger events, but were often, themselves, negotiators. Yearly, they either accepted the revenue settlement, or rejected it and sent their headman back to renegotiate. More interestingly, the ordinary cultivators could and did reject a headman they found unacceptable, either because he was an unknown outsider or an unsuitable insider (perhaps an illegitimate son of the former headman).[45]

[45] Kulkarni, "Social mobility," 109–10.

CHAPTER 2

MARATHAS AND THE DECCAN SULTANATES

In this chapter, we will turn from the more general discussion of deshmukhs and the political texture of seventeenth-century Maharashtra to specific events of the Sultanates of Ahmadnagar and Bijapur. These set the stage for the rise of Shivaji, the founder of the Maratha polity. Here, we will focus on Shahji, Shivaji's father, who rose from minor commander to kingmaker and general in the middle decades of the seventeenth century.

Before embarking on the specifics of the house of Shivaji, we must look at warfare in the seventeenth century. It will be against this background that the innovations of Malik Amber early in the century and Shivaji later in the century will make sense. The following is somewhat idealized, but is drawn from accounts of warfare in Khandesh and Malwa, and warfare between the Deccan kingdoms. Much of it will be familiar from studies of European, fort-based warfare of two centuries earlier, but there were many local, Indian features.

In the seventeenth century, a main-force army (be it Mughal, or from Ahmadnagar or Bijapur) was a moving city. Based on heavy cavalry, the army had at least three horses for every two riders. Each mounted fighter had at least a servant and a groom. Artillery, which supplemented the cavalry, was physically large and required dozens, sometimes hundreds, of oxen for each piece. We must add to this picture infantry and the full bazaar that accompanied the army and supplied it. There were elephants for the commanders and a large store of treasure to pay the troops, who normally bought their provisions in the camp bazaar. Such an entourage, with everything from saddle-makers to dancing girls, rarely moved more than ten miles a day, usually with two stationary days per week.

An "invasion" meant that the invading kingdom had solved a whole series of internal problems, at least temporarily. The king had settled on a commander and had overcome the factional grumbling of whatever groups had not got their representative selected. The king had enough cash to make the initial payment to the troops, so that the army could move out. He had enough cash or credit (more likely the latter) to sustain the army in the field for a campaigning season. There had been a muster of the royal troops; there were enough to hope to win. Some, if not all, of the subordinate polities (petty rajas, deshmukhs, zamindars) had shown up with their required contingents. By the time all this was assembled, there was – in this best case scenario – still time, before the monsoon, to invade another polity.[1]

At ten miles a day, with months of preparation, it was certainly no secret that an invasion was planned. Newswriters stationed at court would have informed their respective neighboring courts that plans were afoot. The only conjecture would be in which direction the army would move. Anyone whose job it was to analyze the political events, such as the newswriters, made guesses that were often entirely correct. In any case, within days of the start of the expedition, the destination would be obvious.

Depending on the size of the expedition, it might be weeks, or even months, before the army reached territory which could inaccurately be called a frontier. This was a broad band between two heartland areas, in which the deshmukh or petty raja might pay taxes and offer loyalty to either side or none or both, depending on the perceived relative strength of the two kingdoms. "Conquest" of this area meant that the invading king sent messengers to these local powers and local officials to attend his camp with a payment and their sanad of authority in hand. Those who came received robes of honor, and had their authority confirmed by fresh sanads in the name of the invading king.

The invading army next sent patrols to coerce local powers who had not attended court. Months might be spent in these outlying areas. Recalcitrant petty rajas and deshmukhs usually retired to their forts. A well-equipped army (with good artillery and enough gunpowder to sap or mine) could take the smaller of the local forts. The larger ones simply defied the invading army. While besieging a local fort, the commander sent messages to village headmen to attend his camp, pay tribute, and receive confirmation of their grants. Some came and, of course, some did not. The commander then sent out patrols to devastate villages whose headmen were truant. These villages usually did not wait for the patrol, but packed up and left – to the surrounding forested area, to a safer pargana, or to a nearby fort.

---

[1] The problems of getting an army into the field were much more successfully solved by the Mughals than the sultanates of the Deccan. They had cantonments, an officer corps, supply arrangements, and a core of professional soldiers.

Meanwhile, diplomacy with the invaded king's court would reach a fever pitch. The invader would state his demands, such as redress for lands lost in a previous defeat; the "invaded" would prevaricate, or make counter-offers. Envoys and newswriters sent gossip, rumors, hints of possible advantages, and formal proposals.

The invading commander and his ministers had constantly to decide the advantage of staying in a more distant area or striking deeper into the enemy's heartland. Often, the "frontier" areas were not paying propositions; the tribute collected did not match the costs of investing forts or tracking down missing villagers. Also, time was against the invader, with the monsoon coming.

All this time, of course, the invaded kingdom was trying to work out the same problems which had plagued the invader – resolve factional conflict to pick a commander, assemble money, muster the royal and deshmukhi troops. Usually, the invaded kingdom would wait, letting the invader advance well into the heartland. This made for longer supply lines for the invader, put the conflict later into the campaigning season, and often placed the invader among villagers and local powers more loyal to the invaded court.

When the invader began collecting tribute from deshmukhs and villages in the heartland area, the invaded kingdom was forced to respond, and its army moved out. Diplomacy reached a new height, as each side secretly tried to detach sections of the opposing army. There were offers to commanders, possible pretenders to the throne, zamindars, and mercenaries. Frequently, the two armies faced each other, in camp, for months. Envoys passed back and forth, spies circulated, and money and rights changed hands.

Finally, one side or the other faced a problem they could not resolve. It was, for example, getting very late in the campaigning season; or they were running out of money to pay the troops; or factional conflict was becoming impossible to control; or the opposing side was detaching too many crucial troops or supporters. If the invaded king had the more serious problems he could pay a tribute. The invading army would then leave and try to solidify its hold on the "frontier" area, hoping to be back in safe shelter before the monsoon.

Fighting represented a much higher risk for both sides, but, of course, represented the only way the invaded kingdom could gain anything from the situation. The typical battle was short, the tactics not subtle. The armies attacked in "wings" (right, middle, and left), the cavalry going for hand-to-hand combat. Last minute diplomacy might result in a whole wing decamping, joining the opposing side, or putting up only token resistance. Reserves would be directed to places where the line was yielding. As the dust rose, battles became more chaotic and strategy more problematic. Battles usually ended with the person of the king or commander. If he was captured, killed, or forced to retreat, the army broke, leaving baggage, guns, and equipment on the field.

Let us assume that the invaded kingdom lost the battle, but the king escaped. He and his immediate followers retreated to the royal fortress, strengthened the defenses, and waited. Most campaigns ended with the invader taking the booty and retiring, especially if the monsoon was starting.[2]

It took yet another level of commitment, financing, and organization to besiege a large fortress. Defensive warfare had distinct advantages. The fortress had an adequate water supply and was stocked with provisions, often sufficient for several years. Some had enough land inside to grow crops. The fortress had stables and barracks. The besieging army had none of these. Local foraging quickly devastated the surrounding countryside. The situation became worse as the monsoon began. The army was in tents; men and horses suffered. It became nearly impossible for long-distance traders to move caravans of grain to the siege site. All the deshmukh and zamindar units, composed of peasant/soldiers, wanted to go home to plant their fields.

From inside the fortress, the besieged king continued every avenue of intrigue and negotiation to weaken the besieging army. The optimum situation for the besieged king placed some of his army outside the fortress. There, they could attack caravans and encourage peasants to leave the fortress area. Thereby, grain prices would go up in the besieging camp; eventually, there would be famine and disease. Since no one, at this period, had the technical means to take a large fortress, the only hope of the besieger was to bribe a defender to open a gate.

If the siege dragged on through the monsoon, there was less and less likelihood that the fortress would be taken. The invading king had mounting problems. Perhaps he was running out of cash. Worse, factions might be forming back at his capital, and he was not personally

[2] Many of these problems are sketchily discussed in I. H. Ghauri, "Organization of the army under the sultanates of the Deccan," *Journal of the Pakistan Historical Society*, 14, 3 (July, 1966), 147–71.

there to counter their influence. There might be rebellions in his own territory. It is, thus, understandable that few fortresses were ever taken until late in the seventeenth century. It is equally understandable why kingdoms could jockey for position for decades, even centuries, without one extinguishing the other.

It is against the background of this style of warfare that we can now turn to specific events of seventeenth-century Maharashtra. It was here that a new style of warfare, known as bargir-giri, developed. Because the rise of the house of Shivaji (founder of the Maratha polity), the development of bargir-giri, and the fortunes of Ahmadnagar kingdom were so closely tied, we must now consider the thirty-five year "fall" of Ahmadnagar in some detail. Focus will always be on the Marathas in service, rather than the arcane factional politics of a declining state.[3]

We know almost nothing about the house of Shivaji Bhonsle before his grandfather, Maloji. The family's only hereditary grant was the headmanship of a village by the name of Verul, near Daulatabad, probably the village nearest the Ellora caves. Maloji's earliest recorded service was under fellow Marathas, the Jadhavs of Sindkhed, who held grants for military service under the Ahmadnagar kingdom. Maloji was a petty horseman in the service of these Jadhavs. Around 1600, cousins of the Bhonsle family, known as the Ghorpades of Mudhol, were well established in service in the Bijapur kingdom, neighbor and rival to Ahmadnagar.[4]

The death of Burhan Nizam Shah of Ahmadnagar (1594) set off a severe factional struggle at court. Broadly, it pitted the "Deccani" Muslims against the "foreign" Muslims, with the queen, Chand Bibi, forming a third faction. Well aware of these problems, the Mughals invaded from Khandesh immediately to the north (which they had conquered more than twenty years before). In spite of resistance organized by Chand Bibi, Mughal forces under Akbar took the town and fort of Ahmadnagar in 1600. The fall of the capital, however, did not mean the fall of the kingdom. Various nobles had troops and lands to maintain them. The invasion was not vigorously pursued because Akbar was already dying, and the succession war for the Mughal

[3] Good short histories of both the Bahmani kingdom and its main successor states – Ahmadnagar, Bijapur, and Golconda – are found in H. K. Sherwani and P. M. Joshi, *History of Medieval Deccan (1295–1724)*, vol. I (Government of Andhra Pradesh, 1973).
[4] G. S. Sardesai, *New History of the Marathas* I (Bombay, second impression, 1957), 51.

throne took more than five years. It was 1608 before the new Emperor, Jahangir, resumed the conquest of the Deccan.

It was in this breathing space that Malik Amber emerged as the leader of the remaining state of Ahmadnagar. He was an Abyssinian slave who had held a minor position in the army of Ahmadnagar. After the initial Mughal invasion (1594) he tried to find service at the courts of both Bijapur and Golconda, but returned to Ahmadnagar in 1597. At the time of the fall of the capital, Malik Amber held the northern portion of the Konkan coast and some territory inland as far as Daulatabad. The main campaigns by the Mughals were against another leader named Miya Raju, who harassed Mughal forts and troops throughout northern Maharashtra and into southern Khandesh. When the Mughal succession dispute shifted to the north, Malik Amber fought Miya Raju across the Pune-Nasik area, defeating him in 1608. Because most Mughal troops were in the north, Malik Amber's troops regularly raided into the Mughal provinces of Khandesh, Berar, and Gujarat.

After ten years of nearly constant warfare, it was in a short interregnum (1610–12) that Malik Amber did his famous pargana by pargana revenue settlement of northern Maharashtra. For our story, this is also the period when he recruited many more of the Maratha families into his army. They were immediately needed; he fought campaigns against the Mughals and the Portuguese in 1613, and another against the Mughals in 1615.

In February 1616, there was a major battle between Mughal armies and the troops of Malik Amber. In the weeks before the final battle, there was much offering of service in the Mughal army to Malik Amber's Maratha leaders. Many changed sides. Malik Amber's forces lost the battle and he retreated to the fort of Daulatabad. Surrounded by major Mughal armies, he surrendered Ahmadnagar fort and kept much of the rest of his kingdom, but formally submitted to Mughal service the following year.

From 1617 to 1619, Malik Amber rebuilt his territory, recruited troops and caused no problems for the Mughals. In 1619, however, all the main Mughal forces were in the north. The Emperor was in Kashmir and Prince Khurram was reducing the hill fort of Kangra in the Punjab. Malik Amber began a successful operation in northern Maharashtra, taking Ahmadnagar and raiding all the way into Khandesh.

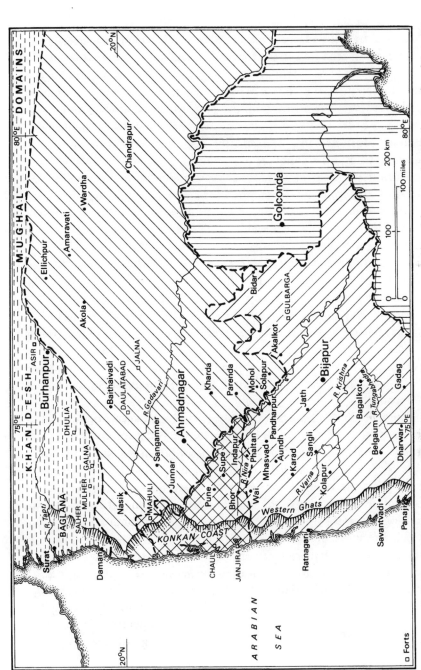

Map 2. Political and military situation of the northern Deccan c. 1615–20 (adapted from Andre Wink, *Land and Sovereignty in India: Agrarian Society and Politics under the Eighteenth-century Maratha Svarajya* [Cambridge, 1986], 87. The boundaries and disputed areas are adapted from Richard Eaton, *Sufis of Bijapur: 1300–1700* [Princeton, 1978]).

Malik Amber's raids deep into Mughal territories finally forced the Mughals to act. The Emperor sent Prince Shah Jahan into northern Maharashtra with a large army in 1620. Malik Amber was defeated in the field, but retreated to the fort of Daulatabad and sought terms. By giving up part of his territory and a large indemnity, Malik Amber was able to carry on the state of Ahmadnagara. Soon Mughal attention again turned to the north, with the succession dispute beginning well before the death of Jahangir, the Mughal Emperor. The Mughal Empire consumed five years in this dispute, before attention could again be paid to the conquest of the south.

During 1621–24, Malik Amber was at war with the neighboring Muslim kingdoms to the south. In a surprise action, he plundered Bidar and laid siege to Bijapur. This is the background to the battle of Bhatvadi in 1624, in which Malik Amber badly defeated the combined forces of the Mughals and Bijapur.

Let us refocus on the Marathas in Malik Amber's army. Maloji, Shivaji's grandfather, served Malik Amber and the fortunes of the remaining state of Ahmadnagar through all of these campaigns. We find only stray references to him, but they are interesting. For example, in 1621 Maloji was serving as an agent for the collection of revenue in the disputed area of Kanad Khore. He died in battle at Indapur, only a year later. By then, his son, Shahji, was also a veteran in Malik Amber's service, and at twenty-six years old, one of the minor commanders of the troops.[5]

There are three important conclusions to be drawn from this period in the history of Ahmadnagar. First, virtually all of Malik Amber's troops were Marathas. This is confirmed both in the Shiva Bharat, a near contemporary Sanskrit poem probably commissioned by Shivaji which lists the units in the battle of Bhatvadi, 1624, and a Tanjore inscription which covers the same material.[6] Second, there was some shifting of service by the Maratha units. This was always the case, but luring the units of the other side with offers of service became an intense part of every pre-battle strategy. For example, before the Battle of Bhatvadi, a few Maratha leaders went over to the Mughal side, including Shahji, who returned to Ahmadnagar's forces just before the battle. The third conclusion to be drawn from this period is the

[5] J. N. Sarkar, *House of Shivaji* (New Delhi, 1978), 27.
[6] P. P. Patwardhan and H. G. Rawlinson, *Sourcebook of Maratha History* (Calcutta, 1978), 5.

importance of Malik Amber's masterful use of guerrilla warfare, which was known as bargir-giri in Dakhni. This consisted of not meeting the enemy main force in the field, but cutting off supplies, maneuvering for the best position, and using superior mobility to strike vulnerable locations far from the battle site.[7] Malik Amber's success in the campaigns of 1619–20, for example, was mainly due to harassing the countryside on which the Mughal army depended for fodder, and cutting off the supply caravans which provided it with food. These tactics were thus common knowledge in Maharashtra a generation before they were elegantly used by Shivaji in the 1650s.

In the period after the battle of Bhatvadi (perhaps because his relatives had been rewarded more than he), Shahji took service with Bijapur, though he apparently retained jagir rights in the Pune region, which was claimed by both Ahmadnagar and Bijapur. Nothing is known of his activities between 1626 and 1628.

Malik Amber died in mid-1626 and the affairs of Ahmadnagar quickly declined into factional chaos. Shortly after, Ibrahim Adil Shah of Bijapur died (September 1627). Without his patronage, Shahji left Bijapuri service. Thus, in early 1628, Shahji returned to Ahmadnagar and entered the chaos of the politics there. We know little of Shahji's service in the court of Ahmadnagar except that he was a higher general than he had been in his previous service. For example, in 1629, Shahji took a force of 6,000 cavalry to create a diversion in eastern Khandesh, but was defeated by a Mughal force.[8]

Towards the end of the 1620s, Mughal attention once again turned to the Deccan and the vulnerable state of Ahmadnagar. The Mughal Emperor Jahangir died in October 1627, and Shah Jahan took the throne in February 1628. His first order of business was to secure the south, particularly to eliminate a powerful Mughal noble who had been an opponent during his rebellion against his father. In February 1630, Shah Jahan crossed the Narmada with a huge army to deal with both recalcitrant Mughal commanders and to extinguish Ahmadnagar.

In the violent factional politics of the court of Ahmadnagar in 1630, Shahji's in-laws and patrons were murdered. Shahji promptly went

---

[7] The Persian term bargir meant a soldier who enlisted without his own horse and thus rode a horse belonging to the king. His status was lower than a silahdar, who brought his own horse and equipment. See S. N. Sen, *The Military System of the Marathas* (Calcutta, new edition, 1958), 4–5. See also J. T. Molesworth, *A Dictionary, Marathi and English*, (Bombay, second edition, 1857), 575.

[8] Sarkar, *House of Shivaji*, 28–29.

into Mughal service with 2,000 cavalry. During the year he was in
Mughal service, he was sent to Junnar and Sangamner (see Map 2),
districts he was ordered to occupy and which were given to him as
jagir. When the jagir was resumed by the Mughal government, Shahji
left Mughal service and began plundering the region around Pune.
The Mughals claimed the area around Pune for several years and sent
an army to defeat Shahji, who fled to safety with the governor of
Junnar.

The period of 1630–32 in northern Maharashtra was quite confused
with frequent changing of sides in the campaign that culminated in the
five-month siege of Daulatabad fort. The countryside was devastated
by the failure of three successive monsoons, culminating in the
Mahadurga famine, which depopulated large areas. Even during this
disaster the war went on. Bijapur sent a large army to the assistance of
Ahmadnagar. It seems that Shahji took service with Bijapur in this
campaign. The combined Ahmadnagar–Bijapur force was, however,
defeated; the Mughals took Daulatabad, and the more powerful
Ahmadnagar generals retired to their lands to continue the resistance.
Shahji retreated from Daulatabad and seized a section of the southern
portion of the fallen kingdom of Ahmadnagar. It consisted of a triangle
formed by Nasik, Pune, and Ahmadnagar. His control was tenuous,
but he was able to offer service to many of the fleeing troops of the
Ahmadnagar state, and quickly formed an army of 2,000–10,000 men.

In the period immediately following (1634–36), Shahji became a
kingmaker. After the fall of Daulatabad, the Mughals sent the nominal
king to prison, but Shahji raised a young boy of the house of
Ahmadnagar to the throne and fought in his name. His forces seized
Junnar fort and much of the northern Konkan within a year. He took
up residence at Junnar fort and increased his troop strength to 12,000.
Late in the year, Shahji began raiding in the vicinity of Daulatabad, and
the Mughals mounted a major campaign to put an end to his resistance.
According to the Shiva-Bharat, the variability of the numbers of his
troops is explained by the coming and going of independent Maratha
contingents – Ghatge, Kate, Gaikwad, Kank, Chavan, Mohite,
Mahadik, Pandhre, Wagh, Ghorpade, and others.[9]

[9] We will return to a detailed discussion of Shahji's son, Shivaji, the founder of the Maratha
polity. Here, we only note the very disrupted conditions at the time of his birth (1630) and
early years. They coincide with the years of the Mahadurga famine, the final collapse of
Ahmadnagar, invasion by the Mughals, and failed resistance by his father. Life throughout
the area east of the Ghats, where he and his mother lived, was precarious at best.

The culmination of this new Mughal campaign was the battle of Parenda (1634) in which many contingents on both sides were Maratha. Families divided. At this time estimates vary on Shahji's strength. A Brahmin newswriter in Bijapur put it as an area yielding 7.5 million rupees, from which he maintained several large forts, including his capital at Shahabad. The same source put his troops at only 3,000 cavalry, with an additional contingent of 2,000 from Bijapur.[10] It is interesting that the areas of Pune and Indapur were not included in these possessions. These areas had been seized by Bijapur from the now conquered state of Ahmadnagar. Shahji's troops were no match for a large main-force Mughal army and were defeated at Parenda. In early 1635, the Mughal forces chased Shahji south from the area of Daulatabad, capturing his supply train and about 3,000 of his men. Within a year, Shah Jahan arrived with a major army to consolidate Mughal control in the Deccan. In three months, the campaign was generally very successful. Shahji and his forces were driven out of northern Maharashtra into the Konkan, losing his cities, including Junnar in the north and Nasik in the center.

We must see the support given to Shahji by Bijapur as the result of a factional dispute which pitted those who favored propping up the failing Ahmadnagar state at all costs against the Mughals versus those who wanted to divide the Ahmadnagar kingdom with the Mughals. As long as the former were in power, Shahji's resistance continued. Power shifted to the latter group in 1635.

In 1636 a peace treaty was concluded between Bijapur and the Mughals. As required by the treaty, Bijapur cut off all support for Shahji. He was finally besieged in Mahuli fort until October, when he surrendered to the Mughals both himself and the Ahmadnagar pretender. As part of the surrender, Shahji was taken into the Bijapuri service and had to surrender the forts of Junnar and Mahuli to the Mughals. Shahji then ceased to be an obstacle to the consolidation of the Mughal conquests in northern Maharashtra. What then was the power situation in 1636, at the conclusion of the treaty between the Mughals and Bijapur? The Mughals held Daulatabad and all the important forts in northern Maharashtra – Galna, Jalna, Ahmadnagar, Udgir – and all the significant forts in Khandesh and Berar. Bijapur

---

[10] Sarkar, *House of Shivaji*, 38–39. The revenue estimate was, of course, the *potential* revenue in the best of times. The area had been badly devastated and the collectible revenue was probably a tiny fraction of that.

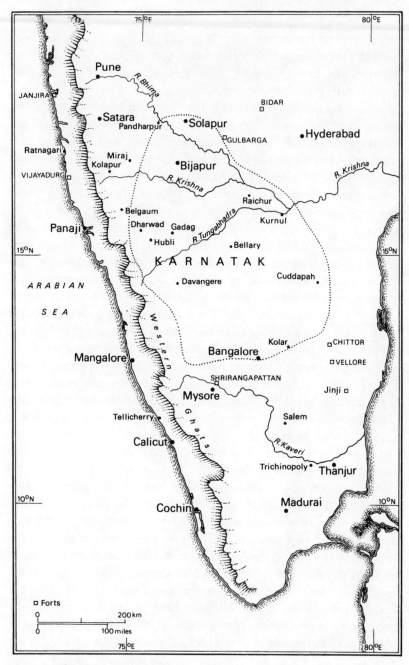

Map 3. The Karnatak region (adapted from *The Times Atlas of the World* [London, 1988], Plate 28).

held the city of Pune, the forts nearby, Indapur, much of the area of central Maharashtra, and all the Konkan.

With Shahji, let us leave northern Maharashtra to the Mughals and shift our focus to the kingdom of his new service, Bijapur. Some specific history of Bijapur is also critical for an understanding of the phenomenon of Shahji and the Maratha movement for independence. It is all too easy to view Shahji in isolation, because he grew up far from the capital in the marginal area of Pune. Still, we must not forget that all the areas involved – Pune, the Ghats – were Bijapuri territory.

As the most vigorous successor to the Bahmani kingdom, we must understand that at the opening of the sixteenth century the Bijapur kingdom was in a phase of conquest. Sultan Ali I (1558–80) had established strong rule over the Bijapur area, developed the bureaucracy, expanded commerce, and built much of the city of Bijapur. Early in his reign, he seized the important forts of Sholapur and Naldrug in southern Maharashtra (see Map 3). After the battle of Talikota (1565), in which the triple alliance, of Ahmadnagar, Bijapur, and Golconda defeated Vijaynagar, Bijapur seized the entire region between the Krishna and the Tungabharda rivers and a large area around Dharwar. In a decade, the kingdom had effectively doubled in size. This conquest provided a partial solution to the king's most important continuing problem, which was the strength of the nobles whose bases were large tracts of alienated land. The king kept much of the new conquests as "crown" lands, increased his bureaucracy to administer them, and used the money to more than double his standing army to 8,000 cavalry.

For our purposes, it is important to know who constituted this new personnel. At the top of both the military and the administration were Muslims. The senior civilian and military post was that of vakil, which later became known as vazier.[11] The top administration was small, and concerned itself mainly with the collection of taxes from the crown lands and the receipt of the fixed tribute from the subordinate states. Beyond these few officials, there were a few major military commanders and the palace officials. Large portions of the best lands in the kingdom were alienated to this elite as "integrity fiefs" (*dar wajh-i-istiqamat*). This elite remained small, in part because the new

---

[11] I. F. Ghauri, "Central structure of the kingdom of Bijapur," *Islamic Culture*, 44, 1 (January 1970), 21. One of the clearest discussions of Bijapur in this period is found in Richard Eaton, *Sufis of Bijapur: 1300–1700* (Princeton, 1978).

Portuguese control of the western coast of India cut off easy immigration from Arabia and Persia; the Mughal Empire likewise limited immigration overland from the north. The result was a major recruitment of local Hindus into both the military and the administration. From this first expansion, Bijapur, like other Deccani states, used local troops in large numbers, not only the levies of the landed families they conquered, but directly recruited main-force cavalry. (This pattern is, as we have seen, equally well documented for the more northerly kingdom of Ahmadnagar.) The new recruits represented a range of local people, predominantly Marathas, but also Lingayats and other fighting groups available after the fall of Vijaynagar. Similarly, Brahmins, especially Deshastas from Maharashtra, and Prabhus, a non-Brahmin writer caste, soon completely dominated the middle and lower levels of the central bureaucracy. They even administered the large "integrity" grants of the Muslim elite of the state.

With the expansion of the "crown" lands and the development of the administrative bureaucracy, we should briefly note an emerging structural problem of the Deccan kingdoms, the ambiguous and difficult relationship of the vazier and the sultan. The vazier was not only the head of the administration, but kept the sultan's seal and could issue orders in his name. The more efficient he was, the more income came to the sultan, but the more the vazier's real power increased. (The parallels to other kingly systems, such as mid-eighteenth-century France should be obvious.) With a vigorous, adult sultan, interested in governing, the vazier would be a loyal official; during a minority rule, or any period in which the sultan was unable to rule (by absence, illness, or disappearing into the harem), the vazier ruled the state. This pattern is clear in Golconda and Ahmadnagar, as well as Bijapur. We note the pattern here because it emerged as a problem when the Maratha polity had lands to administer a century later.[12]

Throughout the reign of Sultan Ibrahim II (1580–1627), we must see in Bijapur a vibrant, syncretist kingdom, its ruler highly interested in Hindu thought and music, its art affected by the many Hindu artisans it employed, and a majority of Hindus in both its army and administration. The capital city, with a population of over 500,000, was cosmopolitan and rich. European traders noted an active export trade in cotton and silk cloth. The cotton came from southern Maharashtra,

[12] I. F. Ghauri, "'Regency' in the sultanates of Bijapur and Golconda", *Journal of the Pakistan Historical Society*, 15, 1 (January 1967), 19–37.

and raw silk was imported from China to be woven and re-exported.[13] At court, even the language reflects this syncretism. The court was dominated by "Dakkanis," that is Muslims who had been living in the south for generations. Their language was a mixture of the Arabic and Persian of their origins, the North Indian Urdu of their past, the Sanskrit of the Brahmins, and the Marathi, Telegu, and Kanada of their subjects. This "Dakkani" language became the official language at court as well as the practical language of the bazaar and the camp. We know, for example, that Ibrahim II spoke better Dakkani and Marathi than he did Persian.

Important to the power structure of the countryside of rural Maharashtra at the time of Shivaji's boyhood were the forts, especially those scattered along the Ghats. Bijapur has been characterized as a kingdom of cities and forts. As a kingdom, this is only partially true. The sultan's direct appointees controlled only the large, strategically important forts. (Many smaller forts and fortified houses were held, as we have seen, by indigenous deshmukh families, mainly Marathas.) The large forts had villages attached to the grant for the maintenance of the fort and its complement of soldiers. This practice was equally true for northern Maharashtra, and had been for the whole period of Ahmadnagar's rule. For example, it was the Maratha garrison troops who turned over Daulatabad to the founder of the Ahmadnagar kingdom at the opening of the sixteenth century.

What of the Bijapuri presence in the countryside? It was thin and infrequent. First, there were the twenty-two tributary states, which paid only a fixed tribute each year; there was no Bijapuri presence inside these areas at all. Much of the best remaining land, as we have seen, was alienated to high nobles. They stayed at court or were on military assignment; their lands were administered by their Brahmin bureaucracy. In the directly administered "crown" lands, there was a unified military/civilian administrator called a havildar whose authority was over several parganas and whose residence was in the largest town in the area. His responsibilities were primarily notifying the villages of any change in the jagir grants that affected them, plus overseeing the tax settlement and collection, examining the forts, and reviewing the troops of the lower military leaders.[14] Even the presence

---

[13] Sherwani and Joshi, *History of Medieval Deccan*, 263–64.

[14] This system is considered in detail in the early chapters of S. N. Sen, *The Military System of the Marathas* (Calcutta, reprinted edition, 1976).

of this administrator was minimized by a policy of frequent shifting of posting. Outside the river valleys, which were the most settled and prosperous areas and kept as crown lands, Muslim Bijapuri presence was even less. In Shahji's father's parganas in the relatively less fertile Pune and Ghats area, there was little, if any, ongoing Bijapuri presence.

In contrast to the more settled area of southern Maharashtra under Bijapuri control, northern Maharashtra had little remaining government infrastructure, as a result of steady warfare between the Ahmadnagar kingdom and the Mughal forces from 1600 to its conquest in 1630. The countryside around Pune, Nasik, and Ahmadnagar had changed hands at least ten times between 1600 and 1635. The only lasting features were villages, often under the walls of some fort, with a citizenry used to "fight or flight." Most other villages had suffered through the long-standing tactic of devastating civilian villages in enemy areas to deny the enemy both grain and revenue, and to draw off attacks from one's own areas. Malik Amber, who ruled the declining state of Ahmadnagar from 1610–25, as we have seen, raised this tactic to a high art in the process of holding off the Mughals for nearly two decades. The remaining villages often yielded revenue and revenue information only by force, and repeated force at that. Village headmen, like the deshmukhs, were never paid from the government treasury. They had tax-free lands in the village and a portion of the harvest. Yet it is important to remember that Malik Amber's land revenue system gave a pervasive pattern for recovery from devastation; also important was the flexibility of the system, the ability to handle cash or kind when there was no cash. The continuity and importance of Malik Amber's settlement is confirmed in the 91-Kalami Bakhar, one of the principal Marathi sources of the period. In the discussion of the measures of Dadaji Kondev to promote recovery in Shahji's devastated lands around Pune, the stepwise increasing taxes end in the eighth year with no specified amount per cultivated bigha, as the earlier years had; they simply specified "Malik Amber's settlement." This was the standard for fully cultivated fields throughout northern Maharashtra. Thus, though the land was devastated, the blueprint for recovery and taxation was common knowledge.[15]

[15] For the details of the Malik Amber settlement, see A. R. Kulkarni, "Towards a history of Indapur," in D. W. Attwood, M.Israel, and N. K. Wagle, City, Countryside and Society in Maharashtra, (Toronto, University of Toronto, 1988), 132.

Let us consider the possible strategies of a Maratha military family in response to this situation, which had the following important features:

(1) A relatively low level of monetization and trade
(2) A declining economy that bottomed out with the region-side famine of 1630, leaving many areas underpopulated or depopulated
(3) The fall of Ahmadnagar to Mughal conquest
(4) A vigorous and growing state at Bijapur
(5) Declining numbers of foreign Muslim recruits in the armies of Bijapur, making the Maratha units relatively more important

Probably the most common strategy was one that combined agriculture at home and loyal service in the army of Bijapur. Both had their potential rewards. In a situation of serious underpopulation, those remaining had the opportunity not only of cultivating the best lands, but also of becoming the local officials with all the attendant rights. Bijapur also offered favorable tax situations for the opening of new cultivation. Consider the advantages of combining this agriculture with service in the army of Bijapur. Service provided ongoing employment in years of agricultural scarcity; service gave the opportunity, even in good years, for some members of the family to make a living outside the region. Service also secured jagir grants over lands in Maharashtra, as well as status. There was also the possibility of grants in more prosperous areas outside Maharashtra, such as the Tunga-bharda valley or coastal Konkan.

Of the many Maratha families which chose to serve Bijapur, we have only a few names (mainly those prominent in later Maratha history), such as the Savant of Savantwadi, the Ghorpades of Mudhol, the Nimbalkars of Phaltan, the Mores of Javli, the rulers of the later Maratha princely state of Jata, and the Shirke, Mohite, and Man families.[16] There were, however, thousands recruited into the Bijapur regular army, whose names we do not know. If we can generalize from the few families we can trace, the Marathas presented themselves alone or in small groups, such as two brothers or several cousins. If this was in fact the pattern of recruitment, then the influence of Bijapuri service would have been widespread throughout Maharashtra and touched most families and villages.

[16] These families are listed in the *Shiva Bharat*, a contemporary Sanskrit poem. It has been translated in Patwardhan and Rawlinson, *Sourcebook*, 5.

During peacetime, the government maintained some long-term control over the families by arbitrating the common, ongoing disputes over rights and service grants.[17] From the government's point of view, families, especially families of deshmukhs, were possible supplemental units to the regular army, which cost almost nothing from the government treasury. The key word here is "possible." Whether the men of a particular family actually joined the main-force army depended on the season of the year, relations between the family and various factions at court, patronage of a particular Maratha general in the Bijapuri army, and the internal politics of the family.

Other strategies opened to families in certain situations, such as a serious factional dispute at the court. This situation was particularly common in the history of Bijapur. Few of its sovereigns lived longer than thirty years, so that a minor was often on the throne. The regency, as we have seen, became the focus of severe factional politics, as the regent asserted power against other groups, frequently also trying to gain the throne. Opposition usually centered on the queen-mother. Courted by one side, then the other, a well-placed Maratha family might extract much more favorable terms in return for their soldiers. Equally likely, the family might fissure, some portion going with each of the factions. Such common crises might end in one of several ways. First, the king might take control and demote the regent. Second, the regent might be assassinated by jealous followers. Third, the regent might be imprisoned after a successful coup by the opposition. Fourth, the regent or the opposition might call in an outside power. It was, for example, this sort of crisis that invited Mughal conquest in the 1680s.

Finally, a Maratha family might take up open rebellion against the state it served; this, however was possible only in special circumstances. The government had to be preoccupied with other matters, such as a succession dispute or repelling a serious invasion. Also, the area of the rebellion had to be easily defended against government main forces, such as in the mountains, where artillery could not be used and supply lines were long. It probably helped if the area was not very productive of either grain or revenue. All these factors came together in Shivaji's movement of independence in the mid-seventeenth century.

With this perspective on other families in Bijapuri service, let us once

---

[17] Many of these are mentioned in V. T. Gune, *Judicial System of the Marathas* (Poona, 1953), 64–65. See also G. H. Khare, "A letter of assurance from Ali Adil Shah I," *Indian Historical Records Commission* (October 1945).

again focus on Shahji, and his service with Bijapur. As part of his initial jagir grant, Shahji managed to get the rights to the Pune region.[18] These districts, as we have seen, had suffered particularly badly in the 1630s, being repeatedly ravaged by Mughal troops. They were almost depopulated by the late 1630s.[19] By the terms of the Mughal–Bijapur treaty, Shahji was himself barred from staying in Maharashtra, so the administration was granted to his son, Shivaji, then ten years old, with Dadaji Kondev as manager. It is worth emphasizing that the rights that Shahji had in the Pune region were a mixture of village headman rights, deshmukh rights, and the jagirdari rights, held subject to satisfactory service with the Bijapur government.

The same treaty which introduced Shahji into Bijapuri service had, of course, much wider effects. By freeing Bijapur from the threat of Mughal conquest from the north, Bijapuri could turn to conquest in the south. Each campaigning season (1637–40), a Bijapuri army crossed the Krishna and the Tungabharda into Mysore. Shahji was one of many leaders in the army of Rustam-i-Zaman, the Bijapuri general charged with the conquest of Malnud. This Bijapuri army defeated the nearby nayaks (local chiefs left after the demise of Vijay-nagar) and took Bangalore in 1639. Shahji was left to hold Bangalore and settle the surrounding area. Shahji's strength was the band of sea-soned veterans who had been with him throughout the wars of the last decade. He also had Brahmin administrators, used to collecting taxes in the countryside. Shahji thus set about creating a whole new estate, based on the city of Bangalore. Bijapuri documents in the India Office Collection show that the first of many conflicts that Shahji was to have with the Bijapuri court happened that year. Muhammad Adil Shah, the Bijapuri ruler, ordered the deshmukh of Lukmeshar to co-operate with the commander Sidi Mooflah, so that the "relations, dependents, servants and horses of Shahji might be arrested."[20] Unfortunately, we have no further details. Shahji's force was, however, unable to hold the area, once the main Bijapuri army moved on. In 1641, there was a general uprising of the Hindu rajahs. Shahji jointed the main Bijapuri army, under the command of Afzal Khan, and, for example, was involved in the assault on the newly fortified

18 Sarkar, *House of Shivaji*, 41.
19 A. R. Kulkarni, *Maharashtra in the Age of Shivaji* (Poona, 1967).
20 Ghauri, "Organization of the army," 46.

Basavapatan, held by Keng Nayak. The fort was taken along with several others, including Velore, in this campaign.[21]

We know little about Shahji's activities between 1642 and 1645. Sometime between 1642 and 1644, Shahji's estranged wife and his son, Shivaji, visited Shahji at Bangalore. Besides arranging Shivaji's marriage, Shahji had the whole family, including Shahji's two sons by his second marriage, presented at the court of Bijapur. Shivaji and his mother returned to Pune after a few months; nothing is known of the conversations between father and son. In 1644, the war was once again renewed, centering on the fort of Ikeri, which had been taken back by the local raja, after conquest by the Bijapuri forces. Throughout, it is possible that Shahji's troops were involved, but they do not appear in the military dispatches of Bijapur; it is also possible that he stayed mainly on his jagir lands at Bangalore.

In order to understand Shahji's arrest by the Bijapuri government in 1648 it is important to understand the continuing tension between the government and powerful nobles, like Shahji. There is little documentation, but a paper found by Jadunath Sarkar in 1930 in a family archive near Pune gives more detail than anything else we have. It is a letter to Kanoji Nayak Jedhe, who was the deshmukh of Bhor (twenty miles south of Pune). He was commanded to assist representatives of government in pursuing and annihilating Dadaji Kondev, who was Shahji's agent in the Pune area. The reasons were explicitly laid out. "Shahji Bhonsle has become a rebel against this court" and his agent, Dadaji Kondev, was campaigning in the Kondana district. The combined government forces were to take control of the district. The order was written in August 1644.[22] We know no further details of the expedition or the immediate results. It does, however, suggest that resistance to Bijapuri control began well before Dadaji Kondev's death, when Shivaji took control of his father's jagir in the Pune region. There is clear evidence in the Bijapuri papers that a similar sequence took place just a few years later in 1646, but again no details are given.

These confiscations (1639, 1643, and 1646) are the background leading to his arrest in 1648. Basically, the nayaks of the south (Madurai, Jinji, Trichinopoly) were trying to gain freedom from their overlord, Sri Ranga III of Vijaynagar. In the process, they courted

---

[21] Sarkar, *House of Shivaji*, 54.
[22] J. N. Sarkar, "An early supporter of Shivaji," *Indian Historical Quarterly*, 7 (1931), 362–64.

Bijapuri help. Forces from both Bijapur and Golconda invested Jinji. It was at this protracted siege that Shahji was arrested. Shahji, as one of the top leaders, was taking an independent course, which angered the commander, Mustafa Khan. Shahji had been negotiating with the various nayaks, and had even asked to go into service with the Golconda government. Perhaps other Muslim nobles were jealous of his growing power in the Bangalore area or his role in negotiating for the Hindu nayaks of the south. It is clear that in 1648 he was one of only two Maratha generals with a very high position in the army. It was also a period in the history of Bijapur when there was a swing back towards orthodoxy after the syncretist reign of Ibrahim II (1580–1627).[23] By the late 1640s, his successor, Muhammad, was already weak from a lingering illness that was to kill him in 1656. Factions struggled for power. In this atmosphere, policy shifts were rapid; it is understandable why Shahji was brought to the capital in chains and forced to give up his two most important forts (Kondana – renamed Sinhagad and near Pune – and Bangalore), only to be pardoned by the ruler within a year. The Maratha histories such as the Shiva Bharat would have us believe that the father was imprisoned for the rebellion of his son, Shivaji. There is plenty of evidence to the contrary, that it was largely, if not exclusively, an internal political problem for the Bijapuri government. The position of Shivaji is never mentioned in Bijapuri descriptions of Shahji's misdeeds, capture, imprisonment, or release.

We have little information on Shahji, from any source on the years between 1648 and 1660. We know that the wars between Bijapur and the Hindu nayaks of the south continued, with Bijapur generally successful. The fall of the fort of Jinji in late 1648 was the beginning of much more pressure on the kings of Madurai and Thanjur. Shahji was apparently no longer stationed at Bangalore, but at Kanakgiri, near the old Vijaynagar capital. His son, Ekoji, remained at Bangalore. Shahji and his forces fought in the war between Bijapur and Golconda. One son, Sambhaji, was killed during a revolt by the Rajah of Kanakgiri (1654).[24] The major events of the period were the death of Muhammad, the ruler of Bijapur, and the subsequent chaos at the court. Many high nobles withdrew their land and loyalty from Bijapur and took service with the Mughals. The Mughals, under the new Emperor Aurangzeb,

[23] Eaton, *Sufis*, 95–96.
[24] Sardesai, *New History*, 87.

immediately made plans to annex Bijapur. This is the context of the Shivaji bid for independence, which became visible and unavoidable by 1655.

In another section, we will consider Shivaji's actions from the inside, looking outward from the Pune region at the surrounding threats and possibilities. For now, let us take the viewpoint of the Bijapur court and see what they tried to do about the "Shivaji problem." The court tried various tactics to bring Shivaji into line. The documentation is scrappy, but the first tactic was to separate father from son. The new ruler "reassured" Shahji that the offences of his son would not reflect on him; all his grants would be continued.

26 May, 1658. At this time it has been reported to His Majesty that owing to the disloyalty and audacity of Shivaji Bhonsle you are alarmed lest his faults should be laid on your head. Be it known to this loyal subject that the improper conduct and acts of Shivaji are evident to His Majesty. Therefore, the faults of Shivaji will not be laid on you, but his offences are being imputed to him only.[25]

In fact, the same reassurance document gave Shahji back the area around Bangalore fort which he formerly had as a jagir.

In the period 1659–62, after the defeat of the army under Afzal Khan sent by Bijapur to defeat Shivaji, Shahji actively mediated between his son and the Bijapur government. Shahji also travelled to Pune to try to work out a peace settlement; it was the first time father and son had been together in twelve years.[26] It was also the last time, as he died in a hunting accident in early 1664.

We will now move from the large scale to the small, from the politics of Bijapur and the invasions of the Mughals to the small town of Pune, from the plains to the mountains; we move from the complexities of service to a more simple life of hunting and horseback, and from Shahji, the father, to Shivaji, the son and founder of the Maratha polity.

[25] Sarkar, *House of Shivaji*, 84.
[26] There has been considerable speculation in the historical literature that Shahji and his son Shivaji were in contact throughout the period, and, in fact, developed joint plans for the independence of Maharashtra. To date, however, no direct documentary evidence of such contacts or plans has surfaced, although the Jedhe Chronology and the later Chitnis bakhar offer indirect hints. We are left with the dominant position in the historiography that Shivaji acted alone and even in opposition to his father.

CHAPTER 3

SHIVAJI (1630–80) AND THE MARATHA POLITY

Let us begin, then, the narrative biography of Shivaji, founder of the Maratha polity. (Throughout, I have kept to incidents corroborated in at least two of the most reliable bakhars or confirmable by outside sources.) The accomplishments of this extraordinarily capable and charismatic leader must always be set against the complex context laid out in the previous two chapters. The most important features of this context were as follows: (1) the near devastation of much of Maharashtra; (2) warfare between the major states of Bijapur and the Mughal Empire; (3) his father's deep involvement in Bijapur; and (4) the presence, in Maharashtra, of powerful deshmukh families whose authority was as legitimate as his.

Shivaji was born in February 1630.[1] He was the second son of Shahji Bhonsle and Jijabai, and he was born in the hill fort of Shivneri in the northern part of the Pune district. Recall that these years of Shivaji's early childhood were ones of constant warfare and famine in Maharashtra, particularly the Pune region. Shahji, his father, was a rebel from brief Mughal service, and a Mughal army pursued him through the Ghats and down to the Konkan. Other campaigns against the Mughals followed, but Shahji's forces, reinforced by Bijapur, were generally unsuccessful against the Mughals. Shivaji and his mother moved from fort to fort. His mother's family had gone over to the Mughal side, and mother and son saw little of Shahji. It was not until 1636, when Shahji was forced to go into service with Bijapur, that Shivaji and his mother were able to settle in Pune.

Shahji, as we have seen, succeeded in getting a grant in the Pune region confirmed by the Bijapur government, the administration of which was bestowed on Dadaji Kondev. The core of the rights was the hereditary patil rights (village headman) to three villages in the Pune

---

[1] Until recently, there was some question about Shivaji's birth date because the near contemporary *Jedhe Chronology* placed it in 1627. The correct date has recently been corroborated by his birth horoscope; a copy taken at the time of his birth was recently found in Rajasthan. Raghubir Singh, "Correct date and year of Shivaji's birth – fresh evidence from Rajasthan collections," in B. R. Kamble (ed.), *Studies in Shivaji and His Times* (Kolhapur, 1982), 11–28.

district and the deshmukh rights of Indapur, some seventy miles south-east of Pune. The family was, thus, a deshmukh family, though not a large one. Beyond these hereditary rights, Shivaji's father also held the mokasa of the Pune region. In Bijapuri parlance of the day this meant a hereditary grant of the government's share of the revenue, whether in cash or kind, for maintenance of troops. Shahji's family was not, for example, the hereditary deshmukh of Pune. This mokasa grant was a triangle bordered by the Nira river on the south, the Bhima river on the north-east, and a portion of the Ghats on the west. It ran almost a hundred miles north to south and the same east to west, and is almost the same outline as the current Pune district (see Map 1).[2] As we have seen, the forts were held separately by families which held grants from the Bijapuri government. Very little is confirmable about Shivaji's early years. The Pune region was largely devastated by two decades of warfare and the famine of 1630. Dadaji Kondev, as steward, set about repopulating and developing the jagir. There is every indication that this was not a peaceful process: "On coming, he [Dadaji Kondev] took possession of the twelve Mawals. The Mawle Deshmukhs were seized and taken in hand, the refractory among them were put to death."[3] We should not be surprised that force was needed; the area's deshmukhs had resisted one claimant to the area, then another, for several decades.

In 1640, Jijabai and Shivaji were called to Bangalore, and Shivaji was married to Saibai, a daughter of the Nimbalkar family, another of the prominent Maratha families. During these early years, Shivaji had not seen his father. In 1642, after formal presentation at the Bijapur court, Shivaji and his mother returned to Pune. All we know of his training was that it included some reading and writing, riding and the martial arts expected of a jagirdar's son, and both the popular and high tradition religious practice of the times. He probably participated in the efforts of Dadaji Kondev, the steward, toward repopulating the jagir and repairing the infrastructure.

In 1644, Shivaji (as we have seen, a high commander in the Bijapur army) was involved in a factional dispute that resulted in his arrest and the sequestering of his estates, including Shivaji's. The Bijapur government instructed two nearby chiefs, the Khopde and Jedhe deshmukhs,

---

[2] G. S. Sardesai, *New History of the Marathas* (Bombay, second impression, 1957), 98.
[3] From the Shabasad bakhar, as translated in S. N. Sen, *Life of Siva Chhatrapati* (Calcutta, 1920), 3.

to seize the estates, but apparently the order was withdrawn before being implemented. During this time, Shivaji explored the hills surrounding his jagir and became familiar with large areas of the Ghats, and – significantly – took the hill fort of Sinhagad, which commands Pune.

In 1647, Dadaji Kondev, the steward of Shivaji's jagir, died, and Shivaji took over the administration. One of his first acts directly challenged the Bijapuri government. Shivaji, through stratagem (or perhaps bribery, depending on the text) took the fort of Torna, and seized the large treasure he found there. In the next two years, Shivaji took another important fort near Pune, Chakan, which guarded the northern road into the city. Meanwhile, he used the money found at Torna to build a new fort five miles east of Torna, on the crest of a hill. He named it Raigad, and it served as his capital for over a decade. All challenges were possible because the Bijapuri government was in crisis due to the illness of the reigning king. Shivaji in these same early years also struck against rival Maratha families in his area.

At a place in the mahal of Supe, was his uncle, his stepmother's brother, named Sambhaji Mohite. The Maharaja had appointed him to the charge of the mahal. Shivaji went to see him on the pretext of asking for a "post" on the day of the Simga festival. The uncle was thrown into prison. He had three hundred horses of his own stable and much wealth. All of his belongings and clothes were taken possession of, and Supe annexed.[4]

Shortly after, Shivaji raided the town of Junnar, capturing three hundred horses and "goods worth three hundred hons," besides clothes and jewels.

In 1648, Shahji was once again arrested, not for Shivaji's activities, but for a conspiracy (which may or may not have been real) involving the kingdom of Golconda; Bijapur, Shahji's employer, was trying to conquer Golconda and Shahji was accused of conspiring with the enemy to at least delay the campaign. There was, in fact, little that Shivaji could do to free his father. He appealed to the Mughals, resident at Ahmadnagar, to invade Bijapur, and offered his services in return. The offer was not accepted. He also repulsed a force from Bijapur, near Purandar fort. Within a year, Shahji had been released, and Shivaji continued his consolidation of his father's jagir. He won over the fort commanders of Baramati and Indapur, and more importantly, took the fort of Purandar (some twenty miles from Pune).

4 Ibid., 3–4.

At that time, died a Brahmin named Nilkantha Rav, commandant of the Adilshahi fort of Purandar. His two sons began to quarrel with each other [about the succession]. The Raje [Shivaji] went to Purandar to mediate between them. And he possessed himself of the fort by imprisoning the two brothers. He established his own garrison there.[5]

It was shortly after the taking of Purandar fort that Bijapur finally sent an expedition to deal with Shivaji as a rebel. This was at the same time that Shivaji's father Shahji was imprisoned at Bijapur for conspiring with Golconda. Without siege equipment, the Bijapuri force was unable to dislodge Shivaji from Purandar fort.

Between 1650 and 1655, Shivaji recruited deshmukhs and soldiers and successfully crushed opposition to his control of the Pune region.[6] During this time, there was little external opposition from Bijapur because the king remained sick, and the only focus was the continuing war with Golconda.

The following year (1656), Shivaji broke out of his father's jagir with new conquests just to the south. Athwart the Ghats was a jagir controlled by the More family. They held long-standing "nested" rights from Bijapur. Shivaji had been steadily undermining their power by courting low level officials (village headmen and other grant holders) by offering better terms. He also offered "aid" to one member of the More family in a succession dispute. The upshot was a full-scale war between the followers of Shivaji and the followers of the Mores. Shivaji gained the Johar valley, and finally the fort of Javali after a siege of a month. The tactics were brutal, including conscious treachery on Shivaji's part. By May, Shivaji had taken Raigad, the strongest fort in the area, and four of the More brothers were killed in battle. This campaign, the bakhars all agree, was pure conquest and elimination of a rival, as Shivaji had no legal rights to the More lands. Shivaji acquired much more than a fort in the campaign. He gained enough treasure to build another fort, which he named Pratapgad, near Raigad. Further,

[5] Ibid., 5.

[6] These events are described in the *Jedhe Chronology*, a near contemporary source, translated in P. P. Patwardhan and H. G. Rawlinson, *Sourcebook of Maratha History* (Calcutta, 1978), 35. It is interesting that Ramchandra Nilkanth, the author of the *Ajnapatra*, a famous Marathi treatise on statecraft, who was an observer of these events simply characterized these recalcitrant deshmukh families – Mores, Shirkes, Savants, the Davlis of the Konkan, Nimbalkars of Phaltan – as "rebels" and listed them along with Shivaji's other enemies, namely the Muslim Deccan kingdoms, the Mughals, the European powers, and chiefs of the Karnatak. "The Ajnapatra or royal edict" (trans. S. V. Puntambekar), *Journal of Indian History*, 8, 1 (April, 1929), 86–87.

he controlled eight important passes that traversed the Ghats from the Desh to the Konkan coast.[7]

This period, 1655–60, was an extraordinarily confused time in both the politics of the Bijapur state and in the larger politics of the whole of Maharashtra. For more than a year, the king of Bijapur lay dying, and factions formed and reformed, trying to seize power. Meanwhile, Bijapur was under attack by a major Mughal army, under the leadership of Aurangzeb, son of the Mughal Emperor, Shah Jahan. In the face of what seemed an unstoppable attack on Bijapur by the Mughals, Shivaji opened correspondence with Aurangzeb, offering to keep passes open and his services in return for recognition of his rights in the Pune region and the former More lands. At the same time, however, he raided several areas in the Junnar and Ahmadnagar regions, which were under the control of the Mughals. The situation abruptly changed, when, in 1656, Aurangzeb left for the north to fight for the throne of the Mughal Empire on the death of Shah Jahan. Shivaji responded to the situation by further conquests. From the More lands which were on the top of the Ghats, he raided down into the northern Konkan and captured the towns of Kalyan and Bhiwandi and the large fort of Mahuli (see Map 2). The exact status of these lands was ambiguous because of the abrupt departure of Aurangzeb for the north. Bijapur, by the peace treaty of 1657, had ceded to the Mughals all territory it had conquered from Ahmadnagar. This included the northern half of the Konkan coast; there was no time, however, to set up an administration. Shivaji could, therefore, claim that he was seizing the territory in the name of the Mughals, on the basis of his offer to serve them.

The raids on the coastal plain were highly successful and first brought Shivaji to the attention of the maritime powers on the west coast of India. In briefest summary, these consisted, first, of the Portuguese based at Goa and holding several smaller ports (Chaul, 20 miles south of Bombay, Daman, 100 miles north of Bombay, and Diu on the south coast of Saurastra) and forts (such as Bassein and Salsette near Bombay). Through superior guns and navigation technology, the Portuguese had been a terror of the western coast (though much less effective on the remaining coast of India) through much of the sixteenth century, forcing the indigenous ships to pay for "passes,"

---

[7] Patwardhan and Rawlinson, *Sourcebook*, translation of the Shabasad bakhar, p. 66. Translation of the 91-Kalami bakhar, p. 67.

and generally attacking and opposing the various Muslim groups involved in shipping. Portuguese trade (mainly cotton textiles from India to south-east Asia) and attempted monopolies (mainly pepper and spices) had, however, never been able to support the required forts and military ships; the practice of taking "enemy" ships had placed the Portuguese in adversarial relationships with every government and family which sponsored shipping. By the mid-seventeenth century, however, the Portuguese power was in decline and their hold on the seas had been successfully challenged. The second power on the western coast was the Dutch; using superior naval technology, they had blockaded Goa and other Portuguese ports in the first decades of the seventeenth century, and, by mid-century, had captured several crucial Portuguese strongholds, both on the Indian coast and in south-east Asia. Simultaneously, the British – a third power – were exploring the same trading territory. They found themselves in a generally weaker position than the Dutch, especially in securing pepper and spices, and were forced into exploring the interstices of trade to south-east Asia and directly to Europe. Large-scale naval warfare between the British and the Dutch began in 1630 and continued off and on for fifty years.[8] On the west coast of India, the British at mid-century were large traders at Surat, the Mughal port at the mouth of the Tapti river. They were developing cloth exports of Indian textiles directly to Europe. Bombay had yet to be given to the British crown.[9] In addition, the strongest actual power on the Konkan coast was not these well-known European trading nations, but the Sidis of Janjira, an Abyssinian Muslim family who held sea forts and some large nearby land possessions, and maintained an extensive navy to protect its merchant shipping.[10] (In general, all these coastal powers were able to establish themselves because the major land powers – the

---

[8] O. C. Kail, *The Dutch in India* (Delhi, 1981), 44–45.

[9] S. A. Khan, *Sources for the History of British India in the Seventeenth Century* (New Delhi, 1978). It is interesting to compare the position of British traders at the same period in coastal China. They were not able to establish their own trading cities or to dominate the coastal trade. They had to trade in existing Chinese arenas and patterns and had almost no impact on the interior. It was strong political opposition which limited their influence.

[10] The Sidis' strongest fort was Janjira, the sea fort about forty miles south of Bombay. In reality, the Sidis held as much legal authority as anyone else in the region. They had been feudatories of the Ahmadnagar kingdom, then switched allegiance to Bijapur when Ahmadnagar was conquered by the Mughals. At mid-century, they controlled much of the coastal area behind Janjira in what is now Raigad district of Maharashtra. See V. G. Dighe, *Peshwa Bajirao I and the Maratha Expansion* (Bombay, 1944), 43–45.

Mughals, Admadnagar, and Bijapur – derived little of their income from and were in the main unconcerned with seaborne trade.) It was this complex coastal world which Shivaji entered, when he invaded the coastal regions of the Konkan in 1657.[11] In spite of campaigning in the northern Konkan, Shivaji was unable to alter the fundamental power relationships. He could neither displace nor defeat the Sidis of Janjira, and needed to maintain friendly relations with the Portuguese as he was at war with both Bijapur and the Mughals.

By the end of 1659, Shivaji was, therefore, in control of the Pune area, the northern Satara district (immediately to the south) and about half of the Kolaba and Thana districts, which form the Konkan coast below the Pune and Satara districts. He controlled forty forts, large and small, led a cavalry of 7,000 regular horse, and infantry of approximately 10,000, and 3,000 independent troopers.[12]

Let us pause to consider the sort of polity that Shivaji was carving out in the Pune region. Many of the major writers on the subject would have us believe that Shivaji was creating a Hindu state, something fundamentally different and in opposition to the Muslim states that surrounded it. The Brahmin historians of the twentieth century, starting with Rajwade, especially wanted to prove that Shivaji was guided by Brahmin advisors from early in his life, and that he had a vision of a state based on something called Maharashtra Dharma. Much of this, if not all, has been shown by later research to be an artifact of the researchers, not a fact of the period. The only articulation of a "Maharashtra Dharma" is in a text that predates Shivaji by four hundred years. Further, it details only the relations between castes, not

---

[11] This discussion relies on much recent research which can only be suggested here. See, for example, M. N. Pearson, *Merchants and Rulers in Gujarat* (Berkeley, 1976). Also, Ashin Das Gupta and M. N. Pearson (eds.), *India and the Indian Ocean: 1500–1800* (Oxford, 1987). Also, K. N. Chaudhuri, *Trade and Civilization in the Indian Ocean: An Economic History from the Rise of Islam to 1750* (Cambridge, 1985). For the specifics of relations between Shivaji and the Portuguese, see P. S. Pissurlencar, *Portuguese Mahratta Relations* (Bombay, 1983).

[12] Shivaji vigorously resisted the common cultural ethos of "gifting" much of his territorial gains to his army. It is interesting to contrast Shivaji's early army, which was mainly recruits riding Shivaji's horses, with armies built up in Tamilnadu at the same period; these were mainly assembled by some sort of "service" to a king, from which the "gift" of a landed income followed. These "inam" grants varied from a few quite large ones to thousands as small as a few acres, for the support of a single trooper; they constituted most of the cultivated area of the kingdom. See N. B. Dirks, *The Hollow Crown: Ethnohistory of an Indian Kingdom* (Cambridge, 1987), 42–47, 168–95.

any sort of a Hindu political program. Finally, there is no evidence of any connection between the text and Shivaji.[13]

Let us consider the alternative, that, initially, Shivaji was not innovating, but only building power much like any other state at the time. First, on the matter of administration, all of Shivaji's appointed officials such as Peshwa, Muzumdar, and Sarnobat were the same as those found earlier in Ahmadnagar or the Bijapur state. In tax collection there were no innovations. He made stepwise increasing settlements, which ended in "Malik Amber's settlement," the famous measured settlement of the late Ahmadnagar kingdom. There is no concrete evidence that he surrounded himself with Brahmin advisors; to the contrary, recent evidence has shown that he did not meet the main candidate for the role of advisor, Ramdas, until 1672. Finally, there is considerable evidence of the Muslims that Shivaji welcomed into his state from the earliest times. For example, the court proceedings of 1657 list the names of the Muslim qazis (judges) who were on salary to adjudicate cases. At the same time, Shivaji welcomed Muslim recruits into his army. The first unit was a group of 700 Pathans, who had left Bijapur after the treaty with the Mughals.[14] Individual Muslims also rose high in Shivaji's army, such as Sidi Ibrahim, who was one of ten trusted commanders at the confrontation with Afzal Khan (to which we shall shortly turn), or Nurkhan Beg, who was Shivaji's sarnobat at this time. It is a question to which we will return at the end of this chapter, but tentatively we see little difference between the emerging polity of Shivaji and the surrounding states. It is only those who must see Shivaji as the perfect Hindu king who will not allow that he learned and absorbed from the Muslim states around him, slowly formulating an idea of freedom and kingship that differed from the surrounding Muslim states.

The events of 1657–59 had been equally important for Bijapur. With the departure of Aurangzeb for the north had come a treaty between Bijapur and the Mughals which secured Bijapur's northern borders from further Mughal invasion. Bijapur's succession dispute had, likewise, been more or less resolved with the accession of Ali Adil Shah

---

[13] For an older articulation of the argument, see Lala Lajput Rai, *Shivaji The Great Patriot* (Delhi, 1980), translated and edited by R. C. Puri, 236–37. The most definitive statement on Shivaji's relationship to Ramdas, in specific, and Maharashtra Dharma, in general, is by A. G. Pawar, "Shivaji and Ramdas," in A. G. Pawar (convener), *Maratha History Seminar* (Kolhapur, 1971), 51–79.

[14] Rai, *Shivaji*, 90.

II. While the king was a minor, leaving open all the problems of a regency, at least there was a king, and some action could be taken. Shivaji's movement for independence was high on the list of problems. Bijapur finally took action in 1659. Afzal Khan led an army of about 10,000 troops into the Ghat region to crush Shivaji. As the representative of the Bijapur government, the local lineages were also required to furnish troops and supplies. Probably the most important event of the campaign came early, even before Afzal Khan met Shivaji's forces. On the march from Bijapur into Maharashtra, Afzal Khan detoured to desecrate Hindu sacred places, especially Pandharpur, the most important pilgrimage site in Maharashtra. This behavior was unprecedented for a Bijapuri force; it reflected the sectarian orthodoxy that was growing in the declining state of Bijapur. It also alienated the local deshmukhs from whom Afzal Khan would have gained invaluable local knowledge. He presumed that he did not need this local support because he had been in charge of the Wai region and knew the area well. From May to November, both sides maneuvered, Shivaji retreating to the fort of Pratapgad and stationing his forces in the jungles of Javli. Afzal Khan's army was much more suited to open plains warfare; the heavy cavalry could not move well in the mountain passes. He also did not have adequate siege equipment. Shivaji on his side knew that his forces could not defeat Afzal Khan's in a battle on the plains. So, Afzal Khan surrounded Shivaji in the fort and waited. There were limits on both sides. Shivaji had limited stores in the fort, but Afzal Khan was getting no supplies from the countryside. Extended negotiations finally produced a solution. Shivaji agreed to meet Afzal Khan, but at a place strategically favorable to Shivaji, beneath the walls of Pratapgad, in a clearing in the dense forest whose trails were known only to the Maratha defenders. It was a locale in which Afzal Khan could only bring his immediate guard of 1,500 men, and the meeting was set up under a truce so that the two leaders would meet in an enclosure virtually alone. Both men came to the truce meeting armed. Shivaji was wearing chain mail under his clothes and a metal skull-protector under his turban. In one hand, he carried a short sword and in the other sharpened iron claws. Certainly, Shivaji had every reason to be suspicious. In a parallel situation, a decade earlier, Afzal Khan had used just such a truce ceremony to imprison a Hindu general. The exact sequence of events in the truce tent will never be known, but the story forms one of the most enduring and stirring stories of Maharashtra.[15] It was long performed as a popular ballad at village festivals, and still is the subject of films, plays, and school text books. The two men fought and Shivaji disemboweled Afzal Khan with the iron claws. After Shivaji killed Afzal Khan, on a signal, his troops fell on the unsuspecting Bijapuri army, which they slaughtered. Incidentally, there is every indication that many of the Bijapuri troops were Marathas, loyally serving Bijapur, as they had for hundreds of years.

Shivaji's defeat of Afzal Khan escalated the conflict with Bijapur. The sultan immediately dispatched another army, under the command of Afzal Khan's son, Fazal Khan. Meanwhile, in the absence of Bijapur authority, Shivaji raided into the south Satara district and further south into the north Karnatak. Also, he managed to take the large fort of Panhala, near Kolapur. The Bijapuri army was generally ineffective until command passed to Sidi Jauhar (another of the Sidi family, this one the subahdar of the Karnul region in the central Karnatak). The considerably reinforced army blockaded Shivaji inside Panhala fort. He and only a small band of followers escaped by night to Vishalgad fort, while a small band held off the pursuing army in a narrow pass. Like the Afzal Khan incident, the defence of the pass is one of the incidents in the life of Shivaji that is celebrated in popular story. The campaign reached no conclusion, with Shivaji safe in his fort, and the Bijapuri army restive to leave the Desh region.

It was in the period after the defeat of Afzal Khan that Shivaji put serious effort into consolidating his hold on the Konkan. He realized the importance of naval power and built a fleet of small fast ships. While they could not challenge a large European warship, they could capture merchant shipping. The main purpose of this fleet was, however, like the construction of several sea forts, to challenge and contain the Sidi of Janjira. Though he expanded control in the Konkan, Shivaji – because of ineffective artillery – was unable to defeat the Sidi in this or any later period of his reign.[16]

Before turning to Shivaji as a problem for the Mughal Empire, let us

[15] This story and other popular ballads are found in H. A. Ackworth, *Ballads of the Marathas* (London, 1894).

[16] G. T. Kulkarni, "The Mughal struggle for occupation of Talkonkan (1660–1662)," in Kamble (ed.), *Studies in Shivaji*, 57–59. A good, older discussion of Shivaji's efforts to build a navy, in order to defeat the Sidis, is found in J. N. Sarkar, *Shivaji and his Times* (New Delhi, 1973), 245–75. The best modern study is B. K. Apte, *A History of the Maratha Navy and Merchantships* (Bombay, 1973).

consider the ways that a state like Bijapur could have disciplined someone like Shivaji and, more generally, strategies for cutting off rebellion. First, there was the offer of service in the army, either personally or with followers. This was, as we have seen, the most effective long-term strategy. It did not work in the case of Shivaji; he never accepted service in the Bijapuri army, preferring to develop his own control of the Pune region. The next level of pressure by a government like Bijapur was to sequester the estates of the offending noble. This was a common strategy; it meant the end, generally temporarily, of employment, income, status at court, the opportunity for booty, the ritual status within the villages of the grant, and the ability to pay troops. For anyone truly integrated into the state system, sequestering required a relatively swift resolution, say six months to a year. This kind of discipline was several times quite effective with Shivaji's father, Shahji, precisely because he was integrated into the Bijapuri army. Only two options were open to a noble like Shahji. If the dispute was not resolved, he either took service with a rival state or retired to his lands, expelled the state officials, and went into open rebellion. Shahji had far too much vested in service with Bijapur and his estates in the Bangalore region to switch to another state or retire to his lands and fight. Shivaji's case could not have been more different. His estates, indeed, were sequestered, but it did not really matter since he was not integrated into the Bijapuri army and did not derive his income and status from service. Knowing the nature of these states and the service involved, it is understandable that Shahji disavowed his son's activities and told the Bijapuris to do what they wanted with Shivaji.

Sequestering an estate was a simple, administrative act; actually seizing it was a different matter. Bijapur had few troops in the countryside, and those were stationed in forts. The next strategy, to put down a rebellion, was to seize the person of the rebel. Again, this was often not difficult when the noble was at court. Shahji was, thus, captured twice. Shivaji, however, never resided at court so this gambit was not possible. The next option for the state was to command a loyal noble in the region of the rebel to actually seize the estate. Bijapur tried this, and the short and decisive war between Shivaji and the More family must be seen in this light.

It was only after these strategies had failed to bring in the rebel that a state like Bijapur would consider sending an army. The rebel had to be not only holding his own estates, but attacking nearby territory, because that threatened other nobles and the tax base of the state. Still, armies were for conquest, which would provide new lands for maintaining nobles. Putting down a rebellion was a purely losing proposition; at best, it regained some territory already assigned. There were other reasons that the state was extremely reluctant to put an army into the field against a rebel. It was categorically more expensive than using a nearby noble. It also involved all the problems we have discussed in the general section on warfare in the period. A successful campaign might well shift the power balance at court; so might failure. In the field, such an army's best strategy was probably to overawe the rebel, simply demonstrating by numbers and strength the futility of the rebellion. This was the approach taken by Afzal Khan when a Bijapuri army finally took the field against Shivaji. Shivaji's strategy, of killing the leader during truce negotiations, while bold, also had an edge of desperation; up to that point, Shivaji knew that the Bijapuri army was, in fact, putting down the rebellion and his army was incapable of meeting Afzal Khan in the field.

For the Mughals, Shivaji was an inherited problem. By the treaty of 1657, as we have seen, Bijapur had ceded all the territory they had taken from Ahmadnagar during the past two decades. Included in the ceded territory were most of the districts that Shivaji in fact held. Nothing could be done about the situation during the long succession war following the death of Shah Jahan. Shivaji sent several letters to Aurangzeb during 1658 and 1659. He asked for his "ancestral" lands in return for providing 500 trained troops to the Mughal armies protecting the imperial boundaries, and rights to any area of the Konkan that he might conquer from Bijapur. Aurangzeb offered pardon and asked for proofs of his loyal service.[17] Aurangzeb finally defeated the other contenders for the Mughal throne in mid-1659 and sent his maternal uncle, Shaista Khan, to the Deccan to put affairs in order. Neither side was prepared to honor any "agreements" of the previous two years. Shivaji raided into the southern Konkan in 1659. Meanwhile, Shaista Khan secured the districts of Ahmadnagar and the North Konkan coast, capturing the fort of Kalyan. Up on the Desh, the Mughal army devastated Shivaji's home districts around Pune. Shaista Khan offered service grants to Shivaji's commanders in return for seizing territories

---

[17] J. N. Sarkar, *House of Shivaji* (New Delhi, 1978), 121–23.

in the Desh and the Konkan.[18] There the situation remained until April 1663, when Shivaji executed a daring night attack on Shaista Khan's camp. Four hundred followers slipped into the Mughal camp, attacked the person of Shaista Khan, killed his son and a number of followers, and escaped into the night.

A letter from Shivaji to Aurangzeb's "officers and counsellors" written in this period gives a clear picture of Shivaji's faith in the difficult terrain of Maharashtra to protect his kingdom from Mughal conquest. Why, Shivaji asked rhetorically, have your officers, in three years of campaigning, been unable to succeed here?

My home, unlike the forts of Kaliani and Bidar, is not situated on a spacious plain, which may enable trenches to be run [against the walls] or assault to be made. It has lofty hill-ranges ... everywhere there are nalas hard to cross; sixty forts of extreme strength have been built, and some [of them are] on the sea coast.[19]

In spite of continuing Mughal pressure, Shivaji launched an attack on Surat within a few months of the night attack on Shaista Khan. The sack of Surat is well documented from European accounts, and, as sacks go, less violent than many.[20] It was, however, cut short when news of an approaching Mughal army reached the city and Shivaji fled with the high-value booty.

The twin insults, the defeat of Shaista Khan and the sack of Surat, turned Shivaji from a minor regional irritation to a major problem for the Mughal Empire. Particularly the attack on Surat had to provoke a response; Surat was the main port of the Mughal Empire. Both the nobles and the Emperor himself backed cargo ships which left from the port, carrying cotton cloth, opium, tin, and the like, and large numbers of pilgrims left for Mecca.

The Mughal response came in the form of a large army, probably 14,000–15,000 trained troops, commanded by Jai Singh, one of the best

[18] Kulkarni, "The Mughal struggle," 59–64. We should recall that it was the Sidis who in fact controlled most of the North Konkan, and both Shivaji and the Mughals were "offering" territory to commanders who would conquer it.

[19] Ibid., 125.

[20] There are several accounts of the sack of Surat in Surendranarth Sen, *Foreign Biographies of Shivaji* (Calcutta, second revised edition, 1977). M. N. Pearson has argued that Mughal "decline" began with Shivaji's twin insults of the attack on Shaista Khan and the sack of Surat which "forced" the Mughal Empire to shift its focus to a major campaign in the south; only the familiar show of Mughal military force could maintain the aura of invincibility and thereby the loyalty of the crucial mansabdari elite and the respect of surrounding empires, such as Persia. See "Shivaji and the decline of the Mughal Empire," *Journal of Asian Studies*, 35, 2 (February 1976), 221–35. It seems, however, that the plan for the conquest of the Deccan kingdoms was a "given" well before the rise of Shivaji.

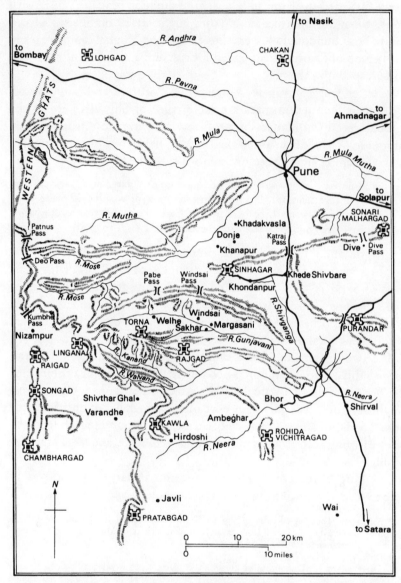

Map 4. Main roads and forts of the Pune region c. 1660 (adapted from Ramesh Desai, *Shivaji, The Last Great Fort Architect* [Bombay, Government of Maharashtra, 1987]).

Mughal generals of the period. Through 1665, Jai Singh pursued a multi-pronged offensive against Shivaji. Columns of Mughal cavalry devastated the countryside of Shivaji's jagir around Pune. Shivaji's army was unable to face these columns in the field. Meanwhile, Jai Singh took a number of Shivaji's important commanders into Mughal service, as well as individual cavalrymen, thus sharply reducing Shivaji's troop strength. When Shivaji broke out into the Parenda region, the Mughal army did not follow, but systematically began to reduce Shivaji's forts. Unlike any previous army in the region, the Mughals had the technical expertise to build siege equipment, and had experience in taking forts by sapping, mining, and by storm. Thus they took the large fort of Purandar, in spite of a gallant defense by the commander. By June 1665, Shivaji was trapped in a fort, effectively surrounded by the Mughal army (see Map 4).

Let us leave Shivaji in his fort and Jai Singh in his siege camp and look at the wider geopolitical perspective. Fortunately, there is wonderful documentation for such a venture with the publication of the detailed dispatches of Jai Singh while he was on campaign in Maharashtra along with the replies of the Mughal Emperor Aurangzeb.[21] From these dispatches, it is clear that the larger objective of the Mughals was the conquest of the two remaining Deccani sultanates, Bijapur and Golconda. There was, however, recognition that Shivaji was an important factor to be dealt with. He had forts and a standing army of at least 10,000 men. Jai Singh's major fear was that he would drive Shivaji into a triple alliance with Bijapur and Golconda, making the conquest that much more difficult. As the military commander on the spot, he was worried about a simultaneous war on two fronts. So, the plan was to first neutralize Shivaji, then proceed with the war against Bijapur.

How, then, did this overall plan devolve into strategy? Jai Singh first isolated Shivaji from Bijapur and Golconda. Both had given Shivaji considerable aid in the campaign against the Mughals. Bijapur had, in fact, offered Shivaji formal recognition of the southern Konkan if he would send his brother's son into Bijapuri service.[22] Jai Singh successfully promoted the idea at the court of Bijapur that Shivaji was a rebel from both empires, and both had an interest in suppressing him. Then,

---

[21] Jagadish N. Sarkar, *The Military Dispatches of a Seventeenth Century General* (Calcutta, 1969).
[22] Ibid., 18.

Jai Singh pursued the military campaign very vigorously, both in the capture of forts, and in the devastation of the lands belonging to Shivaji. This had the effect of showing to other landed elite families the power of the Mughal Empire. With this understanding of the larger perspective, let us return to the siege.

Jai Singh refused many offers of negotiation, demanding Shivaji's unarmed visit to his tent. Finally, Shivaji had to agree to the terms. The Mughals took twenty-three of Shivaji's forts, including most of the major ones, leaving him twelve forts, including his capital, Raigad. The treaty also confirmed that all Shivaji's lands and possessions were subject to loyal service to the Mughals. His son, Shambhuji, was created a high Mughal mansabdar of rank of 5,000. Shivaji was to pay four million gold hons, if he was confirmed in the possession of lands in the Konkan, after the presumed Mughal conquest of Bijapur. These lands were currently of ambiguous status; they had been ceded to the Mughals by Bijapur in the treaty of 1636, but Bijapur had refused to turn them over. They were, in fact, divided between Shivaji (mainly in the South Konkan), the Sidi (mainly in the North Konkan), and remaining Bijapuri nobles and officials.[23] Finally, Shivaji was exempted from attendance at Mughal court. While the Mughals resumed all of Shivaji's lands, leaving him only the twelve forts, the Treaty of Purandar was not a surrender of Shivaji to Mughal imperial might, but the result of extended negotiation which reflected the power realities of Maharashtra and Jai Singh's overall strategy for the conquest of Bijapur and Golconda. Jai Singh also hoped for an immediate impact on the landed families of the region.

Seeing the rectitude in the words given by me, the slave of your majesty, and the granting of leave of Shiva to depart, now all the zamindars of the Karnatak and the wild people of Barkol and Kanul, etc., have sent their agents, just as one captured deer draws many wild and forest deer. And they are waiting for hints or signs and for the sake of the Bijapuri expedition. It is absolutely necessary to conciliate them and give them hope to get their watan [homeland].[24]

After the rainy season, as a Mughal commander, Shivaji was given orders to conquer the Panhala fort and region from the Bijapuris, and the Phonda fort inland from Goa. His troops succeeded in neither

---

[23] Sarkar, *House of Shivaji*, 144. The actual letter from Jai Singh to Aurangzeb is translated in Jadunath Sarkar and Raghubir Singh, *Shivaji's Visit to Aurangzib at Agra*, Indian History Congress Research Series, 1 (Calcutta, 1963).

[24] Sarkar, *Military Dispatches*, 19.

venture. They did, however, take the fort of Phaltan and take some control of the southern Konkan area.[25]

This whole period well illustrates the important differences between Shivaji's army and the Mughal army of the time. Shivaji's army came to be more and more a rapidly moving light cavalry which was backed up by forts as places of refuge. The strength of such an army was its speed, being able to travel fast and light, striking at unexpected places far from home base. Thus, the army was most effective precisely at raids, such as the ones into the Konkan or the major one on Surat. It could cut off supply lines to enemies or generally devastate enemy areas thought to be safe. The army was weak, however, because it had no ability to take forts by storm, sapping, or mining.[26] The armies also lacked provisioning facilities, so they were often forced to "live off the land," a strategy which did not endear them to peasants who had to provide the grain. The final weakness of such an army was the difficulty in establishing regular rule. Shivaji could not provide the protection to cultivation and trade which would have made the area prosper. The area continued the economic decline that had started with the wars of a half century earlier.

On the Mughal side, the army was mainly heavy cavalry, backed by siege equipment and large-scale provisioning facilities. The initial encounter showed the Mughal advantages – the ability to take Maratha forts, the better training of the Mughal cavalry, the loyalty of regularly paid troops, and the ability to hold territory by a well-worked out system of negotiation and treaty with both locally powerful lineages and local officials. In this initial encounter, the Mughal weaknesses were not yet obvious – the fragility of the supply lines, the potential for factional strife in the command of armies, the factionalization caused by bringing into the Mughal army groups like the Marathas, and the need for large amounts of cash, which were not met by a poorly monetized and devastated region like Maharashtra. For example, the cash needs for the capture of Purandar fort were Rs. 30,000 for salaries, plus an unnamed amount for shot and equipment; the occupation of the ceded forts required hiring 5,000–10,000 foot soldiers on a monthly salary. Within two years, an imperial order forbade grants in the

[25] Sarkar, *House of Shivaji*, 153.
[26] The technology of sapping and mining had been used by the Deccan sultanates for at least a century, but was neither routine nor efficient. See I. A. Khan, "Origin and development of gunpowder technology in India: A.D. 1250–1500," *The Indian Historical Review*, 4, 1, 26–27.

Deccan that carried cash salaries; only jagirs based on land were to be granted.[27]

By the end of the monsoon 1665, Jai Singh did not like the drift of the situation in Maharashtra. One of Shivaji's main commanders had been lured to the Bijapuri side, and could only be bought back with an expensive Mughal service grant. Jai Singh worried about Shivaji similarly defecting. This situation set the stage for Jai Singh's suggestion to the Mughal Emperor Aurangzeb that Shivaji be forced to visit Agra, the Mughal capital. After much negotiation and Jai Singh's guarantee of his personal safety, Shivaji, his son, and a small party of 250 troops set out for Agra in early May of 1666.

An eye witness, at the capital, was impressed with Shivaji's contingent.

A large elephant goes before him carrying his flag. An advance guard of troopers also precedes him; the horses have gold and silver trappings. The Deccani infantry too marches before him. In this manner he has come to Agra, with the whole of his contingent moving with great care and pomp. He has two female elephants saddled with haudas which follow him. A sukhpal [i.e., a sort of palki with a dome-shaped top] is also carried before Shiva; its poles are covered with silver plate, and all its tassels have large hanging knobs of silver. His palki is completely covered in silver plates. With this spendour has he come.[28]

Let us pause while Shivaji and his entourage are making their way north to Agra, to discuss chauth and sardeshmukhi, two revenue claims central to the development of the Maratha polity. Both these terms emerged in Shivaji's negotiations with Jai Singh and both have been much discussed in the historical literature. The term chauth, it seems clear, was current in the Maharashtra of Shivaji. In the documents of Daman (on the coast, about 100 miles north of Bombay) the Portuguese, for example, paid chauth to the nearby Ramnagar Raja, in return for his not raiding the territory of the Portuguese. Chauth, a kind of protection money, was contingent on stopping the depredations of other raiders. The Portuguese withheld it when the Ramnagar Raja failed to stop raids by a nearby Koli Raja. The chauth was in 1659 offered to Shivaji, if he could stop the Koli raids.[29]

---

[27] *Selected Documents of Aurangzeb's Reign: 1659–1707 A.D.* (Hyderabad, 1958), 62.
[28] Sarkar and Singh, *Shivaji's Visit*, 31.
[29] S. N. Sen, *Administrative System of the Marathas* (Calcutta, third edition, 1976), 71. A portion of the revenue, given by the king, to the subduer of rebels is also the sense in which the term chauth is used in a much older document from Bidar, see G. S. Sardesai (ed.), *Selections from the Peshwa Daftar* (Bombay, 1935), XXXI, no 1.

It was likely from this source that Shivaji developed his definition of chauth as simply a quarter of the government's share of the produce of an area. It was to be paid in return for not devastating the area. It was protection money, extorted yearly from areas outside Shivaji's immediate jurisdiction, mainly those controlled by Bijapur and the Mughals. This claim was such a direct challenge that no government could concede chauth and retain dominant control of the countryside.

Shivaji's claim of sardeshmukhi was equally interesting. Thereby, he claimed to be head of the deshmukhs, the dominant families in parganas (whose position we have discussed in some detail in Chapter 1). The term appears in the Malik Amber settlement of much of northern Maharashtra. This settlement generally divided the revenue, two-thirds to the cultivator and one-third to the government, plus 10 percent of the government share to the king, as "sardeshmukhi."[30] The position of the sardeshmukh was also well known in the Bijapuri system, and, though occasionally granted to noble families, it was mainly seen as the personal prerogative of the king.

Shivaji began these claims in the early 1660s. For example, he claimed sardeshmukhi rights in Junnar and Ahmadnagar. Shivaji had no legal claim to sardeshmukhi rights anywhere in Maharashtra, as he possessed limited deshmukhi rights and no formal rights of kingship. His claims in the Pune region rested mainly on the military grant to his father from Ahmadnagar (by 1650, absorbed into the Mughal Empire). So, sardeshmukhi, which Shivaji defined as 10 percent of the government's share of the revenue, was – like chauth – an audacious claim to revenue and dominance over the deshmukhi families of central Maharashtra. It allowed him to send agents into the countryside to discover revenue information and make contact with village headmen; perhaps more importantly, it gave him an excuse to invade any nearby region, since sardeshmukhi was rarely voluntarily paid. It must be emphasized how bold and defiant were these claims to chauth and sardeshmukhi for one on his way to Agra to meet the Mughal Emperor.

At the Agra court, things went badly from the very first day. The initial audience provoked a crisis. Shivaji was brought forward in the audience and gave one thousand gold mohars and two thousand silver rupees as expected presents to the emperor. The emperor neither spoke

[30] A. R. Kulkarni, "Towards a history of Indapur", in D. W. Attwood, M. Israel, and N. K. Wagle, *City, Countryside and Society in Maharashtra* (Toronto, Centre for South Asian Studies, 1988), 132.

to him nor acknowledged his presence. Shivaji was then made to stand with relatively low-ranked nobles. He made a scene, refused the honorary robes offered to him, and stalked out of the audience hall. Except for the intercession of a powerful noble, Shivaji and his son would have been killed within days. Even with a high noble's surety bond for his good behavior, Shivaji was confined to his house while factions attempted to influence the emperor's decision regarding his future. All of this well illustrates the difference in Shivaji's position as perceived by Shivaji and by the Mughal Empire. Shivaji already perceived himself as a king with lands, forts, subjects, and an administration. To the Mughal Emperor, however, Shivaji was only a relatively successful rebel zamindar from Bijapur. Jai Singh was quite explicit about this in his letters to Aurangzeb. "Shiva is a zamindar and the pillars of his zamindari [that is, the Bijapur State] will not endure beyond a period of seven or eight years."[31]

Within a fortnight all possibilities seemed grim. Shivaji was running out of money to bribe nobles to work on his behalf. Court gossip said that if he ever left Agra, he would be posted to Kabul; there was a strong likelihood he would be murdered along the way. This posting was confirmed; Shivaji refused to leave, and the order was cancelled, but the situation further deteriorated. In the ensuing indirect negotiation, Shivaji asked for all his forts back, in return for becoming a mansabdar in Mughal service; Aurangzeb demanded all his remaining forts, before even considering making him a mansabdar. Once again, orders to kill Shivaji were only rescinded by the intervention of Jai Singh. In despair, Shivaji asked that his men be allowed to return home, and he allowed to retire to Benares as a sannyasi. This request was also denied. A week later in early July, Shivaji's entourage was, at last, allowed to leave for the Deccan. Finally, Shivaji was able to negotiate a loan of 66,000 Rs. from his patron at court and managed to escape. Aurangzeb's urgent enquiries, over the next several months, uncovered no particular plot or escape route through the three sets of guards surrounding Shivaji's residence. The emperor strongly suspected Kumar Ram Singh, but nothing was ever proven.[32]

[31] Sarkar, *Military Dispatches*, 15.

[32] Sarkar and Singh, *Shivaji's Visit*, 50–61. There is the widely quoted and charming story that Shivaji, feigning illness, began distributing large baskets of sweetmeats to Brahmins of the city. Both he and his son escaped captivity by hiding in baskets of sweetmeats that were sent out of his house. There is, however, no evidence in the contemporary newswriters' reports that this was more than one of many speculations of his escape route. More likely, he simply bribed the guards.

With at least one night's head start, Shivaji was able to elude pursuit by travelling off the main roads in the tribal area east of Malwa. He arrived in Maharashtra in just a month, though seriously fatigued and sick from the trip. At Agra, all his goods and jewels were confiscated.[33]

It is hard to overestimate the opportunity which the Mughal Empire lost at this point. There was much misunderstanding on both sides. Aurangzeb knew perhaps too much of the Deccan, the Marathas, and of Shivaji. He could not conceive of supporting Shivaji, in his attempt to extract loyalty from the deshmukhs, as probably the only way to keep his loyalty. This policy might have treated the Marathas as the Rajputs had been under Akbar. The cultural gulf between the Mughal court and the Marathas made this unlikely, as did Aurangzeb's increasing Muslim sectarianism.

Back in the Deccan, Shivaji did not immediately attack the Mughals. Quite to the contrary, the following three years were ones of peace with the Mughals. Shivaji offered his submission to Aurangzeb, sent his son to enroll as a Mughal mansabdar, and sent a small contingent to serve at Aurangabad. He recognized that a Mughal main-force army of the style of Jai Singh's would once again overwhelm the forces available to him. Until 1669, Shivaji's campaigns were minor, centered on consolidating the Konkan, and failed in their main aim, which was the capture of the sea fort of Janjira.

The peace broke down in the fall of 1669. The immediate provocation was a Mughal demand for recovery of the costs of Shivaji's trip to Agra. Shivaji launched rapid attacks to recover the lost forts in his claimed territories. The first and most spectacular success was the capture of Sinhagad fort. It was taken by scaling very difficult walls by means of rope ladders in a night raid which culminated in hand-to-hand combat inside the fort. The raid was led by Tanaji Malusare, who was killed in the battle. The exploit is the subject of one of the most popular Marathi ballads, still current today. Within six months, Shivaji's forces had taken four more forts – Purandar, Rohida, Lohgad (see Map 4) and Mahuli (see Map 1). In October of 1670, Shivaji sacked Surat for the second time, once again obtaining much booty. Throughout 1670, he raided into Khandesh, Berar, and Baglan. These are the districts immediately to the north of Maharashtra and had been solidly under Mughal control, Berar and Khandesh for more than

[33] Sarkar, *House of Shivaji*, 169.

seventy-five years, Baglan for about forty years. Early in 1671, Shivaji's forces captured both Mulher and Salher forts in western Khandesh (see Map 2); these were crucial for control of the trade routes to Surat and were bitterly fought over in the course of the next few years. At the same time, he was able to expel Mughal forces from Nasik, immediately to the south of these forts and from his home areas around Pune. In 1672 and 1673, the focus shifted to south-east Maharashtra and war with Bijapur. Bijapur was in the midst of another succession crisis, with the death of Ali Adilshah II. Shivaji's forces sacked Hubli and took Panhala fort, one of the strongest forts in the Bijapur area that controlled the main access from Shivaji's area. Meanwhile, other of his forces raided into the southern Konkan, the area below the Ghats in the vicinity of Goa. Further attempts to defeat the Sidi were no more successful than earlier campaigns. Throughout this period, the Mughals were not focused on Shivaji in Maharashtra, but on a fierce war with the Pathans in the north.

Let us complete the narrative of Shivaji's life before turning to the important themes of the Maratha polity. From 1674 to his death in 1680, Shivaji was mainly involved in long campaigns in the south. He was invited by a faction of the Bijapur court to invade Golconda, and led an army all the way across India to Jinji on the eastern coast. There, he both fought and negotiated with Ekoji (his half-brother) and took the major fortress of Vellore. During this period, his son Sambhaji briefly took service with the Mughal Empire, apparently unsatisfied with his prospects for succeeding Shivaji. Shivaji had proposed dividing the polity, his younger son, Rajaram, to get the heartland areas of Maharashtra and his older son, Sambhaji, to get the new conquests in the Karnatak and coastal Jinji. These problems, as we shall see, remained unsolved at Shivaji's death.[34]

THEMES AND ISSUES OF SHIVAJI'S POLITY

At the outset, let us be clear what Shivaji did not do. First, Shivaji did not represent "proto-nationalism." He did not lead a movement of Marathas. His was a polity like others at the time, offering mainly social mobility for Maratha soldiers and Brahmin administrators, as had Bijapur and Ahmadnagar. In revenue administration and social

[34] Ibid., 199.

structure it represented more continuity with these kingdoms than discontinuity. Second, Shivaji did not significantly alter the power of the rural elite families of Maharashtra, especially the deshmukhs. He attacked the largest of these who were rivals, but all the remaining families with "nested" rights were left in peace.[35] It would have been impossible to collect taxes or govern without them. Shivaji's was not a revolt against deshmukhs, but a polity that attempted to integrate them. He was more successful with some than others; many remained partly or wholly loyal to the Mughals or Bijapur throughout his reign. Third, Shivaji was not attempting to create a universal Hindu rule. Over and over, he espoused tolerance and syncretism. He even called on Aurangzeb to act like Akbar in according respect to Hindu beliefs and places. Shivaji had no difficulty in allying with the Muslim states which surrounded him – Bijapur, Golconda, and the Mughals – even against Hindu powers, such as the nayaks of the Karnatic. Further, he did not ally with other Hindu powers, such as the Rajputs, rebelling against the Mughals. In his own army Muslim leaders appear quite early, and the first Pathan unit joined in 1656. His naval commander was, of course, a Muslim. Older Maratha histories asserted that Shivaji was a close follower of Ramdas, a Brahmin teacher, who guided him in an orthodox Hindu path; recent research has shown that Shivaji did not meet or know Ramdas until late in his life.[36] Rather, Shivaji followed his own judgement throughout his remarkable career.

None of this should in any way minimize Shivaji's main accomplishment, which was to carve a small kingdom out of a marginal, frontier area of Bijapur and Ahmadnagar, and hold it against the vastly superior forces of Bijapur and the Mughal Empire. Shivaji was a general of extraordinary personal charisma and ability to motivate his progressively larger armies. Many of his encounters depended on great personal courage; he had it in abundance.

Shivaji was, however, much more than just a successful and courageous leader of men. He evolved a strategy that consistently baffled and defeated armies sent against him. Shivaji realized that the most vulnerable point of the large, slow-moving armies of the time was

---

[35] V. G. Khobrekar (ed.), *Records of Shivaji Period* (Bombay, Government of Maharashtra, 1974). Letters 11, 19, 21, 24, 35, 36, and 43 are all such grants.

[36] Pawar, "Shivaji and Ramdas," 51–80. In Tamilnadu, Dirks has identified the acquisition of a Brahmin spiritual preceptor as a stage in state formation. This is, perhaps, also a useful way to see the relation of Shivaji to Ramdas, Dirks, *The Hollow Crown*, 167–68.

supply. The strategy he evolved was to use knowledge of the local terrain and the superior mobility of his light cavalry to cut off supplies to the enemy. His cavalry attacked caravans and devastated the countryside around the enemy camp. Shivaji regularly refused a decisive plains battle, which tactics of the day demanded. Instead he left the "battlefield" and struck some portion of the enemy territory, perhaps hundreds of miles away, forcing the enemy to chase him. These tactics, it is true, had been developed by Malik Amber in the early seventeenth century, but Shivaji raised them to a high art.

Further, he understood the importance of forts for the geopolitics of Maharashtra. He captured dozens of them and spent much of what he gained on building dozens more. One might question why Shivaji built many forts in areas where forts already existed. Shivaji could never be sure of the loyalty of the families who held existing forts, and they, indeed, often supported the opposing side. Only by building and supplying his own forts could Shivaji staff and maintain them with troops of proven loyalty. Shivaji also well understood that forts had important symbolic value. They were the physical manifestation of supra-local power, virtually the only one in Maharashtra. There were no kingly cities (Shivaji never controlled Ahmadnagar, or Aurangabad, or Burhanpur) and no important roads. Forts were the manifestation of kingly authority. If there is any architectural monument to the genius of Shivaji, it is the many forts up and down the Ghats of Maharashtra.

It must be noted, however, that there were several drawbacks to Shivaji's emphasis on light, mobile cavalry. The first was a limited ability to take forts. Shivaji captured forts by stratagem, but rarely by assault. He did not have the technical means of sapping or mining or artillery which were available to the large Muslim powers. Late in his reign, he did hire foreigners and develop artillery, but the quality was never high.

The other much more serious problem was the way Shivaji's tactics spread warfare across the countryside. To make an army withdraw from central Maharashtra, he attacked the Ahmadnagar region or sacked Surat. To deny the Bijapuri army grain, he devastated a wide area around their camp. Looting their grain caravans forced longer foraging expeditions. There was an intrinsically destructive downward spiral to this style of warfare.

Equally destructive was the ethic of the yearly campaign. As the Shahabad bakhar so eloquently puts it, "As soon as Dasara was over, the army should march out of their quarters. At the time of their departure, an inventory should be made ... and they should start on the expedition. For eight months, the forces should subsist [on their spoils] in foreign territories. They should levy contribution."[37] The claims of chauth simply quantified the demands of these yearly expeditions. In spite of the confident assertion of the Shabasad bakhar that war could be made to pay for itself, it rarely did. Undoubtedly it was the ethic of the time, and Shivaji, his commanders, and the men expected these yearly expeditions. It provided them with spoils and glory, but military expeditions were an extraordinarily inefficient and destructive way to extract either revenue or loyalty from a population. In fact, this kind of raiding is the stuff of local legends; even centuries later, oral traditions which portray the Marathas as destructive raiders are found in several areas surrounding Maharashtra. At the very least, living off the land was hard on the countryside and cultivation began a downward cycle.

Shivaji recognized these problems. He realized that Maharashtra needed time, and peace, to recover from more than thirty years of continuous warfare. Shivaji, from the early years, had a larger vision, one that included welfare and prosperity for his subjects. It is possible that his negotiated treaty with Jai Singh in 1665 was, in part, to allow peace to return to Maharashtra. In the last decade of his reign, Shivaji was fortunate that both Bijapuri and Mughal energies were focused elsewhere. The Mughals fought Pathans and Rajputs; Bijapur was consumed with factional disputes and a Mughal invasion.

In this respite, Shivaji worked to rebuild Maharashtra. He encouraged taqqavi (developmental) loans, low settlements to repopulate devastated areas, and carefully commanded his army when they were in monsoon cantonments not to disturb cultivators. Further, he understood the importance of the administration for tax collection. At the top, was an advisory council; at the bottom, he laid out rules for the measurement of agricultural land. Even with scanty records, it seems that land measurements were carried out in some areas of the Desh, though perhaps not in the Konkan.

Shivaji also realized the potential destructiveness of his large standing army, when they were camped during the monsoon. He admonished his commanders to make sure the supplies lasted through the

[37] S. N. Sen, *Life of Siva*, 31–32.

monsoon. Otherwise, "You will starve and the horses will begin to die."

Then you will begin to trouble the country. For instance, you will go, and some will take some grains of the cultivators, some bread, some grass, some wood, some vegetables and things. When you begin to act like that, the poor peasants, who are holding on to their cottages, and somehow eking out a livelihood, will themselves begin to run away. Some of them will starve. Then they will think that you are worse than the Mughals who overran the countryside.[38]

If we consider the larger picture, peace never came to Maharashtra because Shivaji never worked out a modus vivendi with the Mughals. Perhaps it was inevitable that no treaty would be honored, on either side. We know the depth of Aurangzeb's contempt for Shivaji, often referring to him as a "mountain rat." We also know the depth of Shivaji's commitment to independence. He entirely rejected Bijapuri service and, only briefly and under duress, served the Mughal Empire.

Shivaji's most serious problem, after military pressure from the Mughals, was his relations with the other grant-holding, armed families in Maharashtra. They held rights either from Ahmadnagar or Bijapur which were at least as old, and often larger, than Shivaji's. As we have seen, these families often held "nested" rights in an area – deshmukhi, a local fort, and a saranjam for maintenance of troops. Often, virtually the whole of the government's share of the produce stopped with one family, for example in Wai or Satara or Sholapur.

Over the course of his life, Shivaji tried a series of strategies to woo and subdue these families. As we have seen, his early activities against Bijapur attracted few of these families, and he mainly recruited troops from his father's saranjam area around Pune. He consolidated his hold by winning over the non-deshmukhi commanders of some of the forts in the region. His first campaign was against the More family, holding forts and Bijapuri grants immediately south of Shivaji's. The Mores were ordered by Bijapur to put down Shivaji's rebellion, and a brutal campaign ensued, at the end of which the More family – father and four sons – was largely extinguished. This "solution" was not lost on other elite Maratha families of Maharashtra. The deshmukhs of Supe, the remnants of the More family, the deshmukhs of Utroli, Phaltan, and Wai all joined Afzal Khan and the Bijapuri army in his campaign against Shivaji in 1659–60.[39] After the defeat of the Bijapuri army,

[38] Patwardhan and Rawlinson, *Sourcebook*, 153.
[39] Satish Chandra, "Shivaji and the landed elements" in R. S. Sharma (ed.), *Indian Society: Historical Probings, in Memory of D. D. Kosambi* (New Delhi, 1974).

Shivaji invaded the coastal Konkan, again fighting mainly Hindu and Muslim deshmukhs of the area. He annexed the territory of the Raja of Shringapur.

One of the key assertions in the Shahabad bakhar, and probably the most discussed paragraph in Maratha history, states that Shivaji not only stopped giving out large grants in land (substituting cash payments), but that he broke the power of the large landed families by destroying their forts and making revenue arrangements with village headmen. Clearly, if Shivaji had been able to do this, his problems would have been over. Indeed, in some areas Shivaji was able to establish relations with village headmen and – to some extent – undermine the position of the large families. There are a fair number of village-level documents which show land measurement and revenue information reaching his court. These date mainly from the last ten years of his reign and are mainly from central Maharashtra. Overall, there is ample evidence in both the administrative papers and sanads that large-scale "nested" rights continued, and some new grants were made, especially in the Konkan. The big families, such as those centered at Bhor or Wai, clearly remained strong powers throughout Shivaji's reign, and their loyalty was subject to negotiation between the main contenders – Bijapur, the Mughal Empire, and Shivaji. Another strategy adopted by Shivaji, which recognized the power of these families, was to marry into them. Shivaji thus married into the Shirke, the Mohite, and the Nimbalkar families, all powerful in their areas.[40]

Shivaji's early strategies for dealing with the large landed families of Maharashtra – fighting them, undermining their administrative control, and marrying into them – had not solved the basic problem of legitimacy and authority. The families held long-standing grants from Ahmadnagar or Bijapur. Shivaji could not suspend, alter, or adjudicate these rights. He had no legal power to interfere in succession or even tax collection.

It is likely that the claim of sardeshmukhi arose as yet another potential solution to this problem. We know that the origin of the term in unclear, and that when Shivaji put forth the claim, in the mid-1660s, the only holders of this right – besides the king – were a few of the most powerful Maratha families, who had long served Ahmadnagar. The claim, of course, was not to just 10 percent of the government share of

---

[40] Sardesai, *New History*, 145.

the revenue; it was to be *sardeshmukh*, that is, in some sense "over" or superior to the deshmukhs. If the Mughal Empire had accepted his claim, it would have become a basis for legal superiority over all but a few deshmukhs. These negotiations, however, continued for decades, with chauth and sardeshmukhi of the Deccan never formally granted until long after Shivaji's reign.

In the middle period of his reign, between about 1660 and 1670, Shivaji attacked the problem of legitimacy and loyalty in a manner much like the Deccan sultanates, that is through the expansion of crown lands and development of administration. Both in the Desh and the Konkan, Shivaji was able to expand his personal estates. He recruited many Brahmins, mainly Deshastas, to manage both the estates and the central bureaucracy. He ordered these officials, for example, to keep the accounts of his personal estates (in Kudal, Rajapur, Dabhol, Pune, Javli, Kalyan, etc.) separate from the general accounts of the polity.[41] He also encouraged the development of a small council of advisors; several of the officers had direct parallels in the earlier Ahmadnagar kingdom (sarnobat, peshwa, chitnis, sarlashkar), others were new (amatya, pratinidhi, sachiv). With the money from his raids and estates, Shivaji built up his own forces; troops were paid out of the central government treasury and rode his horses. Again, this is a strategy found in Bijapur during its period of expansion. Both strategies were quite effective in shifting the balance of power from the deshmukhs to Shivaji's central government.

It was in the last decade of Shivaji's rule that he put together his most ambitious plan to establish authority over the large deshmukh families. It began with further strengthening his personal army, relative to the strength of deshmukh forces. Though there is no direct, documentary evidence of the size of Shivaji's army, there is some indirect evidence. From Shivaji's will, for example, we know that he personally owned 30,000 horses. This suggests that his personal forces were perhaps 15,000–20,000 cavalry. This is a big army, by any standards of the day, and was an order of magnitude larger than a typical deshmukh force.[42] He owned the guns and gunpowder to supply the army. In addition, Shivaji was in possession of the largest and most important forts in Maharashtra.

It was from this position of strength that Shivaji undertook probably

[41] A. R. Kulkarni, *Maharashtra in the Age of Shivaji* (Poona, 1974), 29.
[42] Sarkar, *House of Shivaji*, 188–89, 194.

the most audacious act of an admittedly audacious career. He decided
to have himself crowned as a Hindu king, a Kshatriya king, and – at a
stroke – solve his minor problems of authority over Brahmins and
major problems of authority over the large deshmukh families. He
would rule them with an authority sanctioned by Brahmins and
acknowledged by the large families.[43]

Many of the known facts surrounding the coronation support the
view that it was primarily concerned with internal relations in Maharashtra. He called in the families to witness the coronation, the
Brahmins from Maharashtra and other parts of India, but he did notify
the surrounding states or invite envoys.

There were big, controversial problems, which delayed the coronation almost a year. First, there was Shivaji's ancestry. If he was a
Maratha, or worse, a Kunbi-cultivator, he was not suitable material to
be a king. He had to be a Kshatriya. Everyone, however, knew Shivaji's
immediate ancestors – Shahji, his father, who had been in Bijapuri
service, and his grandfather, Maloji, who had been a cultivating village
headman in northern Maharashtra – and they were all Marathas, not
Kshatriyas. If Shivaji was, indeed, a Kshatriya, why had he never had
the sacred-thread ceremony, and why did he he not wear the sacred
thread? Why had his marriages been in accordance with the Maratha
tradition, not the Kshatriya tradition? No one in the Brahmin communities in Maharashtra came forth with answers which would allow the
coronation to proceed.

What was needed was a "creative" Brahmin, with credibility in
Maharashtra, to solve the various problems and perform the coronation ceremony. Such a Brahmin was Gagabhat, a highly respected
writer and philosopher, originally from Maharashtra, but long resident
in Benares.

The initial problem of Shivaji's Maratha past was solved by the
"finding" of a genealogy which connected his family to Rajput origins
in Rajasthan, the family having migrated south to Maharashtra

---

[43] Patwardhan and Rawlinson, *Sourcebook*, 163. This is a translation of the Shabasad
bakhar. Also interesting is André Wink's translation of the *Sivdigvijaya* (a chronicle of
Shivaji's life) on the coronation: "Shivaji was unwilling to share the leadership of the
Marathas with others, and although he had formerly been on one level with many of the other
Maratha sardars as (mere) servants of Bijapur, he could justify his new claims to pre-eminence
amongst them by pointing out that this dependence, through his efforts, no longer existed"
(*Land and Sovereignty in India: Agrarian Society and Politics under the Eighteenth-century
Maratha Svarajya* (Cambridge, 1986)).

following Muslim invasions of the thirteenth century.[44] The genealogy solved the suitability problem, but gave no model for an actual coronation ceremony. Rajputs were, after all, Mughal feudatories. They did not perform ceremonies which seated an independent Hindu king on a throne. Such a ceremony had not been performed in centuries.

One by one, Gagabhat worked through the problems. He, in consultation with other Brahmins, gradually worked out a ceremony based on sacred texts, but unlike any extant ceremony. The opposition was neither very visible nor vocal; this is possibly a problem of the sources, which were produced by Shivaji's court or Gagabhat himself. The only outside observer was the Englishman, Oxinden, who had little idea what was going on beyond the pomp and display.

The actual ceremony took place over several weeks, and we will focus briefly only on those parts which affected legitimacy and loyalty.[45] The first section was homage to the family deity and penance for living as a Maratha, when he was in fact a Kshatriya. The second section focused on the thread ceremony for himself and his son, and new marriage ceremonies for all his wives, based on Kshatriya customs. Thus, Shivaji had become suitable to be a king.

The actual coronation took place over the course of nine days and nights. It began with fasts, a night ritual of offerings at the sacred fire, and the ascending of the smaller of two specially built thrones. Shivaji held durbar from this throne and declared the beginning of a new calendar and era. In the next section, he was ritually cleansed by bathing in water and oil, then hot water, then anointed with earth from sacred places, then bathed in honey, milk, curds, ghee, and sugar. Then there was another bath of hot water and anointing with sandalwood powder. This whole section made him the representative of Indra on earth.

[44] Two pieces of evidence suggest that Shivaji may have thought of himself as a Rajput before this period. The first is a letter from his father, Shahji, written to Ali Adil Shah II, of Bijapur (whom he served) in 1656. In the middle of this letter, complaining of the terms of his service, he says, "I have served several kings, but always maintained my self-respect. We are Rajputs" (in D. V. Apte, *Itihas Manjari* (Poona, 1923), 67). The second bit of evidence comes from the impression Shivaji made on Rajputs, when he was at Agra. The contemporary newsletters, written to the Rajput courts, include the following passage: "One day when Ballu Sah, Tej Singh and Ran Singh were sitting together, Maha Singh Shekhawat said, 'Shivaji is very clever, he speaks the right word, after which nobody need say anything more on the subject. He is a good genuine Rajput, and we have found him just what he was reported to be. He tells us such appropriate things marked by the characteristic qualities (or spirit) of a Rajput that if they are borne in mind they will prove useful some day'" (translated in Sarkar, *House of Shivaji*, 162).

[45] The details of the coronation are covered in V. S. Bendry, *The Coronation of Shivaji the Great* (Bombay, 1960).

The ceremony continued with many Brahmins anointing him with various sacred liquids from pots they had brought. They, thereby, accepted Shivaji as a king and his authority over them. This was followed by another lavish dakshina, distribution of presents to Brahmins. Thereafter, he received kumkum on his forehead, and ascended a specially built chariot of Indra and received blessed bows, arrows, horses, and elephants.

The next sections were perhaps the most crucial for legitimacy and loyalty. Shivaji ascended the main throne – made of gold and covered with lion and tiger skins – and received presents from many of the nobility. Gold coins from his chief administrators were poured over his head. Next was a private darbar, in which he received fealty from many of the powerful families of Maharashtra. Finally, there was a large public darbar, in which his ascension and the era were announced, and he received presents. Another substantial dakshina was distributed to Brahmins and others who came to the public darbar. Perhaps equally significant for the actual ceremony was how it was financed, which was at least in part by a tax on the deshmukhs. The successful collection of this tax and the presence of these families at the ceremony suggests more control over them than ever before.[46]

Shivaji certainly perceived an important change in his own status. During the coronation ceremony, for example, he proclaimed a new era and a new calendar. He set himself above all the deshmukh families, receiving a cash payment from them in honor of the coronation. Shivaji also saw himself as equal to the rulers of the surrounding states. In a letter to Baji Mudhol (deshmukh of the area), for example, written in 1677, Shivaji emphasized that as an independent ruler he could negotiate with the Qutb Shah monarchy of Golconda on a footing of equality.[47]

After the coronation, as expected of a newly crowned king, Shivaji immediately went on campaign, suddenly raiding the Mughal camp on the Bhima river. Later in the year, he attacked north into Khandesh and Berar, along the way burning the English factory at Dharangaon. In the last years of his life, Shivaji mainly returned to campaigning in the south, as well as developing his naval force to control the

[46] Many of these acts and kingly "substances" were part of a much wider tradition of kingship. Dirks' description of eating the kingly rice, plus the regalia and wider ceremony establishing kingly relations with landed families sound very similar. See Dirks, *The Hollow Crown*, 101–04.
[47] Translated in Sardesai, *New History*, 240–43.

Konkan.[48] The real change in the coastal region, however, was the rapid development of Bombay. It had grown under English naval protection into a thriving trading city of over fifty thousand inhabitants, all of this is in spite of low-level opposition from the Marathas.

Overall, Shivaji was fortunate that the Mughals and Bijapur were otherwise occupied, giving a respite to Maharashtra. There is every evidence that Shivaji was grooming his older son Sambhaji to rule. Extant documents show Sambhaji as representative of Shivaji as early as the negotiations with the English factors in 1673. There are several court judgements by Sambhaji from the 1674–77 period, and he led a major campaign in the Hubli area of the Karnatak in 1675–76.[49]

After a lingering illness of two years, Shivaji died in 1680. He left a kingdom with a full treasury, more than a hundred forts in the Ghats, the Desh, and the Konkan, and more tenuous possessions and rights east and south into the Karnatak. Through his charismatic leadership, successful campaigning, and administrative pressure, he had built up his power relative to the large, landed deshmukh families of Maharashtra. For almost a decade, his kingdom had been relatively free from military pressure by both Bijapur and the Mughal Empire. As we shall see in the next chapter, both the internal and external situation were to change radically within a year.

[48] The Maratha ships had not improved in two decades. They were still very small and lacked effective artillery. In an encounter before Khanderi island (just south of Bombay) in 1679, one English frigate routed a fleet of fifty of the Maratha boats. See Sarkar, *House of Shivaji*, 272–73.

[49] Kamal Gokhale, *Chhatrapati Sambhaji* (Poona, 1978), 18–20.

CHAPTER 4

RESPONSES TO FAMILY INVASION
(1680–1719)[1]

None of Shivaji's plans to divide the kingdom prevented the factionalization of the court, which began about the time of his final illness in 1678. One faction supported Sambhaji, the other a much younger son, Rajaram, then eight years old. This factionalization at the center, caused in part by Mughal military pressure, forms the main theme of this chapter. We will look at the shifting and delicate balance between power at the center and power held by the principal commanders; further, we will examine survival strategies and accommodations of various families and the long-term effects of warfare on Maharashtra. Finally, we will look at what government "control" and "conquest" meant in this period, and the problems the Mughals had in integrating Maratha families into the mansabdari system.

Immediately after Shivaji's death, a group of ministers and one of Shivaji's wives crowned Rajaram, who was promptly opposed by several of the most powerful Maratha families and Sambhaji. It took months for Sambhaji to crush the opposing faction, and it was more than eight months before his coronation took place (in December, 1680).[1]

As successions go, this one was not crippling, and Sambhaji's first few years looked much like Shivaji's later strategies. There was, for example, a campaign against the Sidi's sea forts on the Konkan coast, which was not particularly successful. Also in a similar way to the late campaigns of Shivaji, Shambhaji sent a large army into the Karnatak in April 1681. The army was defeated by Chickadevaraja of Mysore; various campaigns there continued with the Marathas involved in the affairs of Mysore, Madura, and Golconda throughout the 1680s – sometimes as allies, sometimes as adversaries, sometimes as tribute collectors.

Throughout these campaigns, Sambhaji was well aware that he lacked the technology to take forts by sapping, mining, or artillery. He pressed the English at Bombay for a defensive treaty, eventually

---

[1] Kamal Gokhale, *Chhatrapati Sambhaji* (Poona, 1978), 39. There is a particularly good discussion of sources for the Sambhaji period in this monograph, pp. 386–99.

concluded in 1684, to obtain quality guns and ammunition. Sambhaji secured, first, the fort of Pratapgad, then others along the Ghats. Administrative records of the period suggest that the administration continued, much as in Shivaji's time, with officials appointed to fill vacant posts.

All this changed abruptly when a rebellious Mughal noble, Prince Akbar, asked for and received asylum with Sambhaji. Let us pause a moment to give Prince Akbar's background. His revolt came after Aurangzeb chastised the prince for non-activity in the war against the Rajputs in 1678. In 1680, he went into open revolt, and early the next year proclaimed himself emperor. After his defeat in Rajasthan, he fled south with about 400 followers and corresponded with Sambhaji, who was then in the Konkan.

Sambhaji was, in those months, involved in problems of his own, specifically a fully fledged plot to poison him and place his younger brother on the throne. Sambhaji was indebted to Prince Akbar when he revealed that the faction opposing Sambhaji had offered much of Sambhaji's kingdom to him for his support. Sambhaji put down the plot; he eventually tried and executed twenty to twenty-five of the main landed elite family leaders of this plot.

Harboring Prince Akbar probably only hastened the inevitable confrontation with the Mughals. Aurangzeb promptly concluded his war with the Rajputs and brought a major army into the Deccan. Sambhaji never gained the advantages he had hoped for from Prince Akbar. He was never able to rally the Rajputs against Aurangzeb or win over possibly dissident Mughal generals. (After several futile campaigns and an attempt to mediate the Mughal–Maratha war, Prince Akbar left India for Iran in 1687.)[2]

Aurangzeb's goals were simple – conquer Bijapur and destroy Maratha power. The Mughal strategy toward Maharashtra was not subtle, just thorough. It consisted of steady pressure on Maharashtra's forts, beating Maratha forces in the field when they could bring them to a battle, and devastating Maharashtra's countryside. The Marathas thwarted a quick victory by the well-established strategy of cutting off Mughal supplies, raiding north into Mughal territories to draw off the Mughal army, and seeking allies – Bijapur, Golconda, the Portuguese, and the English. The fronts shifted quickly – Khandesh and northern

---

[2] Ibid., 68–69.

Maharashtra in 1682, followed by the Konkan in 1683. The Marathas attacked Goa and Chaul in 1683, but could not take the main forts. The degree of conflict in the Konkan had alienated several key families by 1685–86. Overall, the Mughals gradually pushed Sambhaji's forces back to major forts, took some strongholds, and controlled more and more of the agricultural land.[3] As they had for more than twenty years, the Mughals also tried to bring powerful Maratha deshmukhs, who were also the military commanders, into Mughal service.[4]

Diplomacy also shifted quickly. Aurangzeb initially tried to ally with Bijapur against the Marathas, then he supported one faction against another inside Bijapur. Sambhaji tried to ally with both Bijapur and Golconda. This jockeying ended in 1686–87 with the fall of Bijapur and Golconda to the Mughals. Suddenly, there were only two players left on the field, the Mughals and the Marathas.

Before looking at the last years of Sambhaji's reign, let us look at the histories of some sample deshmukh families to see how they dealt with the invasion and crisis. What of the Mane family of Mhasvad, who we considered in Chapter 1? In 1678, two years before Shivaji's death, the Mughals were courting the family. Nagoji Mane received a letter of assurance from Aurangzeb that he would receive sardeshmukhi and zamindari rights in his area if he joined Mughal service. A couple of years later, there was an order from Aurangzeb granting the city of Mhasve and a jagir in pargana Man of 1,350,000 Rs. In 1689, haggling was still in progress over the exact rights of the Mane family. Nagoji wrote to Aurangzeb that his father had inams in sixteen areas (mahals) from Bijapur (all in Satara, Sholapur, and Sangli districts), and he wanted them confirmed by Aurangzeb. Presumably, the negotiation never reached a satisfactory conclusion, because – looking ahead – we find Nagoji in Maratha service within just a few years. Both the Yadavs of Karad (whom we briefly considered in Chapter 1) and their rivals, the Jagdales of Masur, took Mughal service in this period to try to maintain or better their position.[5]

There was much shifting of sides as Mughal pressure increased and families tried to save their rights and their lands. Consider, for

[3] The Mughals were, at this time, routinely using foreign gunners in the forts they captured. See *Selected Documents of Aurangzeb's Reign, 1659–1706 A.D.* (Hyderabad, 1958), 134–35, 138–40.
[4] Ibid., 153, 174–80.
[5] Andre Wink, *Land and Sovereignty in India: Agrarian Society and Politics under the Eighteenth-century Maratha Svarajya* (Cambridge, 1986), 168–70.

example, the Jedhe family of Kari. In 1684, Shivaji Jedhe left Maratha service, joined the Mughals, and began devastating the lands of his brother, Sarjerao, and other members of the family. Rather than seek the intervention of Sambhaji and the Maratha court, Sarjerao sought the help of a nearby Mughal fort commander. When, shortly afterwards, Sarjerao Jedhe wrote to Sambhaji, pledging his loyalty to the Maratha side, Sambhaji's reply was understandably irate; he castigated Sarjerao for looking to the enemy to solve family problems, for allowing his brother to join the enemy, and tacitly serving the Mughals. A year and a half later, however, Sambhaji accepted Sarjerao back into Maratha service, on the intercession of a loyal commander and after a personal audience. After Sarjerao captured Rohida fort from the Mughals, Sambhaji also accepted Sarjerao's son back into Maratha service.[6]

Towards the end of Sambhaji's reign defections were common. In the southern Konkan, for example, Sambhaji had badly alienated the deshmukh families through burning villages to deny supplies to Goa during an extended war with the Portuguese. Families often divided, some members wanting to make accommodation with the Mughals, others wanting to continue resistance. For example, Sambhaji attacked the Shirke family in 1688, though they were his close relatives. We know almost nothing of the circumstances, though several of the Shirkes had gone over to the Mughal side some years earlier.

Let us return to complete the story of Sambhaji. In early February 1688, while moving from Panhala to Raigad fort with a small contingent, Sambhaji was captured by Mughal troops. He was brought to Aurangzeb's camp, tortured and executed. During his reign we find no evidence to support notions, made popular by Marathi drama and ballads, that Sambhaji was constantly drunk or drugged or in his harem. Quite to the contrary; there are extant administrative orders right up to the month of his execution.[7] Shivaji's kingdom was not lost because of the deficient moral qualities of Sambhaji. Rather, the Mughal strategy of conquest was simply working.

After Sambhaji's death, what remained of Sambhaji's kingdom, and

[6] Gokhale, *Chhatrapati*, 295-96. A good reconstruction of the earlier family history of the Jedhe family is found in Wink, *Land and Sovereignty*, 173-76.

[7] There are over four hundred extant administrative documents from the short reign of Sambhaji. The vast majority of them have been published in the Annual Proceedings, Conference Reports Quarterly, and Shiva Charitra Shaitya, of the Bharat Itihas Samshodak Mandal, Pune.

what did "conquest" mean in this period? The Mughals by 1689 controlled most of Khandesh and the forts of northern Maharashtra. The Konkan resisted longer, but the major forts were captured within a year of Sambhaji's death, and the North Konkan became a Mughal district. Shivaji's fleet was burned and dispersed. On the plateau, all of the land including the forts from Pune east was in Mughal control.[8] The main Maratha resistance centered on the southern Ghats and central Konkan. The recent Maratha conquests in the south were lost with the exception of Jinji and Thanjur and the areas immediately around them. The political situation continued to deteriorate; the remaining heir, Rajaram (nineteen years old), and his mother, Tarabai, were besieged in Raigad fort. Maratha resistance continued, however, outside the fort. Two young leaders, Santaji Ghorpade and Dhanaji Jadhav, gained fame and followers by daring raids on the Mughal camps, including a night attack on Aurangzeb's tent, which nearly killed him.

In spite of these attacks by various Maratha bands, the basic Mughal tactics continued successfully. In November 1689, Zulfiqar Khan bought access to Raigad, and Rajaram and a small party just managed to escape. Pursued to Panhala (near Kolhapur), they fled south and east, finally arriving at the estates of Sambhaji's half-brother at Jinji and Thanjur on the Coromandel coast.[9] The main supporters of Rajaram in this flight were Dhanaji and Santaji, who also provided military escort for some members of the inner circle who joined Rajaram at Jinji. (The retreat can be traced on Map 3.) Rajaram was soon crowned and set up a functioning court.[10]

The Mughals followed, and soon Rajaram and his followers were besieged in the fortress of Jinji. The nine-year siege of Jinji is a textbook case of the problems of siege warfare, as discussed in Chapter 2. The most likely time that the fort would have been taken was in the

---

[8] See A. R. Kulkarni, "Towards a history of Indapur," in D. W. Attwood, M. Israel, and N. K. Wagle (eds.), *City, Countryside and Society in Maharashtra* (Toronto, University of Toronto, 1988), 132. The village of Indapur, sixty miles south-east of Pune, was integrated into the Mughal *sarkar* of Junnar in 1682.

[9] One of the deshmukh families which we have been following, the Yadav family of Karad, gave good service to Tarabai and Rajaram during this flight. Arzoji Yadav was sent by Rajaram to get the royal hoard of jewelry out of Raigad, after he escaped. Arzoji was entrusted with this jewelry, when the royal party fled to Jinji. See D. A. Pawar (ed.), *Tarabaikalin Kagadpatra*, I (Kolhapur, 1969), 470–71.

[10] For the major events of the flight to Jinji, I have followed G. S. Sardesai, *New History of the Marathas* (Bombay, second impression, 1957), I, 332–34. See also Grant Duff, *History of the Marathas* (Jaipur, reprinted edition, 1986), I, 265–68.

first six months. The Mughals had supplies, cash, manpower, and spirit; the weather was still favorable, and the Mughals had managed to buy a substantial quantity of good gunpowder from the British at Fort St. George. Jinji, however, was not taken, and within a couple of months the general advantage shifted to the besieged. Jinji was such a massive fortress that even the large Mughal army could not effectively surround it. Provisions were, therefore, regularly brought in, and the Maratha light cavalry regularly came and went.[11]

By the middle of the monsoon, the Mughal camp was suffering. Maratha bands, led by Santaji and Dhanaji and stationed outside the fort, regularly cut off such caravans as made it through the monsoon. Awaiting reinforcements, the Mughal general left Jinji and collected what tribute he could among the petty chiefs in the south towards Travancore.

As the years passed, it is possible that the Mughal commander reached an "understanding" with the Marathas and did not vigorously pursue any attempt to breach the walls. It is equally possible that he could not pursue the siege because of increased Maratha pressure. Rajaram was able to recruit additional Maratha forces outside Jinji, which cut off caravans and produced periodic crises in the Mughal camp. By early 1693, the Mughals were themselves besieged. They had destroyed their artillery through overcharging the volleys. The enhanced Maratha forces, which sometimes numbered 20,000 cavalry, cut off supplies and occasionally captured contingents of Mughal troops, as foraging parties had to go further and further from the Mughal camp. Because of interrupted communication, there were incessant rumors of Aurangzeb's death. The Mughal commander proposed peace with Rajaram in early 1693, but the commander's advisors pointed out that Aurangzeb would never ratify the treaty.

Two years were spent in another Mughal attempt to secure the south coast and inland region. Once again, tribute was collected, but there was no further progress in the siege of Jinji. The French who were in touch with both sides were convinced that the Mughal commander and

---

[11] The long siege of Jinji figures prominently in the English *Records of Ft. St. George*, and in the contemporary French memoir of Francois Martin. See Lotika Varadarajan (trans. and annot.), *India in the Seventeenth Century: Memoirs of Francois Martin* (New Delhi, 1983). John Richards has astutely pointed out that the Mughals were no more successful at recruiting the nayaks of the south than they were in bringing the Maratha deshmukhs into the mansabdari system. See "The imperial crisis in the Deccan," *Journal of Asian Studies*, 35, 2 (Feb. 1976), 327–55.

Rajaram had reached an understanding and were waiting for Aurang-zeb's death.

Meanwhile, the war continued in Maharashtra. Rajaram had left the campaign in Maharashtra to the competent oversight of Ramchandra Nilkanth, who was based at Vishalgad fort (east of Kolhapur). (He had been an official in Shivaji's court, but had lost favor in the intervening reign of Sambhaji.) Initial attempts to recruit leaders were successful – largely based on lavish grants in areas held by the Mughals.[12] The bands grew in size, as leaders recruited Marathas who had been in the service of now defeated Bijapur and brought in new groups, such as Dhangars, a shepherd caste.[13] In 1692, with the forces of Santaji and Dhanaji in Maharashtra, the Wai district and the important forts of Panhala and Raigad were retaken. Santaji led another attack on Mughal supplies along the Godavari river and defeated several Mughal forces sent to contain him. The next year, Santaji's forces returned to Jinji, and were generally successful at cutting off supplies to the Mughal camp and defeating the large forces the Mughals fielded. In spite of Ramchandra Nilkanth's attention to the forts under Maratha control and attempts to regularize revenue collection, and the military successes of Santaji and Dhanaji, Rajaram's control and authority grew more tenuous with each passing year of the siege. The very success of the commanders made them more independent. In a personal appearance at Jinji, Santaji demanded a "suitable" reward and asserted in open court that he could make or unmake the Maratha king. Rajaram immediately instigated Dhanaji against Santaji. This bitter and violent rivalry resulted in a series of battles and finally the murder of Santaji.[14] By 1697, Rajaram was also out of money; he sued for peace, but Aurangzeb accepted none of his proposals.

Finally, in 1698, Aurangzeb sent a new commander, reinforcements, and cash. The siege pushed ahead; outer forts were taken, and an assault planned. Meanwhile, Rajaram escaped to Vellore fort. Within days, the Mughals scaled the walls and took the fort. Thus ended the nine-year siege of Jinji.

---

[12] See Sardesai, *New History*, 337–38, for the translation of one such grant.

[13] Grant Duff, *History*, 270.

[14] After most of his troops had deserted him, both the Mughals and the Mane family were pursuing him. The Mane family had a personal vendetta, because Santaji had executed an in-law of the family. The Manes, apparently, found him first and killed him; Sardesai, *New History*, 347. Mughal documents, particularly the *Mashir-i-Alamgiri*, however, suggest that Nagoji Mane gave Santaji some short-term sanctuary, in spite of their feud, and that he was

In contrast to the Maratha documents, which highlight efforts of Ramchandra Nilkanth, the picture we get from Mughal histories is that throughout the 1690s there was little functioning Maratha polity in Maharashtra. The state that Shivaji had created had ceased to exist. The Mughals controlled almost all of the major forts in Maharashtra and much of the countryside. They had begun assigning land in jagir grants for the maintenance of troops, as they had done in the conquered areas of Bijapur and Golconda.

It is, however, the family documents of the deshmukh families of Maharashtra which show that the situation was, in fact, much more complicated. Some families had indeed sided with the Mughals, such as the Sawants of Sawantwadi and the Dalvis of Kudal. Most, however, vacillated.[15] Let us, for example, again consider the Mane family of Mhasvad. Against what we would expect, Nagoji Mane, who had been in Mughal service for seven years, returned to Maratha service in 1691, towards the beginning of the siege of Jinji. He personally travelled to Jinji, had an audience with Rajaram, and was granted two new villages, in perpetuity, for returning to service. He was also granted the sardeshmukhi rights to all twelve mahals which he had previously held (and two further inam villages within a couple of months).[16] He stayed in the area of Jinji for several years, and was complimented by Rajaram for his service. As we have just seen, in 1697 Nagoji Mane sided with Dhanaji Yadav, and, pursuing a personal vendetta, killed Santaji Ghorpade; he was rewarded by Rajaram.

Within a few months, however, Nagoji Mane was negotiating with Aurangzeb to return to Mughal service. Let us emphasize that this was a negotiating situation. Nagoji Mane, in July 1697, wrote to Aurangzeb the terms under which he would return to Mughal service. He wanted pardon for whatever "bad actions" he had done. He wanted a jagir of 7,000 zat and 7,000 swar; only one-fourth of his horses should be branded. He wanted a large ceremonial drum, robes of honor, an elephant, and a horse with gold tack. He wanted an immediate cash payment of 70,000 Rs. and possession of Sangola fort and seven other

actually killed by a near relative of the man Santaji killed; his head was carried to the Mughal camp by some soldiers who found it, rather than by Nagoji Mane.

[15] Sarjarao Jedhe, for example, left Maratha service in late 1692, after successful military campaigns against the Mughals. He joined Mughal service and was granted the deshmukh rights of Bhor, but returned to Maratha service a few years later. See G. T. Kulkarni, *The Mughal–Maratha Relations: Twenty Five Fateful Years (1682–1707)* (Pune, Deccan College, 1983), 148.

[16] V. S. Khobekar, *Records of Shivaji Period* (Bombay, 1974), 140–47.

forts in southern Maharashtra. He wanted complete jagir rights, including the settling of criminal cases, in all the parganas surrounding pargana Man, plus two new mahals in the area of Bidar and five new parganas in the area of Parendra.[17] About a year later, Aurangzeb came back with a substantially smaller counter-offer – a zat of 5,000 and swar support of about 4,000, all to come from jagirs in Berar. There was no mention of control of forts in Maharashtra, much less the drum or the elephant. Nagoji Mane was to give a substantial present to Aurangzeb and give even more substantial surety for his conduct when he entered service.[18] He actually took Mughal service sometime in 1698, at the level of 5,000 zat and 4,000 swar. The documents do not, unfortunately, tell us much about the "nested" rights of the Mane family in the Mhasvad/Kasegaon area at this time. One document details that Nagoji's deshmukhi rights in Khanapur were continued, and a document of 1700 suggests that the family held several important forts in the area. Looking ahead, Nagoji Mane in 1702, as a Mughal jagirdar, petitioned Aurangzeb on behalf of another Maratha for a suitable position and honors.

The second deshmukh family we have been tracking, the Yadavs of Karad, split in this period. One branch took service with Aurangzeb, another stayed loyal to Rajaram. Later, in 1706–08, the "disloyal" members were welcomed back to the Maratha side.[19] Actually taking possession of the deshmukhi rights involved years of conflict.[20]

We should not assume that either the Mane pattern of switching sides every few years or the Yadav pattern of the family dividing were the only ones. Consider, for example, the records of the Patankar family of Patan, a hilly area of the Ghats. These deshmukhs showed unswerving loyalty to the Maratha cause. After opposing both Mughals and their Maratha allies in the Javli area, Rajaram in 1690 ordered the family and its troops to the Bijapur district; the head of the family received twelve villages in hereditary inam and a ceremonial elephant for his good service. In 1692, we find the family serving outside of Jinji and supporting Dhanaji against Santaji Ghorpade. The family received a total of thirty-seven villages in inam and mokasa in

[17] Ibid., 154–56. Nimaji Shinde, about whom much will be heard later, also left Mughal service in late 1690 with Nagoji Mane and travelled to Jinji. G. T. Kulkarni, *Mughal–Maratha Relations*, 103.

[18] Pawar, *Tarabaikalin*, 154–56.

[19] Ibid., 139–40, 176–79.

[20] Ibid., 183–84.

1693, and rights to transit duties in Patan in 1696. When Aurangzeb besieged Satara fort in 1700, the family looted his supplies.[21]

Both Rajaram and Aurangzeb were competing for the loyalty of the large deshmukh families. Both offered rights and recognition. Though the Mughals had a major army in Maharashtra, they could not control the long-term loyalty of the deshmukh families. Resistance continued at all levels in Maharashtra. In some areas, families continued to hold important forts and towns. In others, there were only roving bands which retreated to the Ghat areas when pursued. Later in the decade, families had recovered a few of the stronger forts in Maharashtra – Pratapgad, Rajgad, Torna, and Panhala – and spread raids south to Mughal-controlled areas around Belgaum and east onto the Bijapur plains. Much of the Desh deteriorated as the warfare continued.[22]

The situation cannot be better summarized than by Ramchandra Nilkanth who was responsible for the Maratha resistance in this period. He wrote, just a few years later, the *Ajnapatra*, the justly famous treatise on politics and statecraft, in which he characterized these years as follows:

Many soldiers ... went to heaven whilst fighting in the cause of their master in accordance with the duties of Ksatra. Some having lost their armies got confounded in their valour and went over to the enemy. Some, seeing their master given up to vices like the enemy, usurped, with the idea of holding them independently, parts of territories and forts which had been made over to their possession ... In various places persons, rising like the crescent moon owing to the weakness of government, began to quarrel against one another. During these adverse times minor chiefs ... got firmly rooted. The remaining parts of the country became desolate, and forts got exhausted of military provisions. Only the idea of the state remained.[23]

After the fall of Jinji, Rajaram and the royal entourage returned to Maharashtra. The combined forces of the king and several leaders of bands attempted a raid on Berar and Surat in late 1699; they collected some chauth and sardeshmukhi in Khandesh, but were forced back

[21] Ibid., 180–95. Overall, the Mughals had been no more successful in either recruiting or subduing the nayaks of the Karnatak, many of whom had been armed elite families of Golconda. See J. F. Richards "The Hyderabad Karnatik: 1687–1707," *Modern Asian Studies*, 9, 2 (1975), 241–60. In the ensuing decades of the seventeenth century, the Marathas had little success either.

[22] See, for example, the kaulnama of Indapur, which mentions that the village was nearly deserted and charged the deshmukh with repopulation, in Kulkarni, "Towards a history of Indapur," 131.

[23] "The Ajnapatra or royal edict" (trans. S. V. Puntambekar), *Journal of Indian History*, 3, 1 (April, 1929), 84–85.

through the central Desh.[24] Several leaders remained in northern Maharashtra – Nimaji Shinde in Khandesh, Parsaji Bhonsle in Berar, and Kanderao Dabhade in Baglana. Typically, these leaders were operating with almost no direction from Rajaram. In any case, Rajaram died at Singhgad within a few months of the Berar raid.

There was no replacement for Rajaram. The most suitable heir was Shahu, Sambhaji's son, but he had been a Mughal captive for years. Rajaram left three sons (one illegitimate), four queens, and one concubine. One queen died and one became a sati; the other two had small sons to promote and hopes of a throne.

In any monarchical system, this situation would be ideal for severe factionalization. All claimants were minors. None had substantially stronger claims by rules of succession. The factions split three ways, one each surrounding a queen and her infant son, and one wanting to continue the war in the name of the imprisoned Shahu. The winner was the elder queen, Tarabai, who ruled for the next decade in the name of her infant son, Shivaji II (and would play a role in Maratha politics for far longer).

In some ways, the coronation of Shivaji II only exacerbated factional problems. Tarabai had to favor the leaders who supported her, such as Parashuram Trimbuk and Shankraji Narayan, at the expense of those who wavered, such as Ramchandra Nilkanth (who had, as we have seen, been leading the effort in Maharashtra) and independent leaders, like Dhanaji Yadav.[25]

Within weeks of Rajaram's death, the Mughal forces under Aurangzeb took Satara fort and nearby Parli fort. The Maratha court fell back to Visalgad (twenty miles east of Kolapur). With the fall of Visalgad in 1702, Tarabai moved the court to the lesser known fort of Ranga or Prasidgad. In the next five years, the Mughals captured fort after fort. Map 5 gives a better idea of the mobile nature of the warfare than any description could.

The Maratha strategy, throughout, was to hold a fort as long as possible, then escape with as much treasure and as many men as possible. Meanwhile, largely independent bands continued to raid the settled Mughal areas of Khandesh and Malwa. Nimaji Shinde, for example, defeated the Mughal deputy governor of Berar, Rustam Khan, and spread raids into Khandesh. There was a raid on the rich

[24] Grant Duff, *History*, 390.
[25] Brij Kishore, *Tarabai and her Times* (Bombay, 1963), 65–66.

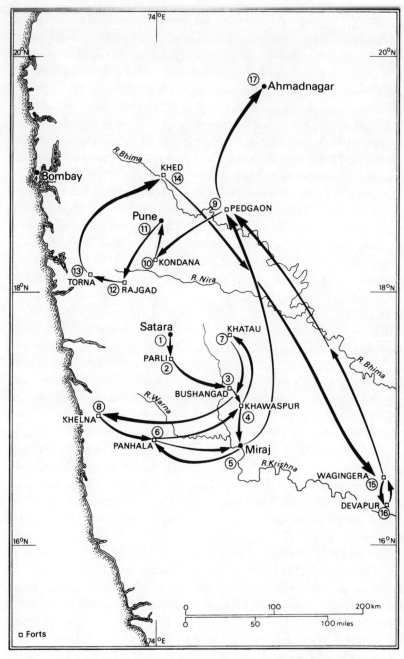

Map 5.   Aurangzeb's campaign against the Maratha hill forts, 1700–07 (taken from Brij Kishore, *Tara Bai and Her Times* [New Delhi, 1963]).

entrepot of Burhanpur in 1702.[26] In the next year, Nimaji set up toll posts along the Burhanpur–Surat road and built several small forts in the Tapti valley (see Map 7). Even though the Mughal commander, Firuz Jang, chased Nimaji Shinde north all the way across Malwa and into Bundelkund, the situation did not improve. Throughout 1704, the transport of grain, cash, and letters from the north to the Deccan was often disrupted.

The war in Maharashtra was devastating to the countryside. Both sides tried to collect taxes and tribute, and foraged for food for men and animals. In 1703–04, there was a severe famine in Maharashtra, accompanied by depopulation and migration. It is not clear that this weakened the Maratha forces; joining a roving band was the only available occupation in a sharply declining economic situation. It is difficult otherwise to explain the rapid recruitment by leaders like Nimaji Shinde or Dhanaji Yadav of thousands of Maratha recruits in a very short time.

By late 1705, the tide had turned. Aurangzeb faced serious problems in the north. He had an exhausted army, anxious to leave the barren hills of Maharashtra. Everyone, Marathas and Mughals, was waiting for the emperor to die. Factions and alliances formed and reformed. Maratha raids continued. Dhanaji Yadav, for example, raided Gujarat in the campaigning season of 1706–07, sacked Baroda, and defeated the Mughal deputy governor of the province and the faujdar of the city. In the same year, there was a major raid on the city of Burhanpur.[27]

After nearly forty years of campaigning in the Deccan, Aurangzeb died (March 1707) at Aurangabad, leaving the Marathas and Maharashtra unconquered. His death set off the succession war for which all the Mughal heirs and commanders had been positioning themselves for years. Of central importance to Maharashtra, one of the earliest events of the protracted Mughal war of succession was the release of Shahu, Sambhaji's son and heir, who had been a well-treated prisoner in the Mughal camp for eighteen years. His "escape" in Malwa was leisurely and arranged, and he ceremoniously visited the tomb of Aurangzeb before proceeding further south into Maharashtra. For the next eight years, there was full-scale civil war in Maharashtra between Shahu's forces and those of Tarabai, the queen who had been ruling in the name of Shivaji II.

[26] Grant Duff, *History*, 399.
[27] Kishore, *Tarabai*, 86.

Before looking at the complex situation in Maharashtra, let us briefly consider the problems facing the Mughal Empire. In the war of succession, several sources suggest that 10,000 seasoned soldiers died, including many generals. By the time Bahadur Shah emerged the victor, a number of structural problems were obvious. The most serious was the decline in the real power of the center. The emperor could no longer simply order an appointee to a new posting. It had become a matter of negotiation, the appointee using his friends at court to reverse or delay any undesirable posting. The center was receiving less and less information from outlying areas, and the financial position of the center steadily worsened. The extended conflict with the Rajputs had alienated the empire's most long-standing and loyal indigenous allies. There was only inconclusive war, but no long-term solution to the ongoing territorial claims of the Sikhs in the Punjab or the Jats in the vicinity of Agra. Law and order and the safety of the roads were questionable in much of the empire except the valleys of the Ganges and the Jumna. Much of the most recent conquests – Bijapur, Golconda, Maharashtra – were losing propositions. The net effect of all the problems was rapid, shifting factionalization at the Mughal court. Groups formed around a policy towards a particular problem or the priorities of problems or a particular individual, who seemed to have the money or the leadership ability to solve some of the problems. It is in this context that the Marathas represented only one of the Mughal Empire's serious problems; vacillating and contradictory policies towards the Marathas were, thus, the norm in the next decades.[28]

Rather than a simple war, we should view the situation in Maharashtra as three-cornered. Shahu, Tarabai, and the Mughals were all competing for the loyalty and support of deshmukh families and leaders of Maratha bands. Mughal policy was inconsistent and expensive, but often temporarily successful at diminishing Maratha raids. The Mughal viceroy of the Deccan at the time of Aurangzeb's death, for example, favored bringing the major Maratha leaders into the Mughal military system. Nimaji Shinde, who had been raiding Malwa and Khandesh, was brought in at the 7,000 level along with his sons and grandsons. This was a very large maintenance grant and Mughal documents suggest that over 1,000 Mughal grantees were displaced to make up Shinde's estates in the Aurangabad area.

[28] Satish Chandra, *Parties and Politics at the Mughal Court, 1707–1740* (Delhi, third edition, 1978) 44–53.

The dominant feature of the war in Maharashtra was the inability of any side to command the loyalty of the leaders of Maratha bands for long periods. When Shahu was released, virtually every leader pledged loyalty to Tarabai. Yet, within months, Shahu had won over several major leaders and defeated Tarabai's forces at Khed and Satara.[29] Shahu's forces pursued Tarabai's army south into the Konkan, taking several major forts, including Panhala. Tarabai took refuge in a coastal fort with the Angria family. Shahu's victory was more apparent than real; as soon as he turned north towards Pune, Tarabai recovered most of the major forts. Both sides sought grants of the Mughal share of the revenue of the Deccan, which included rights to chauth (one-quarter of government revenue) and sardeshmukhi (an additional one-tenth and rights over the deshmukhs). Though the Mughal court delayed the decision, the rights were eventually awarded to Shahu.

As the war dragged on, leaders more and more took wholly independent action, mainly raiding Mughal territory on the perimeter of Maharashtra. Let us look at some of these actions. In Gujarat, for example, we have mentioned several raids before Aurangzeb's death. These continued; in 1707, Kanderao Dabhade attacked southern Gujarat, threatened Ahmedabad, and was bought off with a large tribute.[30] In 1710, Surat was threatened again, and the residents started building the city wall.

In the northern half of Maharashtra, Maratha bands regularly raided the Ahmadnagar area and plundered the suburbs of Burhanpur. In 1710, a band defeated the Mughal governor of Aurangabad and plundered part of the city. The same pattern continued in following years. The Mughal governor of Burhanpur was killed in 1711 defending the city from yet another Maratha band (see Map 7).

To the south and east of Maharashtra, in 1710, Chandrasen Yadav besieged Vijaydurg and attacked Gulbarga. Haibat Rao Nimbalkar invaded Bijapur territory, but was attacked by the local Mughal commander. Mughal sources reported a large band attacking the Junar region. In 1711, Maratha bands attacked Karnul, Sholapur, and many other places in the Karnatak (see Map 3).

By 1712–13, the situation had hit some kind of low ebb. The anarchy

---

[29] For example, see Shahu's courting of the Yadav family in Pawar, *Tarabaikalin*, 187–88, and the shift to Shahu of the Satham family, who had been serving Tarabai. Ibid., 367–80.

[30] V. G. Dighe, *Peshwa Bajirao I and the Maratha Expansion* (Bombay, 1944), 22. Many documents of the conquest of Gujarat are found in G. S. Sardesai, *Selections from the Peshwa Daftar, XII: The Dhabades and the Conquest of Gujarat* (Bombay, 1931).

in Maharashtra was near total. Shahu controlled only the area immediately around Pune. With defections and the inability to pay his troops, the royal forces were substantially smaller than the larger independent Maratha bands. Tarabai's position was much the same. Her base in the Konkan was equally devastated. Even though Aurangzeb's policy of orthodox hostility toward the Marathas had been completely abandoned, the Mughals were unsuccessful at developing loyalty among Maratha leaders. They pursued a policy which remained contradictory – trying to defeat the bands, while offering service to the more successful leaders. Since the main Mughal attention was on the Sikh uprising in the Punjab, followed by Jats, Mewatis, and Afghans raiding up to the walls of Delhi, Mughal policy in Maharashtra tended to devolve on the senior official (the vazier) and changed with each new office-holder.

Let us now turn from the specific political narrative to a discussion of the broad processes by which Shahu brought about a consolidation of power and a strengthening of the monarchy. First, we will look at the composition of the elite military leadership of the Marathas in 1715 and compare it to Shivaji's elite, say forty years earlier. Second, we will look at the Maratha involvement in the factional politics in Delhi which resulted in the granting to Shahu, in 1719, of broad rights in Maharashtra. Then, we shall tie these two themes together in a discussion of power and legitimacy under Shahu.

Let us turn first to the composition of Shahu's military elite in 1715. The initial important point is that few of the families closely associated with Shivaji survived or prospered in the eighteenth century. Some had, of course, died out in the protracted wars and dislocation. Many more declined as a direct result of Maratha factional politics. Sambhaji, Shivaji's son, for example, executed twenty-five members of key families, including top cabinet members in the government, after the 1683 plot to poison him. Two decades later, many other families lost out in the factional conflict between Tarabai and Shahu. Consider some examples. Santaji Ghorpade was a close associate and contemporary of Shivaji. After all the factional strife, the family was given a small jagir by Tarabai at Kaphi in Kolapur State and played no significant part in later Maratha history. Dhanaji Yadav, to consider another example, was one of the principal leaders harassing the Mughal forces outside Jinji in the 1790s. His son, Chandrasen Yadav, led a major band against the Mughals in Khandesh and Malwa in the 1700–10 period. Chandrasen, however, fought with Shahu's new Peshwa, Balaji Vishwanath, and the family rapidly declined. After 1713, they never again played a major role; later in the eighteenth century, they held small estates and were not even sardars of any princely state in the nineteenth century. Consider just two more examples. Mane Thorat was a close associate of Shivaji, with long prior association with the Bijapur court. In the later struggles, the family sided against Shahu and was reduced to a small jagir on the ancestral lands of Kathad. Udaji Chavan was a minor commander during the Shivaji period. The family sided with Tarabai, and – as one of her main supporters – was given the title of Himmat Bahadur. In the eighteenth century the family declined to a small jagir in the Kolapur State. Sometime between 1710 and 1712, Ramchandra Nilkanth (who had been a key figure in the resistance in Maharashtra after Rajaram's flight to Jinji) was brought over to Shahu's side. He got everything he asked for – sardeshmukhi and mokasa rights and rights to a number of forts. His sons were brought into service at high salaries. He was to be in charge of the administration. Two years later, however, he returned to Tarabai's side and extracted large concessions. Within a few years, as Shahu's faction won out, his position was displaced by Balaji Bajirao, Shahu's chief minister.[31] All of these families are examples of the more general principle which we established in Chapter 1. In the Maratha polity, just as in the earlier Deccan kingdoms, rights to shares of revenue were never isolated from the larger politics of court. Factional struggles intensified during disputed successions, and those on the losing side rarely recovered positions of power.

What, then, was the composition of the "new" elite when Shahu's faction was firmly in control in 1718? Three older families remained. One was the Nimbalkar family, whose position of power went back more than a century in the Phaltan area. The family had served Bijapur in the sixteenth century and Shivaji in the seventeenth century; Haibat Rao Nimbalkar was still a powerful figure at the court of Shahu. Another family which remained from the Shivaji period was the Deshasta Brahmin family of Bhor which took their name from the post of sachiv which they had fulfilled ever since Shivaji's original cabinet.[32]

[31] The relevant documents are found in Pawar, *Tarabaikalin*, 274, 291.
[32] Older books on Shivaji's "administration" assigned specific duties to the various "cabinet" members, such as sachiv. More recent research suggests that their position was advisory, their duties vague and overlapping, and that the "cabinet" rarely met as a body. There was an inner circle of powerful men who met in darbar and some were assigned titles,

The third older family which survived into the Shahu inner circle was the Hingnikar Bhonsles. Originally village headmen in the village of Hingni near Pune, the family had provided two leaders, Rupaji and his nephew Parsoji, during Shivaji's reign. Parsoji led an independent band in Khandesh around 1700 and was the first major leader to accept Shahu when he was released in 1707; Shahu rewarded him with a major saranjam grant – six sarkars including 147 mahals in Berar and the title Sena Saheb Subah. After the death of Parsoji in 1709, his son Kanoji apparently mismanaged the saranjam and opened negotiations to go into Mughal service. Shahu ordered his nephew, Raghuji, to defeat and displace his uncle. This done, Raghuji succeeded to the title and saranjam, which formed the basis of the later Maratha state of Nagpur.

The rest of Shahu's elite were leaders of successful, largely independent bands. First was the Dabhade family, which, under Shivaji, had been appointed village headmen of the village of Talegaon. Family tradition has them instrumental in Rajaram's escape from Jinji (1699), but there is no outside confirmation. We find Kanderao Dabhade raiding Gujarat as early as 1701, and his son continuing the raids from a fortified base in Baglan. He was also one of the leaders who shifted to Shahu at a crucial moment in 1713.[33] By 1715, he could assemble as many as 5,000 cavalry for a raid. In 1716, Dabhade closed the Mughal road from Surat to the Deccan and extracted fees from all caravans on the Burhanpur–Surat road. He engaged the Mughals near Ahmadnagar and was raised to the cabinet post of senapati.

A second independent leader was Fateh Singh Bhonsle (no relation to the Hingnikar Bhonsles). Originally, the family held the headmanship of the village of Parad, some twenty-five miles south of Daulatabad, and the head of the family died in a pitched battle with Shahu's forces (in 1707). His widow appealed to Shahu, who promised to treat her only son, Fattesingh, as his own. Later, Shahu granted him a hereditary jagir in Akkalkot in southern Sholapur district.[34] By 1715, he emerged as a major leader.

A third leader was Nimaji Shinde. We first found him serving in the forces outside Jinji in the 1690s, then as an independent leader in Khandesh in the late 1690s. He figures frequently in the raids on

such as sachiv; we should, however, be cautious about attributing too much of a modern structure of government to them.
[33] Dighe, *Peshwa Bajirao*, 25.
[34] A. R. Kulkarni, "The revolt of zamindars in Akkalkot, 1830," in S. B. Bhattacharya, *Essays in Modern Indian Economic History* (Delhi, 1987), 147.

Burhanpur and into Malwa and Khandesh throughout the first decade of the eighteenth century, and was one of the strongest leaders supporting Shahu. It is, however, a measure of the volatility of the times that Nimaji Shinde disappears from the record within a decade, and the family is untraceable thereafter.

Now let us turn to the "new" Brahmins in Shahu's inner circle. First, there was Parushram Pant Pratinidhi. He was a Deshasta Brahmin, the family originally from Karhad. Secondly, there was the Bhat family of Chitpavan Brahmins who were, as peshwas (chief ministers), to become de facto rulers of the Maratha polity for the next sixty years. The family were hereditary deshmukhs of Danda Rajpuri on the Konkan coast about sixty miles south of Bombay.

Because he was so important to Shahu's success, and the family so central to later Maratha history, let us pause a minute to consider the rise of Balaji Vishwanath. In his late teens, he left a post as a clerk in the saltworks of the Siddis of Janjira (in the Konkan) and, around 1700, found employment as subahdar (head administrator) of Pune and later the Daulatabad district.[35] He early declared for Shahu, and militarily, and especially through negotiations, was Shahu's main support. He brought in Dhanaji Yadav, the first major leader to support Shahu. He led the military expedition against Dhanaji's son's revolt. After appointment as Peshwa, in 1713, it was Balaji Vishwanath who negotiated in the Konkan with Kanoji Angria, who was Tarabai's main supporter. When Angria switched sides, Tarabai's support collapsed and she was imprisoned. Balaji Vishwanath also led Shahu's army against the Mughal forces led by the Nizam, in 1713–15. Balaji Vishwanath, thus, embodies the first theme of Shahu's early reign, the disappearance of older deshmukh families and the rise of new Maratha and Brahmin families which chose correctly in the civil war between Tarabai and Shahu.[36]

---

[35] In 1708, he was in the administration of Dhanaji Yadav, the Maratha commander who figured so prominently in the war with the Mughals in the 1690s. See *Maratha Itihasiche Sadhne*, IV, 170. Shortly thereafter, he served as diwan of the senapati, another of the inner circle. See Dighe, *Peshwa Bajirao*, 2–3.

[36] Ramchandra Nilkanth in his *Ajnapatra* (issued in 1716 though written some years earlier), devoted one of his longest sections of this treatise on statecraft to the qualifications of king's ministers and the dangers of a minister too powerful or a king not attentive enough, "The Ajnapatra or royal edict" (trans. S. V. Puntambekar), *Journal of Indian History*, 8, 2 (August, 1929), 207–14. Ramchandra Nilkanth identified another important need of a strong monarchy, a complete army (including artillery and matchlockmen) who were salaried professionals paid by the king. Cavalrymen were to ride the king's horses. Shivaji had had

Let us now turn to the second theme of Shahu's early reign, the events which led to Mughal recognition of Maratha rights in Maharashtra. By 1716 it was clear that Mughal troops in Maharashtra were not winning against the unifying Maratha bands. Various officials in Gujarat, Khandesh, and further south sought piecemeal accommodations. The new Peshwa, Balaji Vishwanath, asked the Mughal Emperor for a sanad, granting Shahu the right to chauth (¼) and sardeshmukhi (⅒) of the government revenue throughout the six Mughal subahs of the Deccan (Aurangabad, Berar, Bidar, Golconda, and Bijapur – including the whole of the Karnatak – and Khandesh). The demand also included chauth of Malwa and Gujarat, and recognition of swaraj (independence) in the Maharashtra heartland, which meant turning over all the remaining Mughal forts. Recent conquests by Parsoji Bhonsle in Berar and Gondwana were to be confirmed, and certain estates in the Karnatak were demanded in the name of Fateh Singh Bhonsle. In return, the Peshwa, on behalf of Shahu, would maintain 15,000 troops for the Mughal subahdar of the Deccan, maintain law and order, and return 10 percent of sardeshmukhi to the Mughal treasury. In addition, Shahu would pay a 100,000 Rs. yearly tribute.

Even though the Mughal subahdar of the Deccan agreed to the terms, the Emperor realized that such a sanad would effectively end Mughal power south of the Tapti river. He prepared for war and repudiated the treaty. Within a year, a Maratha army, under the command of Balaji Vishwanath, travelled to Delhi, and became troops of the Sayyid brothers, one of the factions competing for the Mughal throne. Just a few months after the arrival of the Maratha army at Delhi, a new puppet was put on the Mughal throne by the Sayyid brothers, and the whole treaty was ratified. Balaji Vishwanath returned to the Deccan in triumph in May 1719 with the treaty and Shahu's family (which had been held captive since his release in 1708).[37]

Now let us turn to a more general discussion of legitimacy and the

such an army, but Shahu was only able to build one slowly in the course of the next decade or so. Ibid. 1 (April, 1929), 101–02.

[37] Grant Duff is the only historian to have seen the actual Mughal grant. It has since disappeared. His extract gives several interesting details. The cash revenue of the six subahs of the Deccan was estimated at over 180 million rupees at the time. Sardeshmukhi was calculated at 10 percent of this figure. Shahu was to pay the Mughal court a "gift" of over six times the value of a year's sardeshmukhi in return for the grant, though there is no evidence that he ever paid it. Grant Duff's extract also gives the districts included in the grant of swaraj, and they did indeed cover the areas of the Desh and the Konkan in which Shivaji had held most control. See Grant Duff, *History*, 324–25 n.

consolidation of power in the polity of Shahu. As we have just seen, the turning of titular legitimacy into some real power at the center was, first, a process of bringing men personally loyal to Shahu into the inner circle and quickly rewarding them with saranjam grants for the maintenance of troops. Within a few years, few of the original families which had served Shivaji remained. Second, there was active warfare against leaders who would not submit personal loyalty to the king. We might think that these families simply retired to their "lands," bided their time, and re-emerged at the next opportunity. Such was not the case. From the time of Shivaji, prominent families sank into oblivion, crushed after siding with a losing faction. Most Maratha families had only minimal "watan" rights, that is, rights given in reward for previous service of high merit and really perceived as permanent and inviolate. Most of their income came from other sorts of "nested" rights (sardeshmukh, deshmukh, village headman) of which they could be stripped – leaving the male members of the family as soldiers only or somewhat wealthier peasants. In the most anarchistic times, "nested" rights mattered less, since the band could be maintained by plunder. In all other times, however, such as the consolidation under Shahu, troops required a saranjam grant from the Maratha polity. None of these new leaders had aspirations to replace Shivaji's line; therefore, they needed a king to assign them revenue.

What is also clear is that neither a compact kingdom, nor a series of compact fiefdoms was emerging. One example should suffice. As we have seen, the Dabhade family of this inner circle were originally headmen of the village of Talegaon. Their base for independent raiding in the 1700–15 period had been Baglan in north-west Maharashtra. The new saranjams were to come from Gujarat, not the "ancestral" area of Talegaon.

This leads us to the third theme of consolidation, the clarification of the grant-giving process. As we have seen in Chapter 2, one of Shivaji's main problems was legitimacy. Many families held deshmukh and other rights from the earlier Deccan kingdoms of Ahmadnagar and Bijapur. From his coronation to his death, he attempted to consolidate the grant-giving process, so that all new grants originated with him, and old grants were continued in his name.[38] After his death, and

---

[38] The reality, as we have seen, was much more complicated. Even in Shivaji's life, there were a number of primary grant-givers – Bijapur, the Mughals, even the Portuguese, and the Sidi of Janjira.

especially after the death of Rajaram (1699), the number of grant-givers multiplied. Tarabai, when she ruled, gave out many grants; even some leaders of bands gave out smaller grants.[39] The second process of grant clarification concerns the deshmukhs and patils and the flow of tax and revenue information from the countryside. Balaji Vishwanath fought hard for the Mughal grant of 1719 because it gave full legal status for revenue collection to Shahu's government in much of India south of the Narmada river. No one else, no faction, no leader of a Maratha band, had this recognition. The grant represented moderate real assets and huge potential assets which could be dispensed to loyal followers. Conversely, it was only Shahu's government which could remove disloyal men from saranjams. Though the process was not completed until about 1740, the Peshwa, in the name of Shahu, managed to force all new and continued grants – saranjams, deshmukhi, patil, inam, and others – through the central Maratha government.[40]

Dealing with the junior line – Tarabai's claimant, Shivaji II – also took over a decade, and was finally settled by the Treaty of Warna (1731) which gave them a self-contained state at Kolapur. This division allowed Tarabai to give small maintenance grants to her supporters and a separate field of activity in the Karnatak. We have encountered this solution twice before in Maratha history. Shivaji's father divided his holdings between Shivaji and Ekoji (his half-brother), Shivaji getting the Pune area and Ekoji a kingdom in Thanjur. Shivaji himself tried to divide his holdings between Rajaram and Sambhaji in the last years of his life.[41] For Shahu and Tarabai, this division was largely successful; Kolapur survived as a separate, rarely threatening state throughout the eighteenth century (and as a princely state in the nineteenth and twentieth centuries).

It would have been ideal if Shahu had himself been a charismatic military leader. It would have enhanced his legitimacy and hastened the

---

[39] See, for example, the stream of grants from Sambhaji II in 1716–17, in Pawar, *Tarabaikalin*, 332–39.

[40] Andre Wink, *Land and Sovereignty in India: Agrarian Society and Politics under the Eighteenth-century Maratha Svarajya* (Cambridge, 1986), 240–41. Ramchandra Nilkanth, writing instructions for the king in the *Ajnapatra* (1700) recognized the crucial importance of consolidating the grant-giving process. "They [watan-rights holders] should not be allowed to have any privileges or watan rights without a state charter." "Ajnapatra" (August 1929), 215.

[41] These acts of division raise interesting questions of the kingdom as property of the king. A deshmukh right, for example, could certainly be mortgaged, sold, or divided, because it was perceived as income-producing property. Such treatment of a kingdom, however, had less precedent or scriptural authority.

consolidation. This was not the case, but Shahu had the good judgement to ally with Balaji Vishwanath and, later, his son, who were such leaders. This solution is a common one in many monarchical systems, and was common enough in India in the seventeenth and eighteenth centuries. The vazier, diwan, or peshwa led the armies.

The Maratha case is interesting because the new peshwa brought not just charismatic leadership and negotiating ability, but two other crucial requirements for consolidation. First, he patronized other Chitpavan Brahmins who formed the core of a rapidly expanding literate elite who filled jobs as tax collectors and administrators. Records-keeping was spotty before, but quickly regularized thereafter. This performance-based Brahmin elite was intermarried with and loyal to the peshwas and provided not just administrators, but a surprising number of military leaders in the coming decades. The second requirement which Balaji Vishwanath brought to Shahu was banking and credit facilities. As we have seen, Maharashtra was little monetized in the Shivaji period and had been largely destroyed since. Shahu's government, however, badly needed credit to raise armies and provide for regular government functions from harvest to harvest. Balaji Vishwanath brought in several banking families, exclusively Brahmin, and their credit was crucial to Shahu's bid for the throne. Especially after the Mughal grant of 1719, these families began to advance money against future revenue receipts. As we shall see, within a decade the system had all the elements of a sophisticated government finance system.

None of these should be taken as final solutions to kingship in the Maratha polity. The very patterns of consolidation under Shahu and Balaji Vishwanath were fraught with problems. Here, let us suggest just two. First, the Peshwa controlled patronage into military saranjams. He already controlled the Brahmin administrative and banking elite. It will come as no surprise that he would soon emerge as de facto ruler of the Maratha polity. Second, the creation of Thanjur and Kolapur states furthered the ethos that conquest would be shared, divided between the king and the military leader. Language to this effect was found in the Mughal grant of 1719, and within a decade leaders demanded a division of the new conquests in Malwa and Gujarat.

CHAPTER 5

BAJI RAO I'S NORTHERN EXPANSION
(1720–1740)

Balaji Vishwanath died in 1720. Against the objections of other ministers, Shahu appointed Balaji's son, Bijirao. Here we meet, after Shivaji, the most charismatic and dynamic leader in Maratha history. He was only twenty years old and already had a reputation for rapid decisions and a passion for military adventure. Bajirao had been on the expedition to Delhi in 1719, and was convinced that the Mughal Empire was breaking up and could not resist a Maratha drive to the north into Malwa and beyond. This was the major theme of the next twenty years of his ceaseless military and administrative activity.

This judgement by Bajirao was quite correct. Let us consider the various regions of the Mughal Empire, starting in the north and working south. Ever since his appointment to the Punjab in 1713, Abdul Samad Khan had sent little information to Delhi beyond the yearly tribute. By the time his son succeeded him in 1726, the Punjab was, functionally, an independent, tribute-paying state (with its own problems with the Sikhs). Awadh followed the same course. Sagdat Khan had been appointed governor in 1722, and independently removed mansabdars and changed jagirs. Four years later, the attempt to remove him resulted in his taking possession of Awadh. Thereafter, the province paid some tribute, but there was no Mughal authority inside it. In 1727 in Bengal, the son of Murshid Quli Khan succeeded to his father's governorship, and the province became functionally independent.[1] The Rajput states, always internally autonomous, expanded in the 1720s. Both Jodhpur and Jaipur took over new areas, previously Mughal, on their borders. Even in areas close to Delhi, Mughal control was tenuous. The Afghans from Farrukhabad, between Delhi and Awadh, carved out a small kingdom, and by 1728 were attacking the Bundelas immediately to the south. Jats, in fact, controlled much of the area surrounding Delhi. If we look further south in Malwa, authority was already disputed with the Marathas. In Gujarat, from 1724 onwards, each successive Mughal governor had to

---

[1] J. N. Sarkar, *A Study of Eighteenth Century India* (Calcutta, 1976), I, 167.

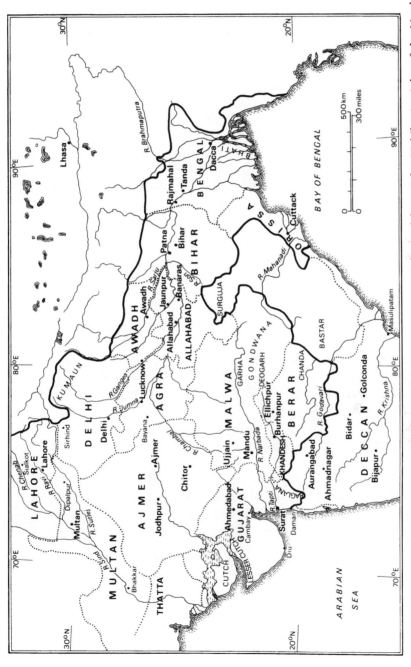

Map 6. Provinces of the Mughal Empire north of the Deccan c. 1720 (adapted from Irfan Habib, *An Atlas of the Mughal Empire* [Oxford, 1982], Plate oA).

displace his predecessor militarily, as each tried to make the province an independent kingdom. By 1724, the Nizam had defeated two Mughal armies, and returned to the Deccan as an independent ruler. The days of huge imperial armies, well-stocked from imperial treasuries, were over. The Marathas would now compete with provincial governors with aspirations of their own and whatever resources they could muster.

All this was, however, not obvious in 1720 and Bajirao had to convince the inner circle on a number of questions. Would the direction of Maratha expansion be primarily north into Gujarat and Malwa or south into the Karnatak? Would Marathas be friend or foe to the Nizam, Mughal subadar of the Deccan? How would the largely independent Maratha forces be controlled? How could a sound administration be set up? How could expansion be financed, since Maharashtra was still largely destroyed?

Within months, Bajirao's answers had caught the imagination of Shahu and the inner circle. Invade Gujarat and Malwa, because the Mughals were too weak to resist. The south could wait. The Nizam could also wait; he had an interest in seeing Delhi weakened. Shahu could regain control of the independent Maratha bands by Bajirao personally leading and organizing the raids on the north. Let the administration develop as new lands were conquered, and let the new conquests fill the government treasury. Push the frontiers to the north and give the heartland of Maharashtra time to recover. It was these policies which prevailed.[2]

Once this plan had been adopted, the following decade saw various Maratha bands attacking on two and often three fronts during each campaigning season. As earlier, bands tended to specialize in the direction of their attack and retreat to safe bases during the monsoon. It thus makes more sense to survey the main leaders than provinces or regions. Let us begin with the Dabhade family (Kanderao, the father, and Trimbukrao, the son), which operated out of bases in Baglana

---

[2] Satish Chandra, *Parties and Politics at the Mughal Court, 1707–1740* (Delhi, third edition, 1982), 190–91. For the period of rapid Maratha expansion, many documents have been printed (in Marathi). See G. S. Sardesai (ed.), *Selections from the Peshwa Daftar* (Bombay, 1931), XIII, XIV. Research on the documents of an individual village in the Pune district suggests that agricultural recovery proceeded rather quickly. In the Maratha system, basic agricultural revenue directly reflected acreage cultivated. In this particular village, revenue and acreage had doubled between the worst period of Aurangzeb's invasions (1698) and 1724. It would double again by 1730. Harold H. Mann, *The Social Framework of Agriculture* (Bombay, 1967), 126–28.

(south-west Khandesh) and soon established bases in southern Gujarat. An especially able leader, Damaji Gaikwad, rose rapidly in the service of the Dabhades and was, early in this crucial decade, leading the Dabhade forces. His son, Pilaji Jadhavrao, succeeded to the command on his father's death in 1721. The Maratha raids on Gujarat encountered a series of ineffectual, short-term Mughal governors, each successor militarily challenged by his predecessor. Maratha leaders were typically courted by both.[3]

The Dabhade–Gaikwad band was far from alone in raiding Gujarat. Two new groups rapidly emerged, one led by Kanthaji Kadam Bande, the other by Udaji Pawar. Both were based in Khandesh, both raided Malwa and Gujarat. The distinctive feature of these two bands was their personal loyalty to the Peshwa, Bajirao, who used their forces to extract a treaty in 1722 for half the chauth of the province from one of the hapless Mughal governors. He assigned a portion of the collection to Udaji Pawar. Pilaji Gaikwad, less tied to the Peshwa, formed links with the local armed elites and the local Raja of Rajpipla and, thus, had safe bases with allies inside Gujarat. There the situation stood at the opening of the campaigning season in 1723.

If we turn to Malwa, there were some differences. Both Udaji Pawar and Kadam Bande, whom we have just met, also raided Malwa from their bases in Khandesh. Two new leaders, Bhikaji Shinde and Malhar Rao Holkar, began in service of these two, but within a couple of years were leading bands of their own.

Let us look, in some detail, at the career of Malhar Rao Holkar for its illustration of the rapid advancement possible in the period. Holkar's early service was under Kadam Bande in Khandesh, starting as a teenager in 1715. He served on Balaji Vishwanath's expedition to Delhi in 1719 and fought in the Battle of Balapur against the Nizam in 1720. At about the same time, he took service with the Raja of Barwani (in eastern Gujarat). This was not uncommon; Maratha soldiers and bands often hired themselves out in local disputes throughout the 1720s.

Holkar petitioned the young Peshwa, Bajirao, to join his service in 1721, citing disagreements with Kadam Bande, and was accepted, first as a simple soldier.[4] A few years later, he was the leader of a small unit,

---

[3] V. G. Dighe, *Peshwa Bajirao I and the Maratha Expansion* (Bombay, 1944), 27. See also Yusef Husein, *The First Nizam; Life and Times of Nizam-ul-Mulk, Asaf Jah I* (Bombay, second edition, 1963), 143–46.

[4] Sardesai (ed.) *Peshwa Daftar* (Bombay, 1934–40), XVIII, letter 1.

and we find him mediating an on-going dispute between the Peshwa and Kadam Bande.

Personal contact with the Peshwa and rapid advancement coincided in the years 1723–29. Holkar accompanied the Peshwa on his campaign in 1723–24, and was deputed to settle the affairs of Bhopal State in eastern Malwa.[5] By 1725, Holkar's command was 500 men. Though the Marathas were relatively unsuccessful in defeating the Mughals in this period, Holkar was given a vague saranjam grant (a military grant for the maintainance of troops) to several unconquered districts in Malwa in August 1727.[6]

It was in the battle of Palkhed (1728) that Holkar particularly distinguished himself by cutting off Mughal supplies and communication. The Peshwa greatly raised his status, in part as a check on the less sure loyalty of the Pawar brothers. Within four years, Holkar was leading a contingent of several thousand cavalry, personally loyal to the Peshwa. His reward was a substantial portion of western Malwa in the "division" declared by the Peshwa in 1732.

If we ask why the Peshwa chose Holkar, the answer is at least in part because of the general situation in Malwa in these years. Except when the Peshwa personally led his troops and assembled bands into Malwa (1723–24), discipline was generally low. Even after this quite successful expedition, discipline rapidly broke down. Three commanders were deputed to collect tribute and set up some sort of administration. Instead, they hired themselves out in the faction disputes of various Rajput zamindars of western Malwa – Amjhera, Jhabua, and Sailana. This situation says much about the Mughal loss of control of their zamindars, but it says as much about the difficulties of the Peshwa in establishing control over the Maratha bands. When he found a loyal leader, like Holkar, he promoted him. The important general point here is that the founders of most of the major Maratha houses of the eighteenth and nineteenth centuries – Nagpur (Bhonsles), Akalkot (the Hingnikar Bhonsles), Dhar and Dewas (Pawars), Indore (Holkars), Ujjain (Shindes), and Baroda (Gaikwads) – were all teenage soldiers whose ability and loyalty were recognized by either Shahu or the Peshwa and were rapidly promoted. This new elite did not, we should emphasize, come from families which had been major commanders under the Deccan sultanates. They cannot really be called "deshmukh"

[5] Ibid., x, letter 27.
[6] V. V. Thakur (ed.), *Holkarsahica Itihasacin Sadhanen* (Indore, 1944), I, 10.

families because their "nested" holdings in Maharashtra were minimal. Rather, this group of leaders should be called – as they were at the time – "sardars" (military leaders), whose power and holdings came from military commands during this period of rapid expansion.

Now, keeping the same time frame (1720–30), let us turn to the Marathas' main rival in the Deccan, the Nizam. We will not attempt here even a summary of this distinguished Mughal general's family and early life. By the 1720s the Nizam was a seasoned general with long senior experience in the Deccan, a powerful army, and substantial ambition. He had correctly sensed the impossibility of controlling Delhi, and had remained largely aloof from the devastating factional struggles. In early 1723, the Nizam met the young Peshwa, near Jhabua in Malwa. No documents remain of these talks, but their brief joint campaign suggests cautious friendship. This policy foreshadows that of the Nizam throughout his long reign – try to circumscribe the Marathas, but provoke no irreparable breach with them. Late in 1723, after granting permission for the Nizam to return to the Deccan as vazier (the senior official), Delhi realized that if the Nizam returned to the Deccan with his army, with or without authority, he would set up an independent state. A pursuing Mughal army caught up with the Nizam near Aurangabad in northern Maharashtra, but was totally defeated, with some help from Maratha cavalry units under the personal command of Bajirao Peshwa.[7]

The imediate results of this victory were that the Nizam became the rival of the Marathas, not only in what were to become his home territories of Hyderabad, but also in the Karnatak (where both claimed revenue rights), in Khandesh (where revenue had been divided between the Mughals and the Marathas by the treaty of 1717), and in Gujarat (where the Nizam's relatives were, briefly, in power). Once again we see that the concept of "boundaries" of these polities is not very useful. The rights of the Nizam and the Marathas not only interpenetrated, but they often collected revenue from the same pargana or village. It is useful to remember that the Nizam's capital was not Hyderabad, as it became in the nineteenth century, but Aurangabad in the middle of northern Maharashtra.

The peaceful rivalry between Bajirao and the Nizam lasted less than two years, during which each had other problems – the Nizam

---

[7] Chandra, *Parties and Politics*, 171–73. See also Husein, *First Nizam*, 131, 150. The best overall biography of Asaf Jah is Husein, *First Nizam*.

solidifying his position in the south, and Bajirao leading expeditions into Malwa. Both were ambitious military leaders with armies, and their rights were totally intermixed. It seems inevitable that each would try to use, subvert, or destroy the other.

The first phase began in 1725. As part of the consolidation of power, the Nizam sent an army into the Karnatak to clear it of Maratha revenue collectors.[8] The Maratha response came within months. Fateh Singh Bhonsle led an expedition, reputed to be 50,000 horse, into the Karnatak. This leader was originally from Akalkot (in southern Maharashtra) and knew the terrain well. Bajirao accompanied him, but did not command. The Maratha forces were outmaneuvered and forced to retreat. A second campaign, after the monsoon, also failed to stop the Nizam's army or its campaign of ousting Maratha collectors. Bajirao used the failures to convince Shahu of the superiority of striking northwards, where there would be no concerted resistance.

Within a year, the war turned to political subversion. The Nizam, as supreme Mughal representative in the Deccan, refused to pay any chauth or sardeshmukhi to the Marathas. His grounds were that he could not decide between the two heirs, Shahu and Sambhaji (of the Tarabai faction). He "offered" to arbitrate the dispute, which, of course, had been fought to a conclusion, with the division of the Maratha polity, almost a decade earlier. Still, there were several leaders of Maratha bands who did not like the rapidly increasing power of Bajirao and the leaders loyal to him. The Nizam's main spokesman at Shahu's court was Parushuram Pant Pratinidhi (a Deshasta Brahmin); he was a direct rival of Bajirao (a Chitpavan Brahmin) in the inner circle at court. The Nizam's main supporter at Tarabai's court was Chandrasen Yadav, who – as we have seen – fought Bajirao's father ten years earlier.

Bajirao convinced Shahu that such "arbitration" actually meant the Nizam taking over the kingship of the Maratha polity by supporting Tarabai's line. War began in August 1727 and ended in March of the following year. On both sides, it was a war of movement.[9] Bajirao (supported mainly by Shinde, Holkar, and the Pawar brothers) raided the Nizam's areas of Khandesh; the Nizam, in turn, struck at Pune. The Nizam picked up an ally in Trimbukrao Dabhade, who wanted

[8] Andre Wink, *Land and Sovereignty in India: Agrarian Society and Politics under the Eighteenth-century Maratha Svarajya* (Cambridge, 1986), 96–98.
[9] Brij Kishore, *Tarabai and Her Times* (Bombay, 1963), 161.

none of Bajirao's attempts to control Gujarat. Bajirao's forces finally trapped the Nizam at Palkhed (twenty miles west of Aurangabad) in the dry hills near the Godavari river, cut off supplies, and forced the Nizam to terms on 6 March 1728.

Before discussing this turning point, let us catch up on events in Malwa and Gujarat, which also yielded important treaty gains within a year of Palkhed. In Malwa, recall that the major leaders were Shinde, Holkar, and the Pawar brothers. The Mughals fought back relatively successfully until the Peshwa brought the army, fresh from the Palkhed victory, into Malwa after the monsoon of 1728. The Marathas defeated the garrison forces of the sarkar capital of Ujjain and all other Mughal forces in south-west Malwa. The Mughal subadar (head of the province) was killed in action. The Peshwa travelled slowly north through the western half of Malwa collecting tribute, reaching Rajasthan in February 1729.[10]

Gujarat was more complicated. In the early 1720s, as we have seen, there was a multi-party competition between leaders of raiding bands, only one or two loyal to the Peshwa. The Nizam negotiated with several Maratha leaders, and, for a time, allied with Kadam Bande. The situation shifted quickly. By 1726, both of the leaders who had been loyal to the Peshwa, Udaji Pawar and Kadam Bande, had sided with the Dabhade/Gaikwad faction which opposed him. (Recall that in these years Bajirao Peshwa was in the Karnatak on fruitless expeditions with Fateh Singh Bhonsle.) The general pattern was that the Mughals controlled the cities and the forts, and the Maratha bands roved the countryside, collecting what they could.[11] Trade at Surat sharply dropped in this decade and was never to recover.[12]

Bajirao sent his brother, Chimnaji Ballal, into Gujarat with a large army. The Mughal governor prepared fresh agreements in 1727 and 1728, which gave the Peshwa and Shahu chauth, sardeshmukhi, and babti – in effect, 60 percent of the revenue. This move, of course, undercut similar independent agreements which the Dabhade family had extracted from the Mughals in previous years. As we have seen, 1727–28 was the height of the attempt by the Nizam to place a rival to Shahu on the throne, and the Dabhade/Gaikwad group from Gujarat

[10] S. N. Gordon, "The slow conquest: administrative integration of Malwa into the Maratha Empire, 1720–1760," *Modern Asian Studies*, 2, 1 (1977), 8–10.

[11] Wink, *Land and Sovereignty*, 114–27.

[12] Ashin Das Gupta, "Trade and politics in eighteenth century India," in D. S. Richards, *Islam and the Trade of Asia* (Philadelphia, 1970), 187–96.

were active Nizam allies, being Shahu's competitors for control of Gujarat. After Palkhed, Shahu withdrew all support from the faction and sanctioned expulsion of Dabhade, Gaikwad, and Kadam Bande from Gujarat. The Peshwa's forces campaigned against all three and defeated their combined forces in 1731.

To look ahead a few years, the Dabhade family rapidly declined and, within two decades, after another rebellion against the Peshwa's authority, disappeared from Maratha history, another victim of factional struggle.[13] The Gaikwad family, however, survived, with half the chauth and sardeshmukhi of Gujarat, perhaps kept by Shahu as a balance to the rising power of Bajirao. By 1737, Gaikwad effectively ruled the province, with Mughal rule reduced to the city of Ahmadabad.[14] Subsequent decades show the family absorbing, bit by bit, all of the Dabhade rights, in return for loyalty to the Peshwa, who himself retained half the revenue of the province. The story of the Kadam Bande family is simpler. The Gaikwads expelled them from Gujarat, and they faded to become a small state (and subsequently a princely state) on the border between Gujarat and Malwa.[15]

What, then, were the results of the milestone period between the battle of Palkhed (1728) and the end of the Dabhade rebellion (1731)? Palkhed resulted in the following concessions by the Nizam:

(1) recognition of Shahu as the sole Maratha monarch;
(2) recognition of his right to chauth and sardeshmukhi of the Deccan;
(3) reinstating the Maratha collectors who had been driven out;
(4) agreement to pay the outstanding arrears of chauth and sardeshmukhi.

The implications, however, were much more important. First, in the military sphere, Bajirao had defeated the best-equipped Mughal army of the day under its best general. The tactics of cutting off

[13] The Dabhades, however, were not reduced to common military service, as they might well have been a few decades earlier. Rather, they retained extensive "nested" rights in the area of Talegaon (about twenty miles morth-west of Pune) which included several village headmanships, a garrison at Induri, and considerable inam land. See Frank Perlin's research on this family archive, in "Money use in late pre-colonial India" in J. F. Richards (ed.), *The Imperial Monetary System of Mughal India* (Oxford, 1987), 274–75.

[14] Dighe, *Peshwa Bajirao*, 42.

[15] The stories of the smaller states on the western rim of Malwa are covered in Raghubir Singh, *Malwa in Transition, or a Century of Anarchy: The First Phase, 1698–1765* (Bombay, 1960).

supplies and rapid movement had defeated the Nizam's far superior artillery.[16] This same theme was being played out in Malwa. The Mughal governors tried to contain the Maratha bands throughout 1726–28, but failed. Periodically, they were cut off from supplies in the field. Second, the victory had settled the issue of Shahu's legitimacy and authority. The treaty of Warna, 1731, created Kolhapur State, the line of Tarabai becoming junior and non-threatening holders of estates and rights in southern Maharashtra.[17] Third, Bajirao's series of victories resulted in a serious challenge to his increasing power. The defeat of the Gaikwad/Dabhade/Kadam Bande faction in 1731, however, meant the end of factional resistance at court for more than two decades. De facto, it meant that the Peshwa ruled the Maratha polity.

In the next decade, we shall see how this consolidation of power resulted in patronage of new leaders (which – as always – had its own problems) and the development of an effective tax-collecting bureaucracy in many areas. Let us, first, summarize the main political and military events up to 1740, then return to a more systematic discussion of trends and patterns.

For Bajirao, the campaigning season of 1733 was spent in besieging Janjira, the extremely strong sea fort on the Konkan coast (see Map 1). Recall that the Sidis (Abyssinian Muslims) had occupied this fort for more than a hundred years and held it against all comers, including Shivaji, the Portuguese, Dutch, and English. In the years after Shivaji's death, the Sidis had expanded their landholdings to include much of the central and northern Konkan coastal plains. (The main competitor of the Sidis was the Angrias, a Maratha family with sea forts and ships, based in the southern Konkan.) Bajirao's forces did not, however, take Janjira, though they captured much of the surrounding area; a favorable treaty in 1736 gave the Marathas some control over virtually all of the Sidi's lands. Major warfare continued in the Konkan in the later half of the 1730s. In a large, multipronged campaign headed by the Peshwa's brother, the Marathas attacked the Portuguese. Salsette, Bassein, and Chaul all fell to the Marathas.[18] The apparent results were

---

[16] Many areas under the control of the Nizam actually began to pay chauth in this period. See Z. Malik, "Chauth-collection in the Subah of Hyderabad 1726–1748," *Indian Economic and Social History Review*, 8, 4 (December, 1971), 395–414.

[17] Kishore, *Tarabai*, 164.

[18] The documents of the Janjira campaign are found in Sardesai (ed.), *Peshwa Daftar* (Bombay, 1934–40), XIII and III. The documents of the Bassein campaign are scattered in XII,

a series of complicated alliances, including the English and the Dutch, but the more important results were a dramatic decrease in the power of the Sidi and the ousting of the Portuguese from the Konkan, reducing them to the enclaves of Goa and Daman. The Marathas and the English were the only remaining powers competing for supremacy in coastal Maharashtra.

Before turning to Malwa and the north, let us briefly carry forward the story of the Hingnikar Bhonsles. In 1720, when Bajirao was appointed Peshwa, Raghuji Bhonsle was the leader of a large Maratha band and was promptly confirmed in a grant for the Berar region (now north-eastern Maharashtra), and he agreed to keep a body of 5,000 horse in the service of Shahu. In the 1720s, he was most likely operating in Berar and eastwards in Gondwana. In the 1730s, Raghuji hired his band out to various factions of the Gond kingdom whose capital was at Nagpur. By 1740, Raghuji had usurped the power, but kept the Gond king a prisoner, as titular head. Thereby, Raghuji claimed status independent from Shahu or the Peshwa, and, as we shall see, was one of the most consistent opponents of the Peshwa. Through the 1730s, Raghuji pushed raiding and tribute collection east and north-east, until the area included coastal Orissa and all of Gondwana. (By the 1740s, his units were attacking Bengal.)[19]

The main front, however, in the 1730s was Malwa and the areas beyond – the Ganges and Jumna valleys, Delhi, and Rajasthan. The Marathas fielded larger armies toward mid-decade; often Shinde, Holkar, Pawar, and the Peshwa's brother were operating separate, but coordinated campaigns. The main Mughal commander, Jai Singh, lost the war of movement and in March 1733 offered terms – cash immediately and the assignment of twenty-eight parganas in Malwa in lieu of chauth and sardeshmukhi. When Delhi would not confirm this treaty, the war in Malwa continued. Holkar's army, for example, passed right through Malwa in 1735, took the fort of Bundi (in north-west Malwa), and extended raids into Rajasthan.[20]

In 1735, the Mughals assembled a huge, unwieldy army, including

XIV, XXX, and XXXIV. The narrative of both campaigns is pieced together in Dighe, *Peshwa Bajirao*, 43–83, 154–91.

[19] Wink, *Land and Sovereignty*, 108–09. The terror which these Maratha raids provoked in Bengal is well described in the Maharashtra Purana, a contemporary Bengali text. See E. C. Dimmock and P. C. Gupta (trans. and annot.), *The Maharashtra Purana: An Eighteenth-Century Bengali Historical Text* (Honolulu, 1965).

[20] See Dighe, *Peshwa Bajirao*, 112–15.

contingents from Rajasthan, and entered Malwa. This campaign showed that the Mughals had not evolved a strategy which could defeat the Maratha wars of movement. As they had for more than four decades, the Marathas cut off grain supplies, prevented the Mughal army from foraging the countryside, and refused decisive battle. The Mughal army starved; finally, the commander bought off the Marathas with a large cash tribute. In these middle years of the 1730s, the Delhi court vacillated between a "peace" party, which wanted to appease the Marathas, and a "war" party.[21] Plans for another campaign against the Marathas, thus, coincided with suggestions for friendly meetings between the Emperor and Bajirao. In 1735–36, Bajirao spent much time in negotiations, through intermediaries, with the Mughal court. All these negotiations failed, because Bajirao kept increasing the demands – finally including a hereditary state for himself, jagir grants for his most loyal leaders, immediate cash payments, full control over Malwa, including the Rajput and Afghan zamindars, the right to nominate all the Mughal officials of the Deccan, and personal rights to 5 percent of the revenue of the Deccan.[22] By May, Bajirao, without a treaty, returned to the Deccan and prepared for war.

The campaign of 1737 was indecisive, though Bajirao attacked Delhi, even briefly holding the Emperor to ransom. It was in the following year, 1738, that the issue was settled. The Mughal Emperor called in the Nizam from the Deccan and supported him with zamindar levies from Malwa, some troops from Rajasthan, and an army from Delhi. The huge force moved from Delhi to Bhopal in eastern Malwa (see Map 7). There – in a pattern perhaps boring by now – it had its supplies cut off, came to a stop, and began to starve. As famine worsened in the Nizam's camp, the zamindar and Rajput contingents melted away. Negotiations ended with the landmark treaty of Bhopal in January 1739.[23] The Nizam granted the whole subah of Malwa to the Peshwa, and ceded complete sovereignty of all lands between the Narmada and the Chambal rivers. The Nizam agreed to try to obtain a large cash tribute from the Mughal Emperor. Note that Bajirao did not get all that he had asked for in the previous year, principally an independent

---

[21] The period of the conquest of Malwa is well discussed in J. N. Sarkar, "The Mughal–Maratha contest for Malwa, 1728–1741," *Islamic Culture*, 6 (1932), 535–52. Also interesting are the letters of the Nizam to the Mughal Emperor, translated in P. Setu Madhava Rao, *Eighteenth Century Deccan* (Bombay, 1963), 139–48.

[22] Sardesai (ed.), *Selections from the Peshwa Daftar* (Bombay, 1934–40), XV, 93–96.

[23] Ibid., 86.

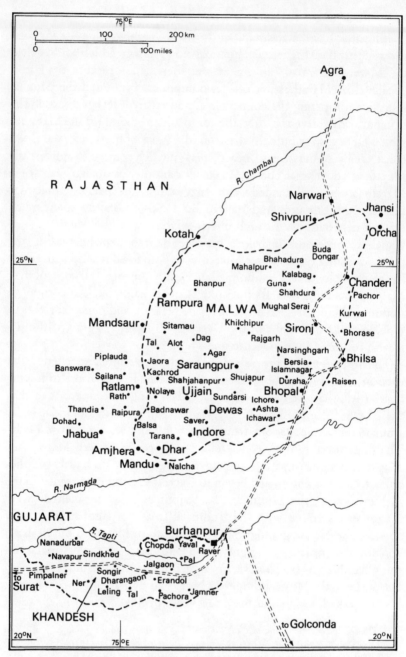

Map 7. Burhanpur, Khandesh, and Malwa c. 1750 (taken from Stewart
Gordon, "Burhanpur: entrepot and hinterland, 1650–1750," *The Indian
Economic and Social History Review*, 25, 4 [1988], 430).

kingdom for himself and large jagirs for his leaders. Bajirao still feared engagement with the Nizam's efficient artillery and settled for cession of Malwa.

The following year 1739 brought the invasion of Nadir Shah (King of Persia), the sack of Delhi with the deaths of perhaps 20,000 local residents, and the loss of 1,500,000 Rs. worth of jewelry and the famous Peacock Throne. When Nadir Shah withdrew from India within a few months, Afghanistan, the Punjab, and the Frontier areas were lost to Delhi's control, and Sikh bands began to raid in the vicinity of the capital, destroying much of the suburbs.[24] This was the end of any leadership, effective or not, from Delhi.

With the thorough success of Bajirao's strategy in Malwa, Gujarat, Konkan, and Gondwana, now let us consider several themes of his twenty years of ceaseless activity. (He was to die within a year at only forty.) First, what do we mean by "conquest" in the context of the Marathas and the eighteenth century? What did it take to convert a revenue-paying Mughal province into a revenue-paying Maratha province? The area best documented is Malwa; it was held personally by the Peshwa, and those documents are found in the Pune Daftar.[25] The early raids, as we have seen, were by largely independent bands, numbering as many as 5,000 cavalry. Like the combined raids under Bajirao in the early 1730s, these certainly did not "conquer" Malwa. They gathered up whatever they could in cash and objects from the villages and cities along their route.[26] After some years of raiding, estimates appear in the Peshwa's documents as to the worth of an area, usually in round sums. Through all the 1730s, the Marathas held no legal rights to collect any part of the revenue of the Mughal subah of Malwa; nevertheless, at Delhi, they kept up claims to Malwa's revenue. On the ground, however, the Marathas were doing a thorough job of undermining Mughal administrative control. We have seen how they rarely met a main-force army in battle, but, instead, cut off its supplies and starved it. They first engaged and defeated smaller Mughal units of the sarkar level, then the larger subah-level units, finally engaging armies specially sent from Delhi. Equally important, Maratha revenue officers established contact with the zamindars all across Malwa, and

---

[24] J. N. Sarkar, *Nadir Shah in India* (Calcutta, 1973), 78–86.

[25] The revenue documents, in the Modi script, are located in the Pune Daftar, Prant Azmas Hindustan Rumals (hereafter referred to as H.R.), witth some additional papers in the Zamau Rumals.

[26] See the receipts of the expedition, in H.R. 154 and H.R. 190.

the Peshwa wrote to them yearly, demanding tribute.[27] By the mid-1730s, many had, in fact, paid tribute for several years, and the regular bookkeeping suggests halting movement towards predictability on both sides. As the Maratha patrols regularly cut off roads and disrupted communications between garrisons and towns, the Mughals were no longer providing basic security of life and property. Some traders and town-based groups began dealing with the Marathas in the hope of restoring it.

After the Treaty of Bhopal, everyone knew the order had changed. Many zamindars were called to witness the Maratha gains. Immediately, tribute was regularized from many of the zamindars of eastern Malwa, with, for example, a Maratha collector resident at his court. Note, however, that the Marathas, at this point, assessed no land, collected no taxes, had no direct contact with the village headmen, heard no court cases, and imposed no fines. The collector's sole job was to "ask" these large zamindars for the negotiated tribute each year.[28] On the whole, the system worked poorly; zamindars were usually in arrears, and generally paid only when threatened with a Maratha main-force army. As we shall see, this system was replaced within a decade by a much more elaborate and information-intensive administration.

Several features of the process of "conquest" are noteworthy. First, conquest began in the countryside, not in the cities or the major forts, which the Mughals held for decades. Second, the early forays, which gathered up "wealth on hand" ended only with the legal recognition of Maratha rights in Malwa (the Treaty of Bhopal, 1738). Third, these rights quickly translated into agreements with local zamindars for a yearly tribute. The Marathas thus made little attempt to displace local powers. We should, in these early years, see Maratha control as very limited, power as diffuse, and local lineages very much in control of their lands and forts. Fourth, there were the beginnings of a centralized, performance-based civilian revenue administration, loyal directly to the Peshwa. Information was starting to come in from the countryside of Malwa. Fifth, this process, which we have examined in Malwa, was typical of all areas of Maratha conquest, though the stages might occur at a somewhat earlier or later date. In Gujarat, for

[27] See, for example, the receipts in H.R. 179 (1731) and H.R. 154 (1732).
[28] See, for example, the tribute agreements in H.R. 165 and H.R. 185. These concern the tribute of the Afghan state of Bhopal in south-east Malwa.

example, this phase of establishing stabilized ties with local lineages was largely completed in the early 1730s. In Khandesh, legal recognition had come much earlier (1719), and the stabilized tribute phase was passed by the mid-1720s.

Our second theme of the 1720s to 1740s is change in the nature of warfare. We have seen the general failure of the Mughal mode of fighting. The Mughals relied on heavy cavalry, large slow-moving armies, and decisive plains battles. Forts were places of strength and retreat, cities the bases of administration. After the Marathas discovered that the weakness of Mughal armies was supply, they raised the art of raiding warfare to a high art. The Maratha bands generally ignored forts, ransomed cities, and drew the Mughal armies into unfavorable areas of the plains, where they cut them off from supplies and reinforcements. The only Mughal response was to raise ever larger armies, which were, in fact, more vulnerable to the Maratha mobile warfare; these grand armies were broken up by the Maratha's raids on the home areas of various commanders.

There were two further changes in warfare, both just beginning in the period. The first was on the Maratha side; armies were getting bigger and more professional. In the 1700–20 period, it was rare for a Maratha band to be more than 5,000 men. In the 1720–40 period, these bands often coalesced to armies of 10,000–20,000. Feeding these numbers was a continuing problem. The old "live off the land" tactics were less possible. Also, more and more of these soldiers were professionals who had to be housed during the monsoon. The mid-1730s was the first time that, for example, major bands stayed in Malwa through the monsoon, rather than returning to Maharashtra. Thus, Maratha military units began to be more expensive, and expenses could only be met with cash, not grants in kind, in the Deccan. As we shall see, all of this pushed the development of revenue administration and banking and credit. The other significant change was on the side of the Marathas' opponents. This was in artillery. The Mughals by the 1740s had long experience in cannon. Developments in casting produced field guns somewhat lighter and certainly more accurate than available in previous decades. The Marathas feared them; they, for example, did not want to engage the Nizam at the Battle of Bhopal (1738), because of his artillery. Developments in artillery were coming quickly outside India. When Nadir Shah invaded North India (1739), his forces used relatively rapid-firing, small-bore guns against cavalry for the first time in India. These swivel guns, mounted on camels, were spectacularly effective.[29] Developments toward more mobile, faster firing artillery were progressing even more quickly in Europe. There is evidence in the Peshwa's correspondence that he was aware of his lack of superior artillery; he was certainly aware that Europeans had it. None of this solved the problem of how to integrate artillery into a cavalry-oriented army.

The final important theme of this period is social mobility. We have already discussed many of the "losers" among Maratha families – the rapid decline of the Dabhades, Yadavs, Kadam Bande, the Pawars – and the Maratha "winners" – Shinde, Holkar, the Gaikwad, and the Bhonsles of Nagpur. The dominant variables (except in the case of the Bhonsles of Nagpur) were personal loyalty to Bajirao and proven military leadership. Advancement came extremely quickly in this period. The other big "winners" were Brahmins, also patronized by Bajirao. To administer the newly conquered areas of Khandesh, Gujarat, and Malwa, the Peshwa needed, quickly, a literate bureaucracy with experience. He called on kinsmen, other Chitpavan Brahmins, and, less so, other Brahmin communities (Saraswat and Deshasta); many of these families had served the Deccan kingdoms for generations in low and medium level administrative positions. Hundreds were recruited in the 1720–40 period, and their wealth built much of what is now the old city of Pune.[30]

The third group to benefit from Bajirao's expansion were the bankers. Most were Brahmins, intermarried with and overlapping the administrative families; they loaned money to the Peshwa against revenue receipts, and made larger loans when the Peshwa needed to raise an army or celebrate a large festival.[31] They also received deposits

---

[29] Sarkar, *Nadir Shah*, 53–54.

[30] Their increasing wealth and position also gave an orthodox tone to the city. Bajirao himself experienced this. Sometime in the late 1720s, Bajirao met and fell in love with a Muslim dancing girl, named Mastani. She was a trained singer and also an accomplished rider. She accompanied Bajirao on all his campaigns, and bore him a son in 1734. The orthodox Brahmin community strongly objected to the attachment (though Bajirao also had a Hindu wife and sons by her) and forced her to live outside the city. The community refused the thread ceremony to Bajirao's son, because of his connection to Mastani. In 1739, Bajirao's son and brother, at the instigation of the Chitpavan community, imprisoned her, when Bajirao was on campaign; this broke his heart and he died within a few months. Mastani died a few days later, whether by suicide is unknown. See G. S. Sardesai, *New History of the Marathas* (Bombay, second impression, 1957), 190–91.

[31] When Bajirao died, he was substantially, though not crushingly, in debt to the banking families. The invasions had been expensive and most provinces were just barely becoming

from private individuals, financed business ventures, and moved money from one city to another.

What were the methods the Peshwa used to build loyalty and keep control of these military, administrative, and banking families? First, as we have seen, he centralized the rights-granting process, pushing aside families which held previous or alternate authority. Second, he tried to scatter and intermix grants so that no leader could use a compact territory as a basis for rebellion. Third, paradoxically, he promptly shared power in the newly conquered areas of Malwa and Gujarat. The most important of the devolutions was the "division" of Malwa in 1732 between the Peshwa, Holkar, and Shinde, with a smaller share to Pawar. Bajirao, however, was the grant-giver of this devolution, and loyalty was the price of receiving such a grant. As a strategy, it worked. Shinde and Holkar remained loyal for decades. Fourth, the Peshwa kept revenue settlement, collection, and division consciously complicated. This placed his Brahmin administrators in a strong position, and kept the Peshwa in the position of arbitrator of disputes. Fifth, the Peshwa regularly appointed inam grants (hereditary merit grants) of villages in Maharashtra to his commanders and others who performed special service. While these represented a stable, personal income, because they were in Maharashtra, they were easily sequestered for disloyal behavior. Sixth, the Peshwa centralized banking in Maharashtra so that administrators yearly had to come to the capital, pay their advance, and receive personal audience with the Peshwa, before proceeding to their districts. Finally, of course, the Peshwa was married into and otherwise related to many of the banking and administrative community.

paying propositions. It would be ten years before the debt was cleared. See Kishore, *Tarabai*, 165.

CHAPTER 6

CONQUEST TO ADMINISTRATION
(1740–1760)

After the death of Bajirao in 1740, there was a short and inconsequential scramble for the powerful office of Peshwa. Shahu, however, overrode the opposition and chose Bajirao's son, Balaji Bajirao, for the office. At the time (and currently in Maharashtra), he was known as Nana Saheb, and will be thus referred to throughout this section. He was only nineteen years old when he assumed office (recall that his father, Bajirao had been only twenty); his experience had been somewhat more in administration than accompanying his father on the yearly campaigns.[1]

We shall divide the period from Nana Saheb's taking office to the watershed Battle of Panipat (1761) into two sections. First, we shall look at the expanding areas controlled by the Marathas, and there were many. Maratha leaders pushed into Rajasthan, the area around Delhi, and on into the Punjab. They attacked Bundelkund and the borders of Uttar Pradesh. Further east, the Marathas attacked Orissa and the borders of Bengal and Bihar. In the south, Maratha armies repeatedly crossed the Karnatak, collecting tribute. Second, we shall look at what sort of polity developed behind these expanding "frontiers." Some of the themes will be the development of largely autonomous Maratha polities, problems posed by the remaining armed, elite groups in the areas conquered, and styles of factional conflict, and we will return to the theme of social mobility.

The Maratha frontier to the east consisted of the raids of Raghuji Bhonsle of Nagpur on Orissa, Bengal, and Bihar (see Map 6). As we have seen, the Nagpur Bhonsles were generally in opposition to the Peshwa, and claimed independent authority because of controlling the Gond king of Nagpur. On Bajirao's death, Bengal and Orissa were functioning Mughal provinces under Alivardi Khan, though separated from Delhi. In 1741–42, Raghuji's troops swept through Orissa and up into Bengal; soon after the rainy season, Alivardi Khan took the field against them and forced them back in the direction of the

---

[1] Jagadish N. Sarkar, *A Study of Eighteenth Century India: Volume I, Political History (1707–1761)* (Calcutta, 1976), 219.

Deccan.[2] The following year, there were negotiations between the Mughal Emperor, Nana Saheb, and Alivardi Khan and a joint expedition against Raghuji Bhonsle. In 1743, Shahu negotiated a compromise between the Peshwa and Raghuji, by which the later was "given" Bengal, Bihar, and Orissa.[3] Each year, between 1745 and 1751, Raghuji's contingents raided Orissa, and, less successfully, attacked Bengal or Bihar, against the determined opposition of Alivardi Khan. The importance of these incidents is a further example of the complexity of the Maratha political system. While Raghuji Bhonsle claimed authority independent from the Peshwa, he still acknowledged the authority of the king, Shahu. Still, Shahu could not dictate a solution to the problem of "spheres of influence," but, instead, negotiated a compromise exactly parallel to the division of Malwa a decade earlier.

By 1751, both Raghuji Bhonsle and Alivardi Khan were ready for peace. Alivardi Khan was an old man, watching factional conflict already forming. Raghuji Bhonsle was also ready to regularize tribute. The treaty appointed a pro-Maratha governor of Orissa, set 120,000 Rs as the annual chauth payment of Bengal, Bihar, and Orissa, and established the boundary between Bengal and Orissa. In effect, Orissa became a Maratha province. In spite of increasing European influence and conflicts in Bengal, there were virtually no Maratha raids on the province in the 1750s.

The second "frontier" of the 1740s and 1750s was the Karnatak. Recall that the Nizam lost the Battle of Bhopal to the Marathas in 1738. Thereafter, he moved south to consolidate his Deccan kingdom. He put down a brief rebellion by his son and – with a large army – set about throwing out the Maratha collectors trying to extract chauth in much of the Karnatak.[4] With the focus of the new Peshwa, Nana Saheb, in the north, through most of the 1740s the only leader operating in the area was Raghuji Bhonsle, who, as we have just seen, soon shifted his focus to Bengal and Orissa. Thus, by the mid-1740s, the Karnatak passed back into the control of the Nizam.

Everyone knew, however, that the death of the old Nizam would

---

[2] In this discussion of Raghuji Bhonsle's raids and the subsequent negotiations, I have followed B. C. Ray, *Orissa under the Marathas (1751–1803)* (Allahabad, 1960), 10–20.

[3] Yusef Husein, *The First Nizam: Life and Times of Nizam-ul-Mulk, Asaf Jah I* (Bombay, second edition, 1963), 209–10.

[4] For a reading of these events different from the English or French records, see the *Tarike Rahat Afza*, a contemporary chronicle, translated in P. Setu Rao, *Eighteenth Century Deccan* (Bombay, 1963), 191–219.

produce an immediate succession crisis which would affect much of South India. On his death in 1748, both the Nizam's son and his nephew raised armies and fought. From 1748 to 1758, the various succession disputes of the heirs of the Nizam became part of a larger war between the English and the French for the control of the Coromandel coast. (So far in the narrative, we have not mentioned the French. This is because they were significant traders only on India's eastern coast and had not – to this point – played any role in Maratha history. Unlike any of the other European powers, the French, in support of the Nizam, approached Maharashtra from the east by land.)

The Marathas fought only one major campaign against the Nizam in this period. It began with the Marathas ransoming Aurangabad, in northern Maharashtra, which was the Nizam's capital. The next year, Bussy, the French general, brought Salabat Jung, his candidate for the Nizam's throne, to Aurangabad and – on the death of Shahu – attacked Maharashtra. Both sides jockeyed for position in the winter of 1751. Bussy advanced through northern Maharashtra, the Marathas falling back to within fifteen miles of Pune. For Bussy, however, problems had started to mount. His high-handed treatment of Salabat Jung, plus jealousy of his power, prevented the cash he needed from reaching him from Hyderabad. Bussy also counted on help from Maratha leaders opposed to the Peshwa; indeed, this faction was plotting against Nana Saheb, but did not join Bussy. In a pattern we have seen again and again, the Marathas cut off all grain supplies to Bussy's camp, and forced him to retreat to Ahmadnagar for supplies.[5] By November, Salabat Jung signed the Treaty of Bhalke, 1751, which ceded the remaining half of the revenues of Khandesh, plus the western half of Berar, plus the small province of Baglan (south and west of Khandesh) to the Marathas. (Salabat Jung kept only the cities of Aurangabad and Burhanpur and their associated forts – Daulatabad and Asir.)[6]

[5] The *Tarikh Rahat Afza* suggests that the Marathas were aided by Muffazar Khan Gardi, a commander with an efficient park of artillery, ibid., 206. The letters of Shah Navaz Khan suggest the same, ibid., 206. The French sources suggest that the Marathas neutralized the superior French artillery by the traditional tactics of moving into more rugged terrain and cutting off supplies. See V. G. Hatalkar, *French Records of Maratha History* (Bombay, 1978), I, 94–95.

[6] The documents of this treaty are found in G. S. Sardesai (ed.), *Selections from the Peshwa Daftar* (Bombay, 1934–40), xxv, no. 149. See also P. M. Joshi (ed.), *Selections from the Peshwa Daftar*, new series (Bombay, 1957–62), I, letter 155. A translated extract from the

And what has all this to do with the Karnatak? As we have just seen, the strength of the Nizam depended through the 1750s on the strength of the French available to him, and varied with the French position in the Anglo-French war. There was, therefore, no regularly available force to oppose Maratha incursions into the Karnatak. As they had for decades, the Marathas treated the Karnatak as a suitable hunting ground for treasure, with some hope of longer term revenue arrangements. Nana Saheb Peshwa ordered campaigns into the Karnatek yearly after the Treaty of Bhalke – Srirangapattan (1753), Bagalot (1754), Bednur (1754–55), Savanur (1755–56), Srirangapattan (1757) (see Map 3). In spite of these expeditions and extensive negotiations between the Nizam and Nana Saheb, the Karnatak, for the Marathas, never became anything more than an occasional area to raise tribute. There were claims, but little real control, and the local lineages always resisted payment. Within a few years, the rise of Mysore State would, once again, change the face of South India.

The third "frontier" was considerably north from Maharashtra. Khandesh, for example, was in no sense a frontier at this period. The Peshwa and the Nizam had been jointly ruling the province for more than twenty years, and it was a prosperous, paying proposition. The Marathas, as we have just seen, gained complete control of the province in 1751 with a minimum of damaging warfare.[7] In Gujarat, also, there had been little fighting since the Dabhade rebellion of 1731. Mughal authority was entirely gone, except for Ahmedabad and Surat, and the revenue was divided principally between the Gaikwad family and Nana Saheb.[8] In Malwa, also, Mughal authority disappeared after the Treaty of Bhopal (1738), and the Peshwa's administration – as we shall shortly see – rapidly developed, along with the new polities of Shinde and Holkar.

The line of conflict, the "frontier," began at the edges of Malwa. To the north and west was Rajasthan. This was not entirely new territory.

---

records of the qanungo (head records keeper) of Aurangabad is found in the papers of Sir Charles Malet, *India Office Library*, MSS European, F. 149.

[7] See S. N. Gordon, "Recovery from adversity in eighteenth-century India: re-thinking 'villages,' 'peasants,' and 'politics' in pre-modern kingdoms," *Peasant Studies*, 17, 4 (Fall, 1979), 61–79.

[8] This is not to say that there had not been considerable change in Gujarat. Industries especially had been affected by the disappearance of Mughal patronage. The new Maratha government at Ahmedabad had by and large not taken up the patronage of these luxury industries, such as weaving, painting, inlaying of ivory and ebony, etc. Many craftsmen migrated to Surat. See James Forbes, *Oriental memoirs* (London, 1813), 257–58.

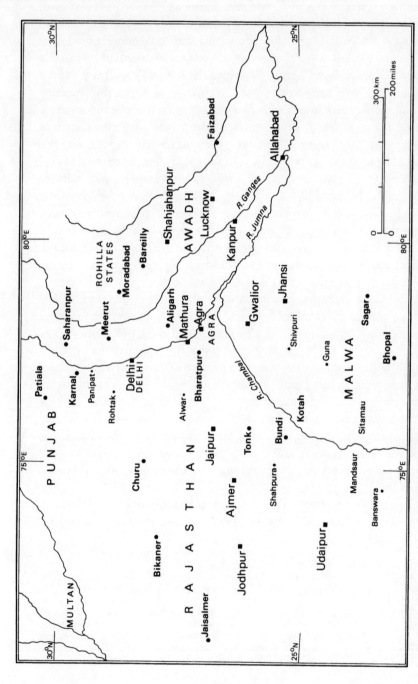

Map 8. Rajasthan, Agra, and Awadh c. 1740–60 (adapted from *The Times Atlas of the World* [London, 1988], plate 29).

As early as 1728, Bajirao had led a tribute collecting expedition north through western Malwa and into Rajasthan. There had been, however, a friendship between Bajirao and Jai Singh (of Jaipur) which lessened the pressure for tribute in the 1730s. After Bajirao's death, Maratha military contingents invaded Rajasthan almost every year.

The strategy of Maratha involvement ran such a similar course, state by state, that it is perhaps worth looking at one state in some detail.[9] On Jai Singh's death in 1743, there were two claimants for the throne, Ishwar Singh and Madho Singh. Both sides hired Maratha leaders in the ensuing war – Madho Singh allying with Holkar and Ishwar Singh hiring Jayappa Shinde. The war dragged on, and eventually the Ishwar/Jayappa group seemed to have the upper hand. At this point the Peshwa intervened and – for a substantial price – offered to mediate the dispute. The Peshwa (then on his way back from Delhi) invaded Jaipur and demanded a huge tribute and division of the state with Madho Singh, who the Peshwa now championed. By August 1748, the Marathas succeeded in forcing a treaty on Ishwar Singh which gave Madho Singh five parganas and themselves a 500,000 Rs. tribute. Madho got his parganas, but the Marathas got no rupees. Two years later, in 1750, the Peshwa ordered another invasion of Jaipur to realize the arrears of tribute. Unable to pay or face the Maratha army, Ishwar Singh committed suicide. The rival, Madho Singh, became king of Jaipur, but he, also, could not pay the tribute. Shinde and Holkar, still in the area, invaded Jaipur city a month later, now demanding one-quarter to one-third of the state. There was a spontaneous, violent uprising in the city of Jaipur against the Marathas and 3,000–4,000 were killed. The Maratha armies retreated after Madho Singh agreed to a 50,000 Rs. annual tribute.

If there is a moral in this, it might be not to invite Marathas into your succession dispute. Yet the appeal of the Maratha mounted troops seemed somehow irresistible. We have noted how Fateh Singh Bhonsle was courted in the succession dispute of the Gond kingdom of Deogarh; within a decade, he controlled the whole kingdom (which became the princely state of Nagpur). Similarly, Maratha bands had been hiring themselves out in succession disputes in western Malwa for two decades, the state doing the hiring always losing revenue and often

[9] The basic facts are laid out in Sarkar's, *Eighteenth Century India*, 255–60. Much more detail will be found in the classic history of Rajasthan, Lt.-Col. James Tod, *Annals and Antiquities of Rajasthan* (London, 1829).

land in the process. Perhaps the important thing to note is that once the Mughal Empire could no longer declare the winner and enforce its decision in the successions of large and small zamindar states, the disputes could easily escalate, using outside troops like the Marathas. The "subsidiary alliance system," thus, was not a brilliant strategy developed by the French or the English, but a common and probably inevitable feature of post-Mughal, eighteenth-century politics.

Succession dispute by succession dispute, we can trace the increasing claims of Shinde, Holkar, and the Peshwa in Rajasthan. Between 1744 and 1751, Holkar installed his candidate on the throne of Bundi, who surrendered territory and an annual tribute of 75,000 Rs. Jodhpur experienced much the same process. After successive wars and peace talks, the state was divided between two claimants, with Shinde promised a 5,000,000 Rs. tribute and Ajmer fort. Through the later years of the 1750s, the Peshwa, Shinde, and Holkar sent armies into Rajasthan to collect the arrears of the large promised tribute. Smaller amounts were collected at Kotah, Bundi, Jaipur, and Udaipur, but nothing like an administration was in place. As soon as the main-force Maratha army left, the Maratha representatives were thrown out, and no tribute paid.

In the 1750s, the "frontier" extended north to Delhi. In this period, the Mughal government directly controlled little territory further than fifty miles from the capital. Even this was fiercely fought over. Jats and Rohillas disputed for the territory; factions fought for the throne, and the Afghan king, Ahmad Shah Abdali, periodically descended on the capital.

The Marathas were frequently asked for help by one faction or another, always extracting land or tribute. Usually, much more tribute was promised than actually delivered, so that the "arrears" issue was always a convenient excuse for invasion. Both Shinde and Holkar fought in the region between the Chambal and the Jumna and defeated the Bangash Afghans; this, in turn, triggered another invasion by Ahmad Shah Abdali in 1752.

For the Marathas, probably the two most significant events of the whole chaotic period in Delhi were a treaty in 1752, which made them protector of the Mughal throne (and gave them the right to collect chauth in the Punjab), and the civil war of 1753, by which the Maratha nominee ended up on the Mughal throne.[10] A large Maratha army

---

[10] The period and treaty are fully discussed in Dharma Bhanu, "The Mughal–Maratha treaty of April, 1752," *Journal of Indian History*, 29–30 (1951–52), 242–57.

plundered Delhi and the nearby areas for the next two years, causing large-scale depopulation.

After yet another Abdali invasion, the Marathas, under Nana Saheb's brother, Ragunath Rao, and Malhar Rao Holkar, returned from Malwa and the Deccan in the campaigning season of 1757–58. A Maratha invasion of the Punjab followed, which coincided with the much more significant Sikh rebellion. The Maratha Punjab adventure was brief; the Ragunath Rao expedition left little administration behind, and the Sikhs successfully resisted any attempt to set up long-term Maratha authority. These events also set the stage for another invasion by Abdali and the crucial battle of Panipat (1761).[11]

Before returning to a discussion of the Battle of Panipat, we must look at developments inside the "frontier" areas. In the 1740–60 period, there were important changes in administration, the style of factional dispute, new groups involved in social mobility, and major changes in warfare. It is to these broad themes that we now turn.

Let us begin with administrative development.[12] Maharashtra was largely secure, but much of it was assigned to military and administrative families serving the Maratha polity. Khandesh was under a dual administration with the Nizam, Gujarat was divided between the Peshwa and the Gaikwad family, and Malwa had just been ceded by the Treaty of Bhopal (1738).

Some of the best documentation for administrative development comes from Malwa, because the Peshwa retained large sections of the province for support of his own army, and these records are preserved in the Pune Archives. Let us look at how Malwa moved from an area of sporadic tribute to a paying, prosperous province. After the treaty of Bhopal (1738), the Peshwa was faced with actually administering the eastern half of Malwa. (He had assigned the western half to Shinde, Holkar, and Pawar, and these parganas entirely disappear from the Peshwa's administrative records.) As we have seen in Chapter 5, the Peshwa tried an arrangement we have termed "stabilized tribute," which consisted of an agreement – generally for several years – signed by both a local armed lineage, termed "zamindar" in the documents, and a Maratha representative.

[11] A clear discussion of Delhi and the Punjab in this period is found in Sarkar, *Eighteenth Century India*, 259–71.
[12] This section may be contrasted with the undocumented assertion that the Maratha revenue system was widely corrupt and without administrative responsibility at least until the mid-1750s. Sarkar, *Eighteenth Century India*, 223–26, 237–40.

Stabilized tribute rapidly proved an unsatisfactory solution. First, large zamindars did not control many areas of Malwa. Some areas had only a deshmukh (termed chaudhri in Malwa) over 15–100 villages; other areas had no functioning local administration above village headmen. Mughal towns were, also, not generally under a zamindar's authority. Second, the Maratha government found itself bound by long-term contracts with the zamindars, and, therefore, did not benefit from ensuing peace and prosperity. The government tried to extract "gifts" and "loans" from the zamindars to augment the contract, but neither worked very well. Third, and by far the most serious problem, was that the zamindars did not pay the contracted tribute. These areas show a cyclical pattern of payment, high for a year or two following the initial Maratha contract, then dropping off until a military expedition forced payment again.[13]

The Marathas quickly tired of the recurrent punitive forays. Their first solution was to place garrisons in some of the zamindaries, but they soon evolved a new strategy. With each necessary foray, the Marathas imposed a more severe settlement on the zamindar. First, the villages constituting the contract were specified, with threats to collect directly if the sum was not paid. When the revenues were not forthcoming, the collector – with troops – collected in the name of the zamindar. Finally, after several years' arrears, the Marathas demanded full administrative control of the areas specified in the contract. In this fashion, Bhopal (in south-east Malwa) surrendered half its territory, which then appeared as parganas directly administered by the Peshwa's collectors. Other places, such as Kutavad (also in south-eastern Malwa), turned over some villages to be directly administered and paid tribute on the rest. Several large zamindaries, such as Bhilsa, Chanderi, and Kurwai (in eastern Malwa) were displaced in the 1740s, and their lands appear in the Peshwa's documents as directly administered areas.

The new administrative system was a simple one. The Peshwa appointed a kamavisdar who had broad powers to settle taxes, collect them, and adjudicate disputes, with some discretion to use funds to develop agriculture. He had a small staff of clerks and messengers, and a small number of troops (typically twenty or less). His reports and records were regularly audited. (Readers familiar with the nineteenth-century British administration in India will find these broadly consoli-

---

[13] See S. N. Gordon, "The slow conquest: administrative integration of Malwa into the Maratha Empire, 1720–1760," *Modern Asian Studies*, 2, 1 (1977), 15–23.

dated powers of the kamavisdar strangely familiar. This is as it should be; the British District Officer was modelled on his predecessor, the Maratha kamavisdar.)

The administration worked on a yearly cycle. The amount of the initial contract between the kamavisdar and the Peshwa was based on the best available statistics. Often, they were quite good (especially if tribute had been collected for some years). This is not surprising, because there were generally local revenue records, kept both at the village and the pargana level, which specified every village and field within the village. This documentation had been essential to the previous Mughal system of revenue settlement and collection. The next event in the yearly cycle was the payment of the first installment or rasad. This rasad, which varied from one-third to one-half of the contract, was, in effect, money loaned by the kamavisdar to the Peshwa. Both principal and interest – between one and two percent per month – were to be recovered from the kamavisdar's district. The Peshwa carefully structured the system to get as much money in advance as possible. The kamavisdar's pay was not a fraction of the total revenue collected, but a fraction of the rasad. The kamavisdar generally raised this rasad in the Pune banking community, and we find many instances of these loans in the papers of the banking families. The few rasad payments which have been analyzed in detail show a variety of backers and that the backers shifted from year to year.

With the first installment paid, the kamavisdar left for the field. He settled in the largest town in his jurisdiction and set up an office and a garrison (which are universal items of expenditure in these early accounts). The kamavisdar next made regular tours through his parganas (as evidenced by the "dinner expenses" charged to various villages). Often, he established secondary small garrisons and posts where transit duties were collected. Within our period (1740–60), the bureaucracy expanded to include rural and urban police (faujdar and kotwal).

Based on the kamavisdar's on-the-ground surveys, the body of information flowing from the district to the Peshwa's clerks at Pune dramatically increased in volume and specialization. The once-a-year accounting gave way to shorter and shorter periods. Six-months accounts were replaced by one-month accounts for the larger and more stable places (like Sironj and Bhilsa), reaching a peak intensity of daily accounts and treasury receipts from several hundred villages. The information in the kamavisdar's reports was in every way the most detailed the Marathas had ever collected. For example, there was a document, termed a dehezada, which listed every village in the pargana, and included those paying through a zamindar and those paying through the village headman, original villages and those lately colonized, deserted villages and those not found by the kamavisdar. Attached documents recorded the name of every farmer in every village, every bigha and fraction of a bigha of land he cultivated, and his kharif (hot season) and rabi (winter season) crops.

The main effect of the bigger and more differentiated bureaucracy was the regulation of a wide range of economic and social relationships, unregulated since the breakdown of the Mughal administration in the 1730s. The Marathas reviewed every major non-governmental demand on revenue, thus scrutinizing each powerful family and religious endowment in the area. Let us pause for a moment and consider one detailed example of this process from Ashta (in eastern Malwa) in 1752. The matter began when Vishnu Mahadev, who had been assigned the revenue of Ashta by the Peshwa, questioned the right of one Pratap Singh, a local Rajput, to an inam grant worth Rs. 200 per year. The assignee's agent asked the Peshwa to examine the existing grant paper from the Mughal Emperor. The kamavisdar of Ashta examined the paper and found it authentic, but questioned why Pratap Singh's name had been entered over his brother's. The Peshwa personally reviewed the kamavisdar's report and heard oral testimony from an agent of Pratap Singh's to the effect that his client's name had been entered because his brother had died. In the end, the Peshwa continued the inam; a new Maratha sanad was issued, specifying the same two villages from which the two hundred rupees were to come. The Peshwa's staff forwarded suitable orders to the assignee, the kamavisdar, Pratap Singh, and the village headmen of the two villages.[14] Note that the pattern here is the same which we have seen in Maharashtra; the Peshwa successfully asserted his right to arbitrate disputes over rights to land revenue, and substituted his grant for a Mughal one.

The new Maratha administration regulated a wider variety of relationships than just financial ones. The new faujdars and kotwals (rural and urban police) produced cases concerning every aspect of life. As one example, let us look at the manufacturing and trading town of

[14] Ibid., 27.

Sironj (in eastern Malwa on the caravan route between Agra and the south) in 1743. Kesari Brami was fined Rs. 114 for failure to pay back a loan; at the end of the year, Sada Ram still owed Rs. 375 of the Rs. 475 he had been fined for using false weights. Hola Bora paid a Rs. 500 penalty for adultery. The thirty-nine cases from Bhilsa (also on the caravan route in eastern Malwa) in 1749 were even more varied. The government seized fifty rupees from the effects of an employee oilman who committed suicide. Fighting between the bride's and groom's families at an intercaste marriage resulted in a Rs. 50 fine. Several persons paid "patdam", the tax to have a widow remarried.[15]

Stepping back from the minutiae of administrative development, let us consider several broader trends. First, throughout much of Malwa and Khandesh, the revenue was boosted in the 1750s to levels of the best of Mughal times. This was without coercion, but by giving out development loans to bring new lands into cultivation. Second, we have a clearer idea of the nature of conquest. Overall, conquest was slow. It began with raids on the movable wealth of villages; it proceeded from countryside to cities, first unhinging the rural administration at the zamindar level. Towns and garrisons were first isolated, then attacked. The final conquest demanded a force of some 10,000 troops, the defeat of a Mughal main-force army, and the extraction of a Mughal grant to the area. This was followed, as we have seen, by stabilized tax collection, development of the administration, and adjudication of disputes on the local level.

By the 1750s, it is important to remember that it was the Marathas who held the towns and roads. It was their garrison troops who walked the ramparts and anxiously watched for marauders. Their civilian officials made surveys, collected revenue, tried cases, regulated bazaars. Now the Peshwa depended on the very communications and trade that his armies had so recently disrupted. He needed to rebuild the provinces which he had plundered; he worried about credit which was based on rural tax revenues.

If this new Maratha administration sounds suspiciously Mughal, it should. Any larger political entity had to be built up out of negotiations with hundreds of zamindars, village headmen and deshmukhs. In the areas of Khandesh, Gujarat, and Malwa, the terms of reference remained severely Mughal. Taxes were called by Mughal terms,

---

[15] Ibid., 28.

assessed in a Mughal manner, paid in the customary Muslim months. The Marathas even retained the Mughal differential transit duties, which charged Hindu traders double their Muslim counterparts.[16] Maratha demands never exceeded the pre-existing Mughal settlement. As we have seen, the Marathas gave replacement sanad papers to various local grantees; the duties and rights were described in Mughal terms. When the Marathas established the basic apparatus of law and order – courts, rural and urban police – both the terminology and function resembled their Mughal counterparts.

Maratha Malwa, however, was not simply an extension of Mughal Malwa. Urban patterns changed considerably. The Marathas did not simply take over the Mughal sarkar towns. Generally, they settled at towns which had not been as important under the Mughals – Bhilsa and Sironj, for example – rather than Mughal Sarangpur and Shahjahanpur. The Mughal trade from Agra never recovered. The Maratha leaders patronized new capitals, such as Gwalior and Indore. The credit network shifted from Mughal Agra to Pune, and the new Brahmin bankers moved the revenue south, rather than north. The new trade route for Chanderi silk (from Malwa), shifted to Pune and Bombay. Rural patterns were more complicated. Many big zamindars suffered; some had been entirely displaced, and many had lost a substantial part of their territory. In contrast, others successfully resisted all Maratha incursions and paid only an occasional tribute. Overall, the pattern of Maratha control remained patchy. When we think of the "texture" of these provinces – Malwa, Gujarat, Khandesh – throughout the eighteenth century, we should be aware that there were many local armed lineages which were not destroyed or replaced. Authority varied from fully administered areas with detailed revenue settlements to areas with a number of small, armed lineages to permanently recalcitrant zamindars defying any Maratha authority from the walls of a strong fort.

During these years of administrative development there were several paths of social mobility. First were the revenue collectors who produced the detailed revenue documents we have just considered. In the Peshwa areas, these men were mainly Chitpavan Brahmins (like the Peshwa), though Saraswat and Deshashtas continued to fill a smaller number of posts. The path was separate from that of military service.

[16] See Pune Daftar, Prant Azmas Khandesh Rumal, no. 196, which contains both the rates and records of actual collection.

For example, the fifty or so Brahmin administrators from the Peshwa's area of Malwa are not found on the list of jagir grants; they, thus, did not move from administration to command of troops.[17] Incidentally, this is one of the important ways that the Maratha administration differed from the Mughal, which had a unified civilian/military rank and pay structure. Very little research has been done on these administrative Brahmin families, so we do not know how much they overlapped, for example, with the Pune banking families.[18]

Outside the Peshwa's area, the situation was different. In the new Malwa "states" of Shinde and Holkar (following the division of 1732), the new administrators were specifically not Chitpavan, but Saraswat, a subcaste originally from Goa, who did not intermarry with Chitpavans. They benefitted greatly from this service and many families emerged as wealthy holders of rights, both in Maharashtra and Malwa, in the nineteenth century. In the other new "states" – the Gaikwad in Gujarat and the Bhonsle family at Nagpur – the administration was, once again, not Chitpavan. Both families used C.K.P.s (Chandrseniya Kayastha Prabhu), a non-Brahmin, Marathi-speaking writer caste, in their bureaucracy, and they prospered throughout the eighteenth century.

What of the cultural expression of these newly wealthy families? Let us start with personal consumption patterns. There was increased demand for luxury items, especially those not produced in Maharashtra. These included Kashmiri shawls, and silks from Malwa, the Ganges valley, and Bengal. We also find examples of inlaid stone, typical of Agra and bidri work from Hyderabad. Objects for personal use in silver, brass, copper, and ivory – mirrors, ink pots, pan boxes, horse trappings – of great grace and beauty were both imported from the north and produced for these families.[19] The families maintained poets, bards, and singers. Whole new schools and styles of painting

[17] Pune Daftar, Zamav section, list of jagirs and inams for 1750–55. For an interesting sketch of a less well-known Brahmin family's social mobility through administrative service to the Peshwa, see Shantaram Suntkakhar, *Ashiahe Shrishantadurga* (Belgaum, 1973).
[18] The materials for this research are, however, readily available in the dozens of kula-vrittana, histories of Chitpavan Brahmin families, which have been printed in Maharashtra in the last four decades.
[19] Many of these are preserved in the Raja Dinkar Kelkar Museum in Pune. Good coverage of the museum's holdings is found in "Treasures of everyday art: Raja Dinkar Kelkar Museum," *Marg*, 34, 2. References to this luxurious lifestyle are found throughout the *Selections from the Peshwa Daftar* and summarized in B. G. Gokhale, *Poona in the Eighteenth Century: An Urban History* (Delhi, 1988), 65–75.

were patronized.[20] This was also an intense period of house building, not only in Pune (mainly in the areas closer to the Mutha river) and Satara, but in many smaller towns. Deshmukh families expanded their houses; retainers and other grantees built new dwellings. All were decorated with wonderful carved pillars, doorways, ceilings, and windows.[21] Religious patronage dramatically increased. Within Pune and in the towns of Maharashtra, many new temples, ghats, and tanks were built.[22] The annual Pandharpur pilgrimage became more lavish and the other sites in Maharashtra – Shridev, Jejuri, Nasik, and others – more popular. Perhaps more striking was the increase in supra-regional religious pilgrimage. From this period Maharashtrians, both Brahmin and Maratha, replaced Rajputs as the main patrons at Benares, both by building temples, bathing ghats, and rest houses, and by on-going support of Brahmins.[23] Thousands made the pilgrimage to Benares (also Gaya and Muthra) each year, and a large community of Maharashtrian Brahmins permanently settled in Benares to serve them. Grants to Brahmins (houses, land, cash, clothes) greatly increased, especially under the direct patronage of the Peshwa.[24]

The second broad theme of the 1740–60 period was the further consolidation of the power of the Peshwa, which occurred at the time of the death of Shahu (1749). In the preceding two years, Shahu recognized that the various Maratha leaders were lining up for a civil war on his death. There was no acceptable heir. Shambhuji, of the Kolapur line, himself an older man, had been Shahu's rival for twenty-five years, and was an anathema to the Peshwa. There were no other heirs.

Into this dilemma came Tarabai, the same Tarabai who had put forward pretenders to the throne in 1707 and 1731. She brought

[20] Several issues of *Marg* have been devoted to this cultural flowering. See "The art of the Chatrapatis and Peshwas," 34, 2. Also, "Maharashtra: traditions in art," 34, 4. Also, "Maharashtra, religious and secular architecture," 37, 1.

[21] The growth of Pune, of course, parallels the other "successor" state capitals – Hyderabad, Lucknow, Farrukhabad. A thorough discussion of the growth of the peths of Pune is found in Gokhale, *Poona*, 16–44.

[22] See, for example, V. K. Bhave, *Peshwekalin Maharashtra* (New Delhi, reprinted edition, 1976), 30–31.

[23] C. A. Bayly, *Rulers, Townsmen and Bazaars: North Indian Society in the Age of British Expansion, 1770–1870* (Cambridge, 1983), 137.

[24] The various volumes of *Selections from the Peshwa Daftar* refer to aspects of this patronage of Brahmins, either on a regular basis, such as the large donations during the month of sravana, or on special occasions, such as a marriage or birth of a son. See, *Peshwa Daftar* III, letter 137; Also, v, letter 26, 36, and XXXII, letter 183.

forward a grandson of Rajaram (named Ram Raja), who she claimed had been raised secretly. In spite of widespread skepticism, Shahu accepted the boy. His will asked all the leaders to accept Ram Raja and placed his care and the running of the polity in the hands of the Peshwa.[25]

Within a year of Shahu's death, the situation became murky. Ram Raja, who had been raised by farmers and had no courtly training, still wanted to rule. Tarabai had expected to rule, and Nana Saheb Peshwa wanted no part of either one of them. Both sides tried to recruit the major leaders – Raghuji Bhonsle, Malhar Rao Holkar, Jayapa Shinde.

An unprecedented summit meeting settled many of the issues. Tarabai came from the fort of Satara to Pune. She was attended by most of her partisans (mainly the holders of the large state offices – senapati, sachiv, and pratinidhi – whose functions had been displaced by the Peshwa's consolidation). The other main leaders were also there – Shinde, Holkar, Bhonsle, Sidashiva Bhau (the Peshwa's cousin), Ramchandra Malhar, Sakaram Bapu, and Mahadoba Purandare.[26] The policies demanded by Nana Saheb Peshwa, and adopted, included the following:

(1) All administration was to move from Satara to Pune, away from intrigues of the court.

(2) The three remaining state officers (pratinidhi, sachiv, and senapati) were to have no independent authority. All grants would only come from the Peshwa.

(3) There would be less intermixing of saranjams, as this had led to much fighting. Henceforth, areas under a leader would be more consolidated.

(4) In pursuit of this policy, the large saranjams of the pratinidhi and the senapati (the Dabhade family whom we have met in connection with Gujarat) were resumed. Raghuji Bhonsle was to get the pratinidhi's rights in Berar, and the Peshwa the Dabhade holding in Khandesh.

(5) Sinhagad fort, formerly loyal to Tarabai, was to go to the Peshwa.

(6) The Peshwa was to make the appointments of the personal staff of Ram Raja.

[25] Brij Kishore, *Tarabai and Her Times* (Bombay, 1963), 170–73.
[26] Documents of this historic meeting are found in Sardesai (ed.) *Peshwa Daftar*, VI. See especially letters 36, 45, 57, 59, 64, 83, 89.

Following this meeting, there were two immediate rebellions. The Pratinidhi family refused to relinquish important forts in the Satara area; the Peshwa sent an army and captured them. In Khandesh, the Dabhade family, displaced by the agreement, raised a major revolt which devastated villages all across Khandesh; it is easy to follow its progress in the disruption of revenue collection.[27] Within two years, however, the revolt was put down, village collection returned to normal, and the Dabhade family disappeared from Maratha history. As part of the same rebellion, the Gaikwad family, which had supported Dabhade and Tarabai, lost a major portion of Gujarat's revenue-paying districts to the Peshwa. The division yielded the Peshwa nearly 3,000,000 Rs. per year in potential revenue.

The last broad theme of the 1740–60 period is the many changes in the strategy, tactics, and personnel of warfare. There were two important structural changes in the period. First, frontiers had greatly expanded. It was no longer possible for Maratha troops to return home and farm. The last fullscale exodus from the north to the Deccan for the monsoon had been in the mid-1730s. The troops were in growing proportion full-time mercenaries, quartered at camps in Malwa and Gujarat. There were several effects of this trend. They had to be paid regularly and provided safe shelter during the monsoon; this enormously increased the cash needs of each of the Maratha leaders. Second, Maratha armies got much larger in this period. Mainly as a result of the centralization of power by the Peshwa and the division of the conquered areas among a small number of loyal leaders, the day of the small, independent Maratha band was over. They either became a unit in a larger army, or the few larger leaders found them a nuisance and suppressed them.

Strategy and tactics changed dramatically. The older Maratha tactics were, of course, avoiding a pitched battle with a major army in the field; instead, the Marathas cut off supplies, communications, and foraging, and let the slow-moving army starve. These tactics, as we have seen, were normally accompanied by forays deep into enemy territory to draw off the enemy army. These strategies had been effectively used by Raghuji Bhonsle in Bengal, Bihar, and Orissa in the 1740s, had been eminently successful against the Nizam in the

[27] Pune Daftar, Prant Azmas Khandesh Rumals. Since these rumals are arranged by place rather than by period, the documents are somewhat dispersed. See nos. 20, 30, 128, 189, 191, 201, 217.

Battle of Bhopal (1738) and, as recently as 1752, at the Battle of Bhalke.

From the 1740s onwards, the main opponents of the Maratha armies were no longer huge Mughal armies, moving slowly on the plains, but recalcitrant armed lineages, often inside surprisingly strong local forts. For a century the Marathas had largely ignored artillery; they could no longer. Technical development came quite quickly in this period. The Marathas hired Europeans – first Portuguese, later mainly French and English – who had expertise in casting and deploying cannon, and built up speciality artillery units.[28] The results were successful assaults on the Jat fortress of Dig (south of Agra), the main fortresses of Rajasthan, and Bassein (a very strong fort on the Konkan coast).[29]

Relying on artillery, however, changed the whole nature of warfare. It tremendously increased the cash needs of a commander. Artillery was expensive to produce. Both guns and shot required a full-time and professional foundry. The metals, especially copper, were imported and expensive. The best gunpowder was foreign-made and only acquired from the Portuguese or the English for cash. Soldiers who operated artillery were specialized, relatively well-paid professionals. Even the support personnel, drovers and such, had to be paid in cash. Equally important, artillery slowed down an army's movements to the pace of a bullock cart; the large pack trains also required both fodder and supplies.

Though the Maratha artillery had proven relatively effective against forts, it was still quite primitive. Guns were large and heavy, and carriages often broke down. The guns were also not cast to a standard bore, so that a limited number of balls could be fired from each specific gun. Perhaps the worst drawback of the Maratha artillery was that the guns were all-purpose weapons. They had to be big enough to knock down fort walls and doors; this made them so cumbersome that they were immobile when used in battle, rather than in a siege. Once the battle began, they could not support ensuing charges or cover retreats. Aiming mechanisms were crude, and volleys often entirely missed the opposing army.

It is worth noting that in Europe, particularly in England, these decades saw the development of light, mobile field artillery. These

[28] An English observer visited the Peshwa's ordinance factory in 1739 and found it generally well run. See G. W. Forrest (ed.), *Selections from the Letters, Dispatches, and State Papers Preserved in the Bombay Secretariat* (Bombay, 1885), 79.
[29] At Bassein, however, it was still mining that played the most important role in breaching the wall, rather than artillery.

pieces were one of the first fruits of categorical improvements in metallurgy, casting, and boring of the early eighteenth century. Artillery was developed under direct, royal patronage by the "scientific" method – standardized castings and bore, stronger carriage design, testing and standardization of charge, thorough training and specialized functions of each member of the gun crew, and a written body of literature on gun testing used to improve design. In field situations, the rate of fire had increased from a few shots per hour to six or even eight shots per minute. These new guns and units had proved enormously effective against cavalry in Europe; these new pieces were just beginning to appear in India in the Anglo-French war of the 1750s.[30]

The period also saw rapid developments in the use of infantry. The Marathas had, of course, used infantry as early as Shivaji. The guns were heavy and the rate of fire very slow. After Shivaji's death, as we have seen, Maratha warfare relied mainly on light cavalry and movement. Infantry, once again, assumed importance in the 1740–60 period. The development of matchlocks and muskets in India is outside the scope of the volume; suffice it to say that there had been many demonstrations of the effectiveness of trained infantry in this period. As with artillery, there had been intense experimentation and battle experience in Europe. Infantry weapons had become lighter, more accurate, and faster to load. The training of infantry included the regular steps of loading, but also firing on command. In India, the first demonstrations of the effectiveness of these trained, combined infantry/artillery units were the English victories at the Battle of Plassey in Bengal and Buxar in Bihar, and the Anglo-French war in the south (1757–63).[31] It is also important to note several failures of this new system. These are illustrated, for example, when the Marathas, using their traditional tactics, defeated the French forces under Bussy at the Battle of Bhalke in 1751. The new armies were even more vulnerable than Mughal armies to shortages of cash and supplies. Unlike the huge Mughal armies, however, they were, because of discipline and training, able to retreat from difficult situations without a complete rout. Other campaigns in the Anglo-French war in the

[30] The story of these developments is told in two complementary books. B. P. Hughes, *Firepower: Weapons Effectiveness on the Battlefield: 1630–1850* (New York, 1975), and D. Chandler, *The Art of War in the Age of Marlborough* (London, 1976).

[31] The recruitment and training of the new English forces is well covered in Philip Mason, *A Matter of Honour* (New York, 1974), 60–116. See also James P. Lawford, *Britain's Army in India: From its Origins to the Conquest of Bengal* (London, 1978).

south showed that these new forces were much less effective in hilly terrain, because the artillery could not keep up with the infantry movements. Also, small units of infantry, unsupported by artillery, could be overwhelmed by cavalry charges.

Like artillery, infantry had effects on every aspect of warfare. They slowed down movement to a walking pace. Infantry were paid professionals, and their equipment (relative to the sword and shield of light cavalry) was expensive. They were only effective as long as ball and powder lasted. Other effects were less obvious. Infantry was ineffective at foraging and living off the land, so that supplies had to be carried along and restocked. Also, Indian-made muskets, even at this period, were relatively slow to load and fire; therefore, there had to be a substantial number of infantry, arranged in lines six, eight, or even ten men deep; this was the only way to sustain enough fire to keep a cavalry charge from breaking through the line. The use of infantry also demanded a disciplined battle plan. Infantry was, especially in these massed lines, a one-directional weapon, and had to have cavalry protecting its flanks from opposing cavalry sweeps around it.

Leading up to the Battle of Panipat (1761), there were three different models of warfare, co-existing uneasily among the Maratha generals.[32] Older leaders, such as Malhar Rao Holkar, favored the traditional Maratha tactics of mobile, light cavalry, shunning a decisive battle. Many of the leaders a generation younger had experience with the effectiveness of artillery, but their armies were much more like Mughal armies than the contemporary armies of Europe – moving cities which included everything from vegetable stalls to dancing girls. Only one commander, Ibrahim Gardi, had built a new army out of trained infantry and artillery. None of the leaders had any experience in integrating Maratha cavalry, which favored the charge and hand-to-hand combat, with the artillery/infantry units, which required the cavalry to protect its flanks.[33]

With this perspective, let us turn to the Battle of Panipat (see Map 8). Because the combined Maratha army was routed by Ahmad Shah Durani's on the plains north of Delhi, this battle has been analyzed as much as any other in India's history – from the psychology of the

[32] Throughout this discussion of Panipat, I am following T. S. Shejwalkar, *Panipat: 1761* (Poona, Deccan College, 1946).
[33] An interesting contemporary Marathi chronicle and papers of this period have been recently translated and annotated by Ian Raeside. See *The Decade of Panipat (1751–61)* (Bombay, 1984).

commanders to the thickness of body armor of the Afghan cavalry. We will, therefore, consider only briefly the movements before the battle, and focus on the battle and its implications.

We left the Marathas retreating out of the Punjab in late 1759, and Shah Abdali slowly advancing toward India through what is now Pakistan, with neither side able to control the Sikh rebellion.[34] The main Maratha force, under Dataji Shinde, besieged Abdali's representative, Najib-ud-daula, but ineffective artillery allowed Najib to hold out. In the next months (January–March 1760), one of Abdali's generals defeated part of Dataji's army and forced a retreat of a second army under Malhar Rao Holkar.[35] Abdali failed in a siege of Dig fort, held by Suraj Mal Jat, and moved off toward Rajasthan to ransom the Rajput states. The Marathas moved to devastate the Rohilla Afghan territories (which were allied to Abdali), causing Abdali to turn north again.

Throughout this hot season and monsoon (June–September 1760), both sides wooed potential allies – Ahmad Shah Bangash (a local Afghan lineage, near Delhi), the Jats under Suraj Mal, the Rajputs, the Rohilla Afghans (another local lineage), and most prized, Shuja-ud-daula, ruler of Awadh. He was known to have a full treasury, a strong army, and regular revenue to maintain the army. On the whole, Abdali was more successful in this local recruiting, allying with Ahmad Shah Bangash, most Rohilla Afghans, and Shuja-ud-daula of Awadh. The Marathas allied with the Jats and some Rohilla Afghans; the Rajputs stayed neutral. In the same period, the Peshwa sent a very large combined army from the Deccan to support the local commanders who – on the whole – were doing poorly against the Abdali forces. This slow-moving army arrived during the monsoon and, without boats, could not cross the Jumna to attack Abdali's camp near Aligarh. Both sides suggested terms, but their negotiating positions were too far apart for a settlement. After the monsoon, the Maratha army moved out to Panipat and built a large fortified camp (October 1760). Including combatants, support personnel, and the bazaar, it probably held 60,000–80,000 people. The monsoon had not been kind to the Maratha forces; disease had broken out among the horses, and thousands died. The vast army was rapidly running out of money. Abdali, when he arrived at Panipat, also had his problems. He was virtually unable to

[34] See H. R. Gupta, *History of the Sikhs* (New Delhi, third edition, 1978), II, 142–56.
[35] Shejwalkar, *Panipat*, 18–23.

communicate with his kingdom in Afghanistan because the Sikhs held the Punjab. Both sides were running out of food, as foraging had devastated everything for miles. The skirmishing, from mid-November to the end of the year, was indecisive.

The main battle took place on January 14, 1761. In manpower, the two sides were about equally arrayed. The Afghan forces were mainly heavy cavalry, men in body armor using muskets; against them were many units of Maratha light cavalry (men in light armor, with sword and shield), the trained infantry of Ibrahim Gardi, and the large, heavy guns brought from the Deccan.

Throughout the morning, the Marathas pushed back the Abdali troops in both the right and the center. The fighting revealed the problems of the Maratha force. It proved impossible to coordinate the infantry and the cavalry. The infantry moved forward in disciplined order, but the cavalry broke off into general engagements with the opposing cavalry. The situation was exacerbated by a weak command structure. The Marathas were a composite army, and the various leaders pursued various tactics. The artillery proved almost useless; it was immobile, slow-firing, and inaccurate. Abdali's light mobile swivel guns were generally much more effective.

In the late afternoon at a crucial moment Abdali was able to put about 5,000 fresh cavalry into the battle, which broke through the Maratha center. Typical of these large battles, capture or death of the main leader meant a general rout, rather than an orderly retreat. The Afghan troops pursued the fleeing Marathas much of the following night. Estimates vary widely, but as many as 50,000 combatants and non-combatants were killed. Abdali's forces captured thousands of horses, pack animals, and whatever could be looted from the bazaar. Over the next six months, surviving units and individuals made their way back to Maharashtra.

CHAPTER 7

CENTRIPETAL FORCES (1760–1803)

Within weeks, Ahmad Shah Abdali retreated from India to his kingdom in Afghanistan. In the north, therefore, the power situation remained much as it had been previously, consisting of armed local lineages (Jats, Sikhs, Bundelas, and Rajputs), and the two major powers (Shuja-ud-daula of Awadh and Najib-ud-daula, the representative of Abdali). The difference, of course, was the Maratha loss of money, credit, manpower, and prestige. These problems were exacerbated by a loss of leadership at the center; Nana Saheb Peshwa died within weeks of the defeat of Panipat. In addition, several major leaders had been killed, and there were succession disputes within these families. Even in the eighteenth century, bad news travelled fast; Panipat produced results in every region that the Marathas controlled or from which they even irregularly extracted tribute. The defeat inspired rebellions by local armed lineages, invasion and subversion by neighboring powers, and factionalization and bids for power at the center. As we shall see, however, the decade after Panipat was, overall, one of recovery of revenue areas, the rebuilding of military strength and prestige, effective leadership, and even some gains in conflicts with neighboring powers. Two themes became dominant in the decades after 1770, first, the shifting power relations between the center and the Maratha "states" (Shinde, Holkar, Gaikwad and Bhonsle) and, second, the emergence of the English as the main competitor on the subcontinent.

Let us begin with the factional problems at the capital, then survey the outlying areas. On the death of Nana Saheb Peshwa, his second son, Madhav Rao, received investiture. As he was only seventeen years old, it was understood that his uncle, Ragunath Rao, would share, or perhaps dominate, power. (It is worth noting that the investiture was received from the Chattrapati – nominally in Shivaji's line – who was, and remained, imprisoned.)

Many leaders, including the Bhonsles of Nagpur, the Nimbalkar family of Phaltan (Satara District), and Gopal Rao Patwardhan (holder of several large estates in southern Maharashtra), opposed the whole dominance of government by Chitpavan Brahmins. Within a few months, they joined the Nizam (grandson of Asaf Shah, founder of the line), who invaded Maharashtra from the east.[1] Supported by these disaffected leaders, the Nizam's army pushed to within fifteen miles of Pune; he was bought off, however, by a large tribute, paid from the Maratha possessions in the area of Aurangabad and Bidar. Little was lost, as the promised forts were not returned, nor was any but a small amount of tribute paid. The Nizam withdrew to Hyderabad.[2]

The factional problems became worse as Madhav Rao, the young Peshwa, began to assert power. He selected new men for senior offices, and gathered a small group of very competent personal clerks, who were to emerge as major forces a decade later. Ragunath Rao, the Peshwa's uncle, accepted none of this, left Pune, raised an army, and, with the assistance of one of the Nizam's commanders, marched on Pune. The young Peshwa's forces were sure to be routed. In a diplomatic stroke, the young Peshwa dispersed his forces and appeared alone before his uncle, conceding him power as the only way to avoid war and a divided state.

As soon as Ragunath Rao reached Pune, he dismissed many of Madhav's Rao's appointees and sent an expedition south against Gopal Rao Patwardhan of Miraj (a holder of large jagirs for military service), who had been one of Madhav Rao's strongest supporters (see Map 1). The expedition reduced the Patwardhan forts and seized the family saranjams. It was only a matter of weeks before a new faction formed around the dispossessed Patwardhans. Allies were easy to find. Prime among them were the Bhonsles of Nagpur (who had generally opposed the increasing power of the Peshwa), the Nizam (as always), and many of the high officers who had been removed by Ragunath Rao.

Through 1763, the forces loyal to Ragunath Rao (and Madhav Rao, who now fully supported his uncle) were limited to two leaders and insufficient to meet the Nizam–Bhonsle–Patwardhan army in the field. Instead, they plundered various districts belonging to the Nizam and Bhonsle. Using the same tactics, the Nizam burnt and plundered the area around Pune and regions as far west as the Bhima river.

Both sides needed to find shelter during the monsoon. The Nizam's army moved toward Aurangabad. A good offer from Ragunath Rao detached the Bhonsle from the Nizam's forces; Ragunath's forces

---

[1] P. M. Joshi (ed.), *Selections from the Peshwa Daftar*, new series (Bombay, 1957–62), III, letters 1–6.

[2] James Grant Duff, *History of the Marathas* (Jaipur, reprinted edition, 1986), II, 119–20.

defeated the Nizam's in a major battle on the banks of the Godavari river at Rakhshasbhuvan (August 1763). Only the portion of the Nizam's army which had already forded the river survived. Effectively besieged in Aurangabad, the Nizam surrendered several territories in the Bidar area; some additional tracts went to Jankoji Bhonsle (for switching to the Ragnath Rao side at a crucial moment).[3] This treaty basically settled the relations between the Peshwa and the Nizam for more than thirty years. More importantly, it was the first settlement of a successful campaign in which the largest share of the gains did not go to the central government, but to other nobles. This event marks the beginning of a shift in power between the center and the periphery which was to become much more serious in a decade.

Ragunath Rao, wisely, became reconciled to some members of the opposing faction. Patwardhan was reinstated in his holdings in Miraj. The Madhav Rao appointees to high posts returned to them, and the loyal and competent personal clerks of Madhav Rao, especially Nana Phadnavis, assumed higher positions in the administration. As a divisive issue, the rivalry between Madhav Rao Peshwa, and his uncle Ragunath Rao did not go away. Just a few years later, when the uncle was returning from an expedition to the north, the Peshwa imprisoned him; there he stayed until Madhav Rao Peshwa's death in 1772. Likewise, the issue of the independence of the Bhonsles of Nagpur remained. Madhav Rao Peshwa even joined the Nizam in a joint campaign in the late 1760s, which seriously reduced the territory and power of the Bhonsles and established the supremacy of the Peshwa.

The more important, larger question is how much this factional conflict in the Deccan affected the functioning of the rest of the areas which the Marathas controlled. Let us undertake a brief survey of the periphery, beginning with Gujarat and proceeding in a clockwise manner around the subcontinent.

Damaji Gaikwad survived Panipat and returned to Gujarat with much of his forces intact. After putting down several rebellions by both Hindu and Muslim groups, he took part in the factional warfare in the Deccan during the 1760s, emerging as a major "loser" because of his continued support of Ragunath Rao.[4] By the late 1760s, the Peshwa had forced the Gaikwad family to pay a large tribute. The death of Damaji set off a long succession dispute between his sons with the

---

[3] A. C. Banerjee, *Peshwa Madhav Rao I*, (Calcutta, 1943), 32–33.
[4] Joshi (ed.), *Peshwa Daftar*, letters 210–20.

Peshwa often able to assert authority (later, the East India Company was also involved). On the ground, the result was warfare in Gujarat through much of the remaining eighteenth century and a consequent decline in trade, agriculture, and textile production.[5]

Looking north and east of Gujarat, Rajasthan also threw off Maratha authority after Panipat. Malhar Rao Holkar, escaping from Panipat with much of his force, attacked the Rajputs in late 1761 and defeated them at the Battle of Mangrol. The battle largely restored Maratha power and reinforced the tribute-paying relationship established five years earlier at the Treaty of Nagor. Marwar, for example, paid a regular lump-sum tribute and had some areas directly administered by Maratha collectors. This pattern stayed stable for several decades, and Rajasthan was not the scene of warfare until the end of the eighteenth century.[6]

In the area around Delhi, between the Ganges and Jumna rivers and south as far as the Malwa plateau, local landed lineages and remaining Muslim powers fought incessantly through the decade after Panipat (see Map 8). There was, in fact, little the Marathas could do to retain any control. After Malhar Rao Holkar's Rajasthan campaign, he – and all other major leaders – were in the Deccan for the next six years. Lesser Maratha leaders, with smaller armies, were generally unable to defeat the Jats, Rohillas, or the large Muslim forces under Najib-ud-daula. At best, they occasionally took sides in a family feud or allied with one group against another.[7] The only major Maratha initiative of the middle years of the 1760s was an inconclusive campaign led by Ragunath Rao; it spent more time on the succession dispute in the Holkar family than on conquering territory.[8] A large Maratha expedition came from the Deccan in 1769, and restored Maratha control to the area. Through 1770, under the leadership of Mahadji Shinde, the

[5] An experienced observer, St. Lubin, who was in Surat in the mid-1770s, thought that the trade of the city had dropped by half in the previous twenty years. V. G. Hatalkar, *French Records of Maratha History* (Bombay, 1978), 71–74. Surat and its problems have attracted a good bit of recent research. A sampling would include Ashin Das Gupta, *Indian Merchants and the Decline of Surat* (Wiesbaden, 1979), and M. Torri, "In the deep blue sea: Surat and its merchant class during the dyarchic era (1759–1800)," *Indian Economic and Social History Review*, 19, 3–4 (July–December 1982).

[6] G. R. Parihar, "The political impact of the Marathas on Marwar," *Quarterly Review of Historical Studies*, 6 (1966–67), 148–52.

[7] Joshi, (ed.), *Peshwas Daftar*, letters 77–130, for example, concern the inability of the Marathas to control the Jats.

[8] A. C. Banerjee, "Revival of Maratha power in the north (1761–69)," *Indian Historical Quarterly*, 17, 3 (September 1941), 311–23.

army defeated the Jats, the Rohilla Afghans, and took Delhi (which remained basically under Maratha control for the next two decades).

In Bengal, the situation shifted after the Battle of Plassey (see Map 6). The British became heirs to the agreements of 1751, by which Alivardi Khan had agreed to pay chauth to the Bhonsles of Nagpur. Nothing, however, was paid, and the Marathas in 1760 invaded the province from Orissa.[9] The dynamics of the situation were little affected by the Panipat defeat. The general appointed from Nagpur defeated chiefs in Orissa, collected tribute, and routinely demanded chauth from Bengal. The British regularly demanded that the Nawab of Bengal finance an expedition against the Marathas; he regularly refused. Through the mid-1760s, the Marathas stayed in Orissa, the British in Bengal. Various British initiatives, thereafter, mainly followed attempts by Bombay to gain some advantage from the conflict between Madhav Rao Peshwa and his uncle, Ragunath Rao.[10]

The last peripheral area was the Karnatak (see Map 3). The main event of the region was the rapid usurpation of Mysore State by a high military leader, Haidar Ali. The Maratha loss at Panipat gave him time to consolidate a shaky position, since he had been under Maratha attack in the late 1750s. Between 1761 and 1763, Haidar Ali reduced many of the local rajas to paying regular tribute. Madhav Rao Peshwa, however, took the Karnatak as a sphere of personal military interest and led four expeditions before he died in 1772. They all had a similar pattern. Haidar was generally unable to face the Marathas in the field, fell back to one or another strong fort, burned the provisions needed by the invading Maratha force, and paid some tribute. The Marathas generally left a small force and a minor leader to collect the tribute, who was generally pushed out of the area by Haidar's forces. Then, the cycle started again. Only in the last campaign did the Peshwa begin to garrison captured forts. In the only large plains battle in 1771, Haidar lost badly. Yet, the Marathas, as much because of Madhav's Rao's lingering illness as any other reason, were never able to control more than the border areas and extract some tribute from the rest. This position was little different from what it had been for decades.[11]

And what of the non-peripheral areas? Maharashtra, except for the

[9] K. K. Datta, "The Marathas in Bengal after 1751," *Journal of Indian History* (1937), 389-90.
[10] Joshi (ed.), *Peshwa Daftar*, letters 25-71.
[11] A. C. Banerjee, "Peshwa Madhav Rao I's last Carnatic expedition," *Journal of Indian History*, 20, 3 (December 1941), 1-11.

Nizam's invasion of 1763, remained peaceful and generally prosperous. On the Desh, for example, the documents of Indapur show that 1773–95 was the most prosperous period of its history. Those assigned to its revenues, as soldiers, lived in the village and lived well.[12] It was much the same in the Konkan. In 1770, for example, an English sea captain named Forbes visited Ragoji Angria, a sardar family who held lands and rights near Bombay. The country was fertile and prosperous, and the Englishman was treated to quite lavish hospitality.[13] Study of the family archives of the Dabhades of Talegaon show the development by this period of widespread credit and cash networks which crisscrossed Maharashtra with nodes at all major cities and towns. Unlike a century before, cash not only circulated in the countryside, but was used in the most minor and local transactions and for the pay of even servants and laborers.[14] Very large sums, millions of rupees, were routinely raised in family firms which formed the banking community of Pune, usually borrowed against future tax collections.[15]

Khandesh and the Aurangabad area had brief disruption early in the 1760s, but were well administered and productive. Malwa had some warfare between Shinde and Holkae and the local armed lineages (Ahirs, Rajputs) in the first five years after Panipat, but this was not seriously disruptive; Malwa was basically doing well, and would do even better, under the benevolent administration of Ahilyabai Holkar in the coming decades.[16] In all the areas directly controlled by the Peshwa, detailed revenue information came into the capital on a

[12] A. R. Kulkarni, "Towards a history of Indapur," in D. W. Attwood, M. Israel, and N. K. Wagle (eds.), *City, Countryside and Society in Maharashtra* (Toronto, University of Toronto, 1988), 131.

[13] James Forbes, *Oriental Memoirs* (London, 1813), 223–25.

[14] Frank Perlin, "Money use in late pre-colonial India" in J. F. Richards, *The Imperial Monetary System of Mughal India* (Delhi, 1987), 279–85. See also Frank Perlin, "Of 'white whale' and countrymen in the eighteenth-century Maratha Deccan: extended class relations, rights, and the problem of rural autonomy under the old regime," *Journal of Peasant Studies*, 5 (1978).

[15] A thorough study of the banking community in Pune in the eighteenth century remains to be done. A good study of a single family is G. T. Kulkarni, "Banking in the eighteenth century: a case study of a Poona banker," *Artha Vijnyana*, 15, 2 (1973), 180–200. A broader survey is found in B. G. Gokhale, *Poona in the Eighteenth Century: An Urban History* (Delhi, 1988), 131–37. Some families – such as the Naik Joshis of Baramati, the Naik Joshis of Chas, and the Rastes – had moved to Pune when the Peshwa moved his residence there in the 1730s. All were related to the Peshwa family by marriage. Others, such as the Bhides, the Omkars, and the Dikshit-Patwardhands, became prominent bankers in the period before 1760, but their pattern was the same. The were Brahmins, married into the Peshwa's family. This near monopoly was in the last decades of the eighteenth century challenged by Gujarati and Marwari banking houses based outside Pune.

[16] See M. W. Burway, *Ahilyabai (Devi) Holkar* (Indore, 1920).

monthly (and sometimes daily) basis, and most areas were predictable enough so that the banking community loaned money at relatively low rates of interest against future collections.[17]

Before carrying on the political narrative, let us pause to consider Ahilyabai Holkar, one of the most extraordinary rulers of eighteenth-century India, and the wider problem of women rulers of the Maratha polity. In normative terms, women were excluded by the strict rules of succession and could not succeed to kingship. Only sons fought for the throne after their father died. Still, there are several examples of women, in fact, ruling within the Maratha polity. We have, for example, met Tarabai, who led the resistance to the Mughals in the early years of the eighteenth century and played a central role in Maratha politics for decades thereafter. Her case shows that a woman could rule de facto as a wife (or widow) or as a mother (and regent) of a potential heir. For a queen to rule required both extraordinary talent and energy and fortuitous circumstances. In the case of Ahilyabai, the circumstances included the death of her husband in battle in 1754 (leaving her with a young son). Thereafter, the father-in-law, the great general Malhar Rao Holkar, seems to have trained her both in military affairs and administration. A number of letters from Malhar Rao Holkar to Ahilyabai show that she was (besides being literate) fully involved in military and diplomatic activities well before her father-in-law's death. In 1765, he wrote her the following instructions:

... proceed to Gwalior after crossing the Chambal. You may halt there for four or five days. You should keep your big artillery and arrange for its ammunition as much as possible ... The big artillery should be kept at Gwalior and you should proceed further after making proper arrangements for its expenses for a month. On the march you should arrange for military posts being located for the protection of the road.[18]

Malhar Rao Holkar assumed that she was competent to handle both civil and military affairs and occasionally favored her with overall military advice: "Whenever you reduce a fortress of the Gohad chief,

---

[17] See, for example, the documents in the Pune Daftar, Prant Azmas Hindustan Rumals, for these decades. These sophisticated financial transactions have generated a number of attempts to explain the growth and movement of money in the countryside. See, for example, H. B. Vashishta, *Land Revenue and Public Finance in Maratha Administration* (Bombay, 1975). Also, V. D. Divekar, "The emergence of an indigenous business class in Maharashtra in the eighteenth century," *Modern Asian Studies*, 16, 3 (July 1982), 427–44.

[18] M. V. Kibe, "Fragments from the records of Devi Shri Ahilyabai Holkar," *Indian Historical Records Commission: Proceedings*, XIII (1930), 133.

send adequate number of artillery. In no case should you be entrenched before a fort. As far as possible get the object by means of prestige."[19] A few weeks later, he advised Ahilyabai, on her arrival at Indore, to arrange the administration of two districts in eastern Malwa and assumed her competence to do so. Thus, when Malhar Rao died, and Ahilyabai's son – the nominal heir – went insane and died within a year of succession, she (already thirty years old) had an established record of both military and administrative competence. Rather than adopt an heir, she petitioned the Peshwa to take over the administration of the Holkar lands herself.[20] She was fully prepared to lead her troops into battle against the faction in the central government which opposed her, when a letter from the Peshwa granting her authority settled the issue.[21] In a novel and ingenious solution, she chose Tukoji Holkar, commander of the "household" troops (but no relative), to head all military aspects of her rule. The stable division of power lasted three decades, until both their deaths in the 1790s.

Ahilyabai turned her attention to just administration, peace, and prosperity within the Holkar estates, especially Malwa. (Tukoji Holkar seems to have administered Holkar estates in the Deccan, where he was resident for long periods, and in North India at other periods.) Since Marathas had little tradition of veiling or secluding women, Ahilyabai held daily public audience.

Her first principle of government appears to have been moderate assessment, and an almost sacred respect for the native rights of village officers and proprietors of land. She heard every complaint in person; and although she continually referred causes to courts of equity and arbitration, and to her ministers, for settlement, she was always accessible; and so strong was her sense of duty, on all points connected with the distribution of justice, that she is represented as not only patient, but unwearied, in the most insignificant causes, when appeals were made to her decision.[22]

In spite of wars to the north and the south, Ahilyabai's territories in Malwa were not attacked or disrupted by local armed lineages during her entire thirty-year reign, proof of her diplomatic and administrative skill. She was more successful than any previous administration in

---

[19] Ibid., 135.

[20] There is a strong suggestion that Ahilyabai also wrote to the Peshwa's wife and she was helpful in getting the crucial grant. See Burway, *Ahilyabai Holkar*, 22–24.

[21] J. Malcolm, *A Memoir of Central India* (London, third edition, 1832), I, 161–62.

[22] Ibid., 176. Malcolm based his history on oral reports of people who had actually been at Ahilyabai's court.

halting the raids of the hill tribes, Bhils and Gonds, on agricultural settlements. She kept virtually the same set of ministers and administrators throughout her reign. She developed Indore from a small village to a prosperous and beautiful city. She was a legend in Malcolm's time (the 1830s and 1840s), as she remains today, for the help she gave widows in keeping their husband's wealth, rather than surrendering it to the state or greedy relatives or managers. Her monuments are forts and roads in Malwa, and a wide variety of religious endowments (temples, rest houses, tanks, bathing steps, and the like), both in Malwa and far beyond – Varanasi, Dwarka in Gujarat, Rameshwaram, Gaya. She also sponsored festivals and gave donations for regular worship in many Hindu temples. Her reputation in Malwa today is that of a saint; such are the results of a good, honest administration.

Let us return to the more disrupted areas outside Ahilyabai's benevolent control. I hope the reader will bear with me through the account of one more period of disputed succession, which we need for discussion of patterns of successional conflict developed in the conclusion. We begin with the death of Madhav Rao Peshwa in 1773. There was only one suitable candidate, Narayan Rao, the younger brother of Madhav Rao. The second contender, Ragunath Rao, the Peshwa's uncle, we have met throughout the previous decade. Early in the decade he shared power; later, he was a state prisoner at Pune. Within nine months of investiture, Narayan Rao was dead, victim of overt political murder. He was cut down by infantry demanding arrears of pay, the murder instigated by his imprisoned uncle, Ragunath Rao. The subsequent investigation proved only that Ragunath Rao wanted the new Peshwa seized and confined. Therefore, Ragunath Rao shortly became Peshwa. He quickly replaced the whole inner circle who had served Narayan Rao and before that Madhav Rao. The new appointees were men personally loyal to Ragunath Rao, who came from fairly obscure origins; they never appeared before or after in Maratha history.[23]

Ragunath Rao then launched a combined campaign against the Nizam that was militarily successful, but brought no tribute or territory. As Ragunath Rao planned a Karnatak campaign, important leaders left camp for Pune and formed a faction supporting the soon to

[23] The rapidly shifting situation is thoroughly covered in Grant Duff, *History*, 173–92.

be born son of the murdered Peshwa, Narayan Rao. Ragunath Rao moved towards Pune, won a battle, but turned north towards Burhanpur. The opposing faction picked up the lukewarm support of the Nizam. Ragunath Rao received support from Shinde and Holkar (of Malwa), and hoped for support from the Gaikwad family of Gujarat and one branch of the then divided Bhonsle family of Nagpur, not thus far involved.

Ragunath Rao's position steadily deteriorated. The opposing allies held Pune and the administration and, shortly, both Shinde and Holkar declared against him. Ragunath Rao retreated westward, hoping to find a solid ally among the warring brothers of the Gaikwad family of Gujarat.

After extended negotiations, Ragunath Rao found a new ally in the English in Bombay. Their conflicts had been, as we have seen, with the coastal powers, indigenous and foreign, and the English had been, in fact, up to this point quite isolated from Pune's main concerns or campaigns. A new, ambitious policy of the Bombay government, with the enhanced military remaining from the Anglo-French wars quickly made them a major contender for territorial conquest. Their strategy was in use throughout India at the time – support one candidate in a succession dispute, in hopes of extracting major territorial gains if he won. In this spirit, Bombay formally allied with Ragunath Rao. The terms ceded a large tract in Gujarat, the islands near Bombay, and 150,000 Rs per month for the maintenance of 2,500 regular troops, including artillery.

By March 1775 Ragunath Rao's forces had been defeated in Gujarat; he fled to Surat, the British his only remaining ally. An East India Company army assembled from Bombay and Madras. In the next few months prospects looked good. The Company received large concessions from Ragunath Rao and the hoped for member of the Gaikwad family joined with his forces. The war of movement in Gujarat generally favored the English–Ragunath Rao side.[24]

Once again, power quickly shifted. The Bengal Government, recently elevated over Bombay and Madras, strongly opposed Bombay's forward policy and appointed their own negotiator, who started from Calcutta. When the order was received, in May 1775, the

---

[24] There was, however, by no means a total collapse of the administration of Gujarat. See the important local documentation in V. G. Khobrekar, *Gujratetil Marathi Rajvat* [Maratha Administration of Gujarat], *1664–1820* (Pune, 1962).

British forces went into cantonment in Gujarat. Negotiations began in December 1775 and produced the Treaty of Purandar (March, 1776). The treaty ended hostilities, returned the cessions in Gujarat, awarded the British Salsette and Bassein and the revenues of Broach and some immediate cash. The British, in return, withdrew all support from Ragunath Rao. He was to receive a yearly stipend.[25]

Neither Bombay nor the Governor-in-Council in Bengal approved the treaty, so war was resumed in 1777. Ragunath Rao waited in Bombay with the British force. (A much larger force was marching across India in support from Bengal.) Severe internal problems weakened the party at Pune, and positions shifted several times. The arrival of Holkar, with his 10,000 man army, changed the situation. He initially opposed the Nana Phadnavis group, but was soon brought in. This support dramatically strengthened the faction opposing Ragunath Rao, and most key Ragunath Rao supporters at Pune were jailed.[26]

In late 1778, the British expedition of over 3,000 trained troops (with 19,000 bullocks dragging guns and supplies), finally moved out (not yet joined by the force coming from Bengal). Meanwhile, the group in Pune, under Shinde, Holkar, and Nana Phadnavis, assembled a large army, stocked the Maharashtra forts, and raised cash. The British force reached the top of the Ghats, marching less than a mile per day. By the third week, the British force had run out of supplies, and the commander decided to retreat. The Maratha army attacked and surrounded the British force at Wadgaon (February 1779). Shinde negotiated the treaty, by which the British gave up Ragunath Rao and every bit of income and territory they had been promised since the death of Madhav Rao in 1773. Leaving hostages, the British army returned to Bombay.[27]

The end of this affair involved Colonel Leslie's force which was marching overland to Bombay from Bengal. It got involved in taking Maratha forts in Bundelkund. The commander was replaced, and the force pushed on. They passed through Malwa, waited for the Narmada river to drop after the monsoon, and negotiated their way through the Bhonsle territory of Nagpur. The force reached Burhanpur on the Tapti river about the time the Bombay expedition was defeated, and

[25] A. Macdonald (compiler), *Memoir of the Life of Nana Farnavis Compiled from Family Records and Extant Works* (London, reprinted edition, 1927), 26–29.

[26] Ibid., 30–34.

[27] Ibid., 39–41. See also R. Wallace, *The Guicowar and his Relations with the British* (Bombay, 1863), 55.

arrived at Surat about a month after the treaty had been signed.[28] The main effect of this large English force was on the troubled politics of Gujarat. The English forced Fateh Singh Gaikwad to cede to them much of the revenues of southern Gujarat, which had been paid to the Peshwa. During the campaign, the rapid breach of the walls of the city of Ahmedabad showed, once again, the effectiveness of British artillery.[29]

There are several long-term trends to be noted in this period of factional warfare. First, we have seen a considerable shift in power from the center to the peripheral Maratha states. Recall how the position of the anti-Ragunath Rao force was strengthened by the arrival of Shinde and Holkar's troops from the north. From military saranjams in the 1730s, the Shinde, Holkar, Bhonsle, and Gaikwad families had built up regular administrations, including tax collection and judicial functions. In the decades discussed, Holkar had the best administered territories, Shinde was the strongest militarily and most active diplomatically, while the Gaikwad and Bhonsle families were factionally divided.[30] The Pune administration needed at least two and preferably three of these families to mount a large-scale offensive against a serious external threat. Second, we should note the progression of power at Pune. Power was defined by control over the actual revenue-producing bureaucracy. We have watched the shift from Shivaji's line to the Peshwa, and, in this period, from the Peshwa's line to Nana Phadnavis, who rose from being a clerk in Madhav Rao's service to controlling the government. Third, we should note the British attempt to control the Maratha polity through the vehicle of Ragunath Rao. This tactic is the same as the subversion of Bengal and Awadh a decade earlier, and no different from the British "protection" of the Peshwa a quarter-century later in 1803. It failed, in this period, partly because they could not control Ragunath Rao, but mainly

---

[28] The manuscript letters and reports of the Goddard expedition are housed mainly in the British Museum. See Add. 29119, 38402, 28403. The political and military letters from Goddard when he arrived in Gujarat are in the India Office Library, Orme MSS Vol. 197, 7–9. See also Raghubir Singh (ed.), *English Records of Maratha History (Extra Volume): Selections from C. W. Malet's Letter-Book, 1780–1784* (Bombay, 1940).

[29] Wallace, *Guicowar*, 60–63.

[30] Based on documents no longer extant, Grant Duff made an attempt to quantify the military strength of the center and the periphery for the early 1770s. He put the cavalry strength of the Peshwa at 50,000 of which forty thousand were stationed in forts and garrisons, leaving him about ten thousand troops for campaigning. He calculated that the Bhonsle and Gaikwad families could muster 15,000 cavalry together. Shinde and Holkar could muster 30,000 together, and the Pawar family, 3,000. Grant Duff, *History*, 171–72.

because the Marathas defeated the Bombay army. Though the new artillery/infantry combinations of the Europeans were clearly superior in the best of circumstances, they were not – at this point – invincible. The Bombay army lost because of problems of terrain and supply – the same two strategic advantages which had allowed Shivaji to resist Bijapur and the Mughals. Even in the 1770s, it remained hard to drag guns and food up the Ghats. Every month, the army cost more than the revenue an average pargana produced in a year. As these new forces became the norm, the power with the most credit would win.[31]

As much as possible, we have avoided burdening the narrative with the names of the inner circle of power at Pune, but thumbnail biographies are important for understanding the patterns of factional politics, perhaps the most interesting feature of this period.[32] What, then, are we to make of this group of leaders? The main point to notice is that there are no new Maratha families on the list. By this period, not only were the main administrators Brahmin (Nana Phadnavis, Khasgiwale, Tulsibaghwale) and the bankers (Baramatikar) – this we would expect – but so also were the military commanders (Raste, Patwardhan, Phadke, Purandre). The Brahmin dominance of the grant-giving process had made opportunities available to Brahmins, as never before in the Maratha polity.[33] The second point is that none of this new group of commanders succeeded in establishing a large, independent area of control, like Shinde, Holkar, Gaikwad, and Bhonsle had done in the 1730–40 period. In spite of almost yearly campaigns in the Karnatak, Maratha control never matched that of Gujarat, Malwa, or Nagpur. Most of the tribute extracted from the local armed lineages went to the Peshwa and later Nana Phadnavis. We shall elaborate on these themes in the concluding section on the Maratha polity.

Let us now carry the political narrative to 1803. The main themes of the period were the increasing separation of north and south as spheres of activity and the elimination of major polities. There was a constant

[31] In a wider context, it is worth noting that these same factors – supply, difficult terrain, and credit – were decisive in another theater of the Anglo-French conflict, known as the American Revolution. The British had considerable trouble moving artillery in the forests of New England; George Washington was in despair at Valley Forge because he had no more cash to pay crucial trained mercenary infantry. At the critical battle of Yorktown, the issue was decided largely by problems of supply.

[32] See Appendix, p. 173.

[33] Grant Duff located an official list of the officers in Madhav Rao's army. Of the 449 men, there were 93 Brahmins, 8 Rajputs, 308 Marathas, and 40 Muslims. Grant Duff, *History*, 172n.

round robin of treaties between the major players – Tipu Sultan of Mysore, the Nizam, Nana Phadnavis and the British – as each tried to better his position. Detailed analysis of these events, policies, and battles, has been given in numerous histories of the British conquest of India, and will not be repeated here. Rather, we will consider only trends which were important for the Maratha polity.

We left the British retreating toward Bombay in 1779–80. Within a year, a grand alliance to drive out the British had been formed; it included the Nizam, Haidar Ali of Mysore, the Bhonsle family, and the Peshwa. It lasted only a year, because the treaty of Salbai (1782), which was negotiated and dominated by Shinde, committed the Marathas and the British to friendship and joint conquest of Haidar Ali. (The same year, Haidar died, succeeded by his son Tipu.)

This treaty is an important marker for changes in the Maratha polity. Certainly, there had been direct negotiations between outside powers and the Maratha "states" before. For example, both Fateh Singh Bhonsle and the Gaikwad family had frequently negotiated and allied with the Nizam. What changed here was that Shinde, formally subordinate to the Peshwa, was, in fact, guaranteeing the behavior of the whole Maratha polity. With the largest and most modern army in the polity, the tail was wagging the dog. The treaty also reflects the direct rivalry of Shinde, who wanted freedom from the English threat in order to expand his territories in the north, and Nana Phadnavis, who wanted to expand in the south. Shinde won.[34] The English were very sensitive to these changes and were willing to give up much

the Maratha polity to their side.[35] As we might predict from the whole of the previous Maratha history, things did not work out as neatly as the English hoped.

The treaty of Salbai allowed Shinde to use his regular infantry and artillery to reduce many local armed lineages in northern Malwa and the Delhi area. In the next five years, he attacked Rajputs, Ahirs, Kichis, and Bundelas, winning the Battle of Lalsot against Jaipur. Nominally successful, the process actually bankrupted Shinde, who largely lost control of Delhi and the surrounding area. The new infantry/artillery units were proving crushingly expensive, even for the largest of the Maratha states.

[34] Macdonald, *Nana Farnavis*, 48–49.
[35] Wallace, *Guicowar*, 66–67.

In the south, Tipu forced the British into a "friendship" treaty at Mangalore, separating them from Nana Phadnavis, who carried on the war against Tipu, now allied with the Nizam. By 1784, Tipu with his trained infantry and artillery had defeated the Nizam and extracted tribute and territory. Through 1786–87, Maratha forces campaigned against Tipu; the British withdrew, under orders from London to refrain from any forward adventures. The war remained inconclusive, the Marathas taking forts in Tipu's territory, but gaining little tribute or rights; a peace treaty was finally concluded in March 1787.

Through 1788–89, all parties jockeyed, knowing that the wars in the south would resume as soon as the British re-entered the situation. The British allied with the Nizam and allied with the Marathas in 1790. Throughout, the Marathas were reluctant partners, not wanting to see Tipu destroyed. They thus did not join Cornwallis on the disastrous bid to take Srirangapatan, Tipu's capital, in 1791. The combined army did, however, take a whole series of Tipu's forts along the Tunga-bhadra river, and in 1791–92 captured more forts between Bangalore and Srirangapatan (see Map 3). Tipu sued for peace in February 1792 and gave up large areas. The Marathas received Savnur, Lakshmeswar, and Kandgol in Dharwar, and all the territory up to the Tungabhadra river. The Nizam gained Cuddapah, Gooty, and the districts between the Krisna and the Tungabhadra. The British were the biggest gainers – Baramahal, Dindigul, Salem, Coorg, and much of the Malabar coast.

Meanwhile, in the north, Shinde – with the battalions of infantry and artillery trained by the Frenchman De Boigne – continued to gain military victories over Jaipur (May 1790) and Jodhpur a few months later. These two battles settled Shinde's dominance of Malwa, Rajasthan, and the Delhi area until his death four years later. The reduction of the huge fortress of Chittor by Shinde's artillery, in a few weeks, signalled the end of the traditional role of forts as places of refuge. Shinde solved some of the problems of the cost of the new forces by giving a large personal estate to De Boigne to cover the on-going costs of the troops; the arrangements worked well for a number of years.[36] Through 1792, Shinde slowly moved south toward

[36] Shinde's problems and strategies are covered in P. M. Joshi (ed.), *Persian Records of Maratha History*, Vol II, *Shinde as the Regent of Delhi (1787 and 1789–91)* (Bombay, 1954). It is important to note the size of these trained, uniformed units. Initial recruitment in 1790 was of ten batallions of 750 men, backed up by 60 pieces of artillery and 500 cavalry. Within two years, the force was expanded to 24,000 troops with European officers and backed up by 130 pieces of artillery.

the Deccan, bearing numerous Mughal insignia to be bestowed on the imprisoned Peshwa. There was much speculation that Shinde would displace Nana Phadnavis and take control of the central structure of the Maratha polity. Though he succeeded in presenting the insignia, Mahadji Shinde was very sick throughout his stay in Pune and died there in early 1794 – succeeded by his adopted son, Daulat Rao Shinde.

If the period from 1790–95 proved the superiority of infantry and artillery, it was the 1795–1800 period which removed major polities from the field. The Nizam was the first. In effect, he had been a tributary of the Marathas since 1773, with no attempt to break free. The new territories acquired at the conclusion of the war with Tipu spurred attempts at independence. The Nizam's actions raised Maratha counter-claims to the chauth of Berar, Bedar, and Adoni. A large combined army, including Shinde's forces from the north, defeated the Nizam at Kharda (April, 1795) and forced major concessions. This defeat would have in all probability meant the final absorption of the Nizam's territory. Events intervened, however, to make the Nizam a valued ally for a few years.

After the Battle of Kharda, the major commanders returned to their respective areas – Daulat Rao Shinde to Malwa, Purushuram Bhau Patwardhan to Tasgaon in southern Maharashtra, Raghuji Bhonsle to Nagpur. Only Tukoji Holkar remained at Pune, though his health was declining rapidly. This was the peak of Nana Phadnavis's power – enemies defeated, commanders contentedly returning to their own areas. It was a brief moment.

In late 1795, the Peshwa, rendered helpless by the policies of Nana Phadnavis, committed suicide; this act set off a succession dispute that was to engulf the Maratha leaders in a civil war for the next five years.[37] The succession was "flawed" in every way. There was no son, no direct heir to the Peshwa. The only collateral line contained the two sons of Ragunath Rao, who had been Nana Phadnavis's arch-enemy for more than a quarter of a century. As the conflict began, through 1796, Daulat Rao Shinde played the major role, advancing south with a large army. By the time he arrived at Pune, the factional situation had shifted several times. The initial agreement between the elder of Ragunath Rao's two sons, Bajirao, and Nana Phadnavis broke down. By June, Bajirao was a prisoner in Daulat Rao Shinde's camp and the younger

---

[37] Only a brief summary is possible here. For the details, see Grant Duff, *History*, 61–110.

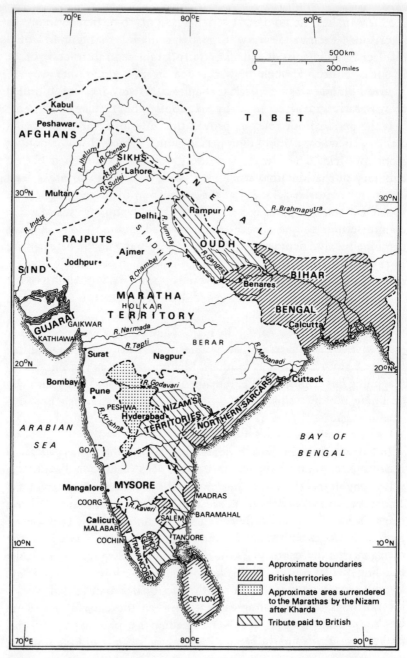

Map 9.   India in 1798 (adapted from C. C. Davies, *An Historical Atlas of the Indian Peninsula* [Calcutta, 1963], 55).

brother was invested with the office of the Peshwa. Nana Phadnavis retreated to Satara and tried to raise allies, including Bajirao, the elder brother, still imprisoned in Shinde's camp. From Raigarh, Nana Phadnavis built a coalition supporting Bajirao, which included Raghuji Bhonsle, the Peshwa's household troops, and the Nizam – who was brought in by the offer of all the territory which had been taken from him after the Battle of Kharda. By late 1796, Nana Phadnavis had returned to Pune with enough backing to install Bajirao as Peshwa.

Events moved even more quickly in the next two years, and it was Pune which suffered. Both Shinde's and Holkar's troops were cantoned just outside the city and were in arrears of pay. There were several serious battles on the streets of Pune and authority declined quickly. When Tukoji Holkar died in late 1797, a succession dispute between his sons was already in progress. Simultaneously, the new Peshwa, Bajirao II, made a bid for freedom from Nana Phadnavis. He instigated a Neapolitan adventurer serving Shinde to capture Nana Phadnavis and his whole immediate group in January 1798. This was followed by a sack of Pune to pay Shinde's troops. Finally, Holkar's troops moved north to Malwa, and Daulat Rao Shinde's attention was demanded by a revolt, centered in northern Maharashtra, involving the remaining queens of Mahadji Shinde. The areas around Ahmadnagar and Kandesh suffered, as both armies fought each other, and pillaged (see Map 1).

The civil war widened, as both Shinde and the Peshwa sought allies. The Peshwa brought in the Nizam. Shinde courted Tipu Sultan, released Nana Phadnavis, who had been a prisoner in his camp for nearly a year, and tried unsuccessfully to find a settlement with the queens of Mahadji Shinde. The conflict spread to Malwa, with both the army of the queens and Holkar's troops attacking Shinde's territory.

Into this confused situation came the British. Their policy abruptly changed with the arrival of Wellesley in April 1798. There was to be a forward policy of engagement and subsidiary alliance with the remaining powers to prevent associations between the French and the Nizam, Tipu, or the Marathas. The Nizam was most eager to call in the British, as a counter to Maratha pressure, and signed a subordinate treaty in 1798. The Marathas were much more cautious. Nana Phadnavis had always been suspicious of the British and opposed any treaty or formal engagement.

With Tipu, the process was much more direct. As soon as the British could marshall sufficient force and credit (1799), they attacked and defeated Tipu, ending with the taking of his capital Srirangapattan. His territories were largely absorbed into the British domain, a small part going to the Nizam, a smaller part yet going to the Peshwa. By 1800, thus, there were only two independent powers left on the field – the British and the Marathas. Every other polity (with the exception of the Punjab) was a subsidiary to one or the other. Observers knew that a conflict was inevitable.

The major event of 1800 was the death of Nana Phadnavis, who had controlled the Peshwa, the administration, and diplomacy for the past quarter-century. He was the last of a whole generation of leaders who had become prominent after the Battle of Panipat – Tukoji Holkar, Mahadji Shinde, and perhaps the best of all Maratha administrative leaders, Ahilyabai Holkar. All died between 1795 and 1800.

With the death of Nana Phadnavis, the factional situation simplified. The Peshwa, freed from restraint, looked for allies and independent action. From 1800 on, he regularly negotiated with the English, but did not really need them as long as he was sure of Shinde's backing. The situation shifted, however, when Shinde was forced to leave Pune to deal with Holkar, who was raiding and plundering his territory in Malwa (see Map 7). Through 1801, Shinde and Holkar fought in southern Malwa. Some of Shinde's regular battalions were defeated in the Ujjain area. Later in the season, battles were fought in the Burhanpur region. Still later in the campaigning season, Shinde's forces defeated Holkar's troops and plundered Indore, his capital. Holkar decided to abandon Malwa and carry the war to the Deccan, hoping to carve out a new sphere of influence.

Not until well into 1802, with Holkar's army coming south, did negotiations between the Peshwa and the English become serious. On October 25, 1802, Holkar's army defeated the combined forces of the Peshwa and Shinde's forces in the Deccan in front of Pune. Pune was once again plundered and the Peshwa fled to British territory at Bassein, where he finally submitted to a subsidiary alliance. In 1803, by this treaty, the British acquired territory Surat, the Peshwa's person, and a commitment that the Peshwa would bear the expense of the British force and consult with the British resident at Pune. Holkar ran out of money and turned north. A British army brought the Peshwa back to Pune and installed him in office. This act represented the end of the Maratha polity as an independent power. The rest of the story is one of British conquest, largely with funds from conquered territories.

APPENDIX

The following are thumbnail biographies of the inner circle of the Maratha polity in the 1770s:

(1) Shinde (of Gwalior), Tukoji Holkar (the forces of Ahilyabai Holkar of Indore), Gaikwad (of Baroda), and Bhonsle (of Nagpur). These are the well-known, large, relatively independent states, all dating from the 1730s. Their influence varied with their proximity to Pune, and the resolution of their internal factional conflicts.

(2) Nana Phadnavis. A Chitpavan Brahmin and extraordinarily able administrator and negotiator, in control of the revenue administration. He had been present at Panipat (1761) and had served in the administration of Madhav Rao for ten years.

(3) Morobada. Cousin of Nana Phadnavis, close in age and a direct rival to Nana. He was jailed in 1777, when the Nana/Shinde faction defeated Ragunath Rao. The family survived with a small jagir and a large house in Pune.

(4) Bapuji Naik Baramatikar. This Chitpavan Brahmin family had been in Adil Shahi service through most of the seventeenth century, mainly in banking and finance. They held "nested" rights in the area of Baramati. Bapuji Naik briefly joined the inner group as a backer of Ragunath Rao, but apparently returned to Baramati after the faction was defeated. The family later changed its name to Sowkar (banker), reflective of its main occupation.

(5) Sakharam Hari Bokil. He was a Kanada Brahmin, mainly a diplomat, and was of the Madhav Rao generation. He emerged, in the 1770s, as a supporter of Ragunath Rao and was jailed along with others of the faction; he died in jail in less than a year. There is no subsequent mention of the family, other than that the lands were confiscated.

(6) Bajaba Purandare. This family of Deshasta Brahmins came originally from the Saswad area. They provided commanders and administrators to the Peshwas, going back to the 1730s. Though Bajaba backed Ragunath Rao and was jailed, the family recovered favor, served in the campaigns in the Karnatak in the 1780s, and emerged as a large sardar under the British in the nineteenth century.

(7) Trimbak Rao Mama. A Chitpavan Brahmin, surnamed Pethe, from the Konkan coast. He fought at Panipat and served as a military leader and diplomat. He died opposing Ragunath Rao's advance on Pune in 1774. The family never again gained prominence, and ended up with a small estate in southern Maharashtra in the nineteenth century.

(8) Anand Rao Jivaji (Khasgiwala). After Panipat, this Chitpavan Brahmin family formed the personal administration for Madhav Rao Peshwa. They settled and collected revenue from the Peshwa's personal inams. The family retained holdings in both Pandarpur and Pune and were small jagirdars in the nineteenth century.

(9) Hari Pant Phadke. A Chitpavan Brahmin. At this time, he was about twenty years old, an army commander, just coming up. He was a strong supporter of the Nana Phadnavis group and advanced rapidly in the next decade.

(10) Murarrao Rao Gorpade of Gutti. This was an established Maratha family whose lands were far from Pune on the border of Andhra. As an army commander, he appeared briefly in the civil war of the 1770s as a supporter of Ragunath Rao. He returned to Gutti and – with two sons – was killed in battle opposing Tipu Sultan in the 1780s.

(11) Anand Rao Raste. In the seventeenth century, this Chitpavan Brahmin family had been collectors on the Ratnagiri coast under the Nizam Shahi kingdom. As administrators and soldiers, they rose rapidly in the 1740s, under the patronage of Nana Saheb Peshwa. Members of the family fought at Panipat. In the civil wars of the 1770s, the family first sided with the Nizam, but returned to the Nana Phadnavis faction (1775). The family served as military commanders, mainly in the Karnatak, and emerged with extensive holdings in Pune and south Maharashtra.

(12) Govind Rao Patwardhan. This Chitpavan Brahmin family migrated from the Ratnagiri coast to the Desh in about 1725. The family name was changed from Bhat to Patwardhan after Sriwardhan, where they settled. Later, five sons took service in Madhav Rao's army (1760s). The family initially supported Ragunath Rao, but was later won over to the Nana Phadnavis side; in the 1780s and 1790s, the brothers were prominent military commanders in the south. The family emerged with six small states in southern Maharashtra in the nineteenth century.

EPILOGUE (1803–1818)

After the Peshwa took refuge with the British, the pattern followed the familiar course of a disputed Maratha succession. The British offered support to an otherwise weak candidate, in return for substantial grants of revenue-producing land. More important, the British asserted the legitimacy and authority of their candidate over the Maratha houses. (This sequence is structurally no different from the British attempt to set up Raghobadada a half-century earlier, or the Nizam's parallel attempts in the same period.) Just as predictably, Holkar and others at Pune set up a rival candidate and sought allies. What differed this time were the resources and organization of the British. Lord Wellesley and Lord Lake organized a vast, comprehensive set of coordinated campaigns, which put 60,000 trained men in the field on widely separated fronts. The aims were to divide the Maratha houses, break Shinde's modern army and regular income, and seize income-producing territory. During the monsoon of 1803, the British neutralized Holkar, the rival Peshwa, and several of the smaller houses (such as Patwardhan) with treaties.[1]

In the months that followed, the war was fought on several fronts. One British army engaged Shinde and the Bhonsle forces in northern Maharashtra, the major battle costing thousands of casualties on both sides. With the defeat of the Maratha army, the British took Burhanpur and its nearby fortress, Asir. They also succeeded in stopping the traditional raiding tactics adopted by the Bhonsle forces. Simultaneously, another British army moved on Delhi, Agra, and Shinde's lands north of the Chambal river. They were also successful, largely because Shinde's European officers (mainly French) deserted and disbanded their troops. Without officers, some of Shinde's best troops fought on,

[1] The period of the British conquest of the Maratha polity has been extensively covered, both in original records and later histories. I have followed mainly G. S. Sardesai, *New History of the Marathas* (Bombay, second impression, 1968), III. See P. C. Ghosh, *Baji Rao II and the East India Company, 1796–1818* (New York, second edition, 1964); Also, M. P. Roy, *The Origin, Growth, and Suppression of the Pindaris* (New Delhi, 1973). For the specifics of the final campaign, see R. G. Burton, *The Maharatta and Pindari War* (Delhi, reprinted edition, 1975).

but were defeated. At the same time, other British units fought Maratha forces in Gujarat, Orissa, and Bundelkond. All were successful.

By December 1803, the British forced on the losers a series of crippling treaties. The Peshwa was functionally replaced by the British Resident at Pune, who took over the administration and all important government functions. The British signed treaties of subordination with all the Rajput states, plus the Jat, Rohilla, and Bundella states on the northern rim of the Malwa plateau. All of these had previously paid tribute regularly or irregularly to the Marathas. The British also took control of Orissa, thereby securing control of the entire eastern coast of India and much of the rest of the eastern territories of the Bhonsle family. The treaty with Shinde conceded to the British all of his possessions north of the Jumna (including Delhi and Agra), control of the Mughal Emperor, all his possessions in Gujarat, and all claims on other Maratha houses. The treaty also made the British arbiters of disputes between the Maratha houses (rather than the Peshwa), and forbade Europeans from taking service in any Maratha army.

The campaigns of 1803–04 virtually bankrupted the East India Company. The army was in arrears, and the Directors, more interested in profit than in conquest, recalled Wellesley, replacing him with Lord Cornwallis (whose specific charge was the negotiating of an end to the expensive Maratha wars). There were three main results of this change in policy. First, Holkar and Shinde recovered little of their lost territory and were reduced to possessions on the Malwa plateau. Second, the British repudiated alliances with the Rajasthan states and others on the rim of the Malwa plateau. Third, and probably most important, all the Maratha houses were directly tied to the British for any claims. The effect of this series of treaties was to separate further the Maratha houses and drastically reduce the power of the Peshwa. All the forms of power, but none of the substance remained. The Peshwa could not collect his own taxes or even discipline his own recalcitrant deshmukh families without the consent of the British Resident.

This situation – forms of power without substance – remained stable for more than ten years. Some areas, such as Maharashtra, did well and prospered; others, such as Malwa and Rajasthan, were often plundered by the irregular troops of Shinde or Holkar, known as pindaries. The situation began to shift in June 1817, when a new treaty was forced on the hapless Peshwa, which effectively stripped him of all power. He would no longer have any representation at other courts in India or even formal overlordship of the Maratha houses. Within months, the British Residencies had been attacked and burned both in Pune and Nagpur. British armies, however, quickly defeated the Peshwa's forces and the Bhonsle forces at Nagpur. By the end of 1817, a large, multi-front campaign reminiscent of 1803–04 had crushed the pindari forces (which had been raiding into British territory) and Holkar's forces, which were the only remaining effective army.

The end of the Maratha polity came with a British proclamation in February 1818, which formally removed the Peshwa. Within a few months, he surrendered and his army was disbanded. The British began the long process of settling and administering the territories which they had conquered. The remaining Maratha houses received treaties of subordination which turned them into princely states.

CONCLUSIONS

How, then, might we describe the Maratha polity? At the outset, let us dispose of several notions prevalent in the historical literature. The Maratha polity was not an empire, if, by that, we have an image of imperial Rome or the Mughal Empire. There was no graded civilian/ military ranking with attendant symbols of authority. Those in the military were not, until late in the eighteenth century, full-time professionals. The Maratha polity did not, and could not, impose a uniform legal or revenue system. It never minted a uniform, high-quality currency;[1] neither did it build the straight roads which were the pride of the Roman Empire. Large parts of the Maratha polity, unlike Rome or the Mughal Empire, were permanently alienated to military commanders. There was no grand, imperial architecture.

Another term, in favor since the nineteenth century in writings on Marathas, is "confederacy." This term, also, fails to describe many central aspects of the Maratha polity. Confederacy implies a long-term shared power among groups or individuals of more-or-less equal power for mutual benefit or gain. The models which come to mind are the co-operation between the Swiss cantonments or the pre-Revolution American colonies. Confederacy implies a long-term cast of characters (the confederates) to make and execute plans. In contrast, as we have analyzed, it was characteristic of the Maratha polity that the inner circle of power changed with each generation, sometimes as frequently as each decade. Men joined or left the inner circle, depending on the stability and strength of the ruling family. Most critically, those who left did not remain some sort of loyal opposition, later to rejoin the inner circle. Rather, the families were most frequently crushed for their opposition and subsequently disappeared from the historical record. This was, clearly, a different dynamic from a confederacy.

---

[1] The Marathas adopted a very open attitude toward the minting of currency. Whoever had bullion or older coins simply brought them to a Maratha mint and, for a fee, new coins were produced. Even late in the eighteenth century, the most common silver coin, for example, made in the Burhanpur mint was the sicca rupee, a coin much predating the Maratha rule. See Pune Daftar, Prant Azmas Khandesh Rumal, no. 196.

Closer to a satisfactory formulation is Andre Wink's emphasis on the role of deshmukhs as "co-sharers" in the polity, the structural tension within families holding rights, and the use of the granting of rights to build the kingdom.[2] Overall, however, it is as one-sided to see the Maratha polity as "typically" riven by factional politics as the older histories which saw only kingly authority and "traitors." The published documents are, indeed, full of factional conflict and lead one to this view. All the famous series – *Selections from the Peshwa Daftar*, treaties, engagements and sanads, Poona Residency Correspondence – are full of these problems. Yet, one must strongly question whether this printed record is "typical" of the Maratha polity. We must remember that the documents were selected as "interesting" more than seventy-five years ago by a handful of historians of Maharashtra, because of their concerns with political history. Meanwhile, hundreds of thousands of routine revenue documents were deemed "uninteresting" and remain unprinted. To prove the pervasiveness of factional conflict, one must show quantitatively that most of the rights were under active dispute most of the time. This sort of research is possible in the unpublished records of the Pune Daftar. The burden of proof is to show that such conflict – at the central government level, at the village and pargana level – was "typical," that is that it consumed a dominant portion of the polity's resources and energy, leaving little for other activities.

We have every reason to doubt that factional conflict was the dominant activity of the Maratha polity. If we look back over its history, there were only three periods of fully fledged civil war, the Tarabai–Shahu conflict of 1708–16, the period after the murder of Narayan Rao (1772–78), and the period following the suicide of the imprisoned Peshwa (1795–1801). These were, indeed, heavily factionalized times, with much of the polity's resources consumed in strife, limiting the ability to expand the polity, even destroying heartland areas. Nevertheless, these three periods were relatively brief. (All were triggered by imperfect successions, the patterns of which we will soon discuss.) To these we must add several rebellions, all of which lasted only a few years and were of limited geographic scope. The Dabhade/ Gaikwad rebellion, for example, was confined to Khandesh and northern Maharashtra and part of Gujarat. The revenue documents of

[2] See Andre Wink, *Land and Sovereignty in India: Agrarian Society and Politics under the Eighteenth-century Maratha Svarajya* (Cambridge, 1986).

the areas show only a two-year drop in revenue, plus considerable short-term disruption, but recovery was complete within a couple of years of the defeat of the rebelling families.

The situation was much the same for "disputed" deshmukh or village headman rights. The printed papers regularly mention these kinds of feuds and just as regularly show the families seeking the intervention of the central power (whether Adil Shah, Nizam Shah, or later, the Peshwa) to resolve them. Yet, if we track these families through their own family papers or – even better – through detailed revenue documents of the area, these conflicts rarely disrupted even the most local area. They were usually settled by fiat or negotiation with the central power with a clear winner and loser, at least until the next succession. There is no doubt that the loyalty of the deshmukh families was essential to the Maratha polity, but this was, at most times, a routine face-to-face oath made by the head of the deshmukh family to the king or, later, the Peshwa. Only when the polity was deeply divided or the polity endangered (such as in the 1690–1705 period) did the inner circle have to reach down for support from the smaller deshmukhs. The limited number of times that a few hundred troops or a few thousand rupees made a crucial difference, only proves the rule. After these critical moments, the deshmukhs – almost invariably – disappeared from the inner circle.

The Maratha polity was more complicated than any of these formulations. There are several contexts in which it could be conveniently placed – as a successor state to the prior Muslim kingdoms of the Deccan, or as an on-going colonial discourse with the non-Maratha, local landed lineages, or as a distinctive example of hereditary, monarchical systems. It was all of these. We will look for continuity, multi-year cycles, and long-term change in three aspects of the Maratha polity (1) authority and personal loyalty (2) revenue and other sorts of information (3) military power.

Let us begin with authority and personal loyalty. If we look, first, at the inner circle, there were many continuities through the 150-year history of the Maratha polity. The inner circle remained small, never more than a dozen men. Through much of the history, all members of the group returned to Maharashtra, and the capital, at every monsoon. It was truly a face-to-face court. Throughout, the reward for loyal and competent actions was the same – a right to a portion of the revenue collected from agricultural production. No other source of revenue was found or sought. The duties and rights of these various portions – saranjam, deshmukhi, inam, patil – remained unchanged. The forms of reward for loyal service also remained unchanged; they included robes of honor, palanquins, ceremonial elephants and horses, and drums. All required face-to-face award at the court, whether at Pune, or Jinji, or Satara. All of these forms of honor and the personal style of the ceremony came directly from the prior Deccan kingdoms and continued unchanged throughout the Maratha polity. Another continuity throughout the Maratha period was that reward did not necessarily mean entrance into the inner circle. Many a deshmukh or a commander, as we have seen, was rewarded and sent off to home lands or distant duty.

We find several strategies of promoting loyalty common to the whole of the Maratha period. For example, every peshwa or king, on his succession, brought in young men of his generation. With some success, these new leaders were promoted very rapidly. Thus, we often find men in their late teens leading units or bands of cavalry. By their early twenties – as in the case of Shinde, Holkar, or Ranoji Bhonsle – they were leading thousands of cavalry. In factional disputes, these younger men, as we might expect, showed much greater loyalty to their patrons (whether peshwa or king) than older men who had been appointed by the previous sovereign. Another strategy that both those of Shivaji's line and the Peshwa used to build loyalty, was to marry into other families in the inner circle. This strategy was not particularly successful at building loyalty. The marriage enhanced the prestige of the in-law family and created rivals – especially cousins and uncles. Some of the most bitter factional conflict arose from exactly these unions within the inner circle. (The tension between trying to concentrate power through marriage and creating rivals was, of course, also a regular feature of European monarchies.) Another constant feature of loyalty in this face-to-face milieu was the importance of charismatic speaking ability. It seems clear that several in Shivaji's line and several of the Peshwas launched whole new strategies from debates among the inner circle at court.

If we look outwards from the court, the patterns of loyalty formed mainly around short- and long-term cycles. For example, there was the yearly cycle of authority/loyalty when the army assembled at Dassera (after the monsoon) for the beginning of the campaigning season. At the designated place of assembly, there would be the Sirpau ceremony

– a special turban distributed to the leaders, accompanied by a vow of loyalty. This ceremony was accompanied by an examination of horses and equipment and a blessing of the guns.

Other demonstrations of loyalty were, however, expected. One pattern of these followed the life-cycle of the king or peshwa. Accession, of course, required attendance and nazar (presents) from both the court and a quite wide circle of deshmukh families of Maharashtra. We find that this pattern of special taxes and audience also accompanied the birth of a son, thread ceremony, marriage of either peshwa or king or their sons, or adoption. All of these were occasions for face-to-face contact between the king or peshwa and the most important landed families of the polity. In a similar pattern, authority and loyalty were periodically asserted in the life-cycle events of these families, right up to most powerful military commanders. The king or peshwa was needed for the transferring of "nested" rights on the death of the grantee. Any relative or sharer of the revenue (such as a saranjamdar supported from the area) could dispute the right of a son to receive revenue when it was his father's name on the grant. Only the king or peshwa could, on receipt of a present and oath of loyalty, transfer the grant to the son.

Another cycle was the pattern of disputed authority. It appeared at every succession, but was most fully played out in the periods of civil war (1708–18, 1772–78, 1795–1801). The cycle began when the inner circle prepared for a succession. Recall, for example, how factions had already formed several years before Shivaji's death. The contenders reached out for alliances, first among the inner circle, then outside powers (earlier the Mughals, later the Nizam of Mysore). At the same time, the contenders courted bankers in the Pune community.[3] The importance of holding a stable, loyal, revenue-producing area creditable with a banker cannot be overstated.

After the death of the king or peshwa, the cycle moved from a preparation stage to military conflict. First, there was assembling of armies and attempts to gain position, using advantages of the terrain or loyal forts or the season. We should note that one side or the other would hold the capital, and certainly proclaim its candidate king or peshwa, but that act did not end the cycle; it was not even a significant marker in the process. As both contending armies moved in the field,

[3] This community, of course, included the Dikshit/Patwardhan family which was based at Nasik, but had representatives in Pune.

much more significant was the reaching down to deshmukh families for immediate help, safe cantonment during the monsoon, money, or additional troops. This meant that the conflict would be a longer and more bitter one than usual. The military cycle had more periods of devastating the revenue-producing areas of the rival than large-scale battles. If the cycle carried on without resolution for more than a campaigning season, one side or the other would likely call in an outside power, which made the situation more precarious; the outside power's "help" cost a promise of tribute and land. This phase of the conflict cycle ended with the capture of one or the other of the candidates, usually after a decisive battle re-establishing an authoritative office-holder. One consistent feature of the process is the variety of outcomes possible for the loser. He might end up in prison, but just as likely not. He might get a portion of the kingdom (the end of the Tarabai episode) or a small estate (the family of Ragunath Rao).

In the immediate aftermath of such a battle, loyalty was demanded of every grant-holder, whether directly involved or not. The direct opposition was not demoted, it was crushed. The families which had been the core opposition did not somehow go back to their "estates" and wait for better times. Most rights, especially the lucrative saranjam rights for maintenance of troops, were quickly resumed. Often, even the older "nested" rights – deshmukh, inam, and patil – were resumed and the family essentially returned to the status of leader of a small, family-based military unit. We have seen how several of the prominent families after choosing the wrong side in this sort of succession conflict simply disappeared from Maratha history. For those outside the core opposition, there does not seem to be a clear trend in what constituted treasonous behavior, not to be forgiven. Throughout the period, leading an attack on the capital was serious business, as was turning over a large fort to the opposing side or switching sides in the final battle. Simply taking service with the losing side was usually not grounds for dismissal; such "errors" were routinely forgiven. The new king or peshwa probably needed the support of the deshmukhs who had joined the opposing side. For the supporters of the winning candidate, there was very rapid promotion – including grants, and offices with power and salaries.

Now let us consider the long-term trends in authority and loyalty during the Maratha period. From the low ebb of the Jinji period (1690s) through 1720, there was a steady centralization of authority and demand for loyalty by Balaji Bajirao and Shahu. Independent bands became parts of larger armies, led by the peshwa. In the Bajirao period, the grant-giving process for inams, saranjams, even desh-mukhs, was gradually taken over by the peshwa, in the name of the king. In the 1730s, the "division" of Malwa and Gujarat actually consolidated the centralization. Initially, the areas under Shinde, Holkar, and the Gaikwad family were not, in any sense, "independent" states. They were ruled by men who had come up with the patronage of the peshwa, and were personally loyal to him. Especially in the case of Shinde and Holkar, there is little evidence of independent action until after the battle of Panipat (1761).[4] From the 1740s onward, the peshwa successfully asserted authority over quite ordinary groups and individuals far from Maharashtra. We have seen, for example, how his administrators adjudicated caste disputes in eastern Malwa. All of these cases ultimately could be appealed to the peshwa. Also in this period, Bajirao Peshwa personally led the army and received personal pledges of loyalty from local zamindars and rajas, when the army was on the march. For this issue of centralization, the period of 1770–95 is more problematic. In some areas, it looks like the process of consolidation and centralization was developing. For example, the Gaikwad in Gujarat was sharing power with the Peshwa; the small states of Satara and surrounding estates were not real rivals. At the same time the beneficiaries of the "division" of the 1730s were rapidly developing institutional and functional independence. Holkar had extensive, well-managed lands on the Malwa plateau; the Peshwa received neither revenue from them nor information about them. Shinde was, however, the biggest gainer in these decades. To his lands in Malwa, he added much of the area north of the Chambal river, the area around Delhi west into what is now Harayana, and tribute from much of Rajasthan. By the mid-1770s, the delicate balance of power between the center and these peripheral "states" had shifted, and the Peshwa (or his keepers, such as Nana Phadnavis) held estates and income only marginally larger than these two families. By the 1780s, the center needed these families to face any serious outside threat. Equally interesting, however, was the fact that no new large landed powers grew up in the

[4] Recall that Shinde and Holkar were also granted estates in Maharashtra, which were an important source of prestige. Both families demonstrated great attachment to them. This made the peshwa's threat of sequestering these estates an effective means of disciplining both families. In the later eighteenth century, the large holdings in Malwa and beyond made the estates in Maharashtra less important.

period. The Patwardhans, the Rastes, and Hari Pant Phadke – the successful military commanders of the late eighteenth century – never had opportunities in the Karnatak like those of Shinde, Holkar, and Gaikwad in an earlier period in the north. None of the newer leaders were able to carve out even semi-independent areas.

Overall, by the late period, power was consolidating in three centers. The center remained fairly strong. The Peshwa's areas had a full, intact administration; the documents from the local districts were the most detailed and comprehensive which the Maratha polity ever produced. Though the Peshwa had lost some areas (such as the city of Burhanpur to Shinde), the Gaikwad and Bhonsle families were courting the British to keep from being absorbed into the Peshwa's domains. Thus, at the end of the period, there were only three significant powers in the Maratha polity – Shinde, Holkar, and the Pune court. We must see this overall trend as one of consolidation and centralization, not somehow chaos and anarchy. Recall that the British were able to conquer the Maratha polity a few years later by subverting the center, a situation only possible when a strong, centralized bureaucracy was in place.

In considering the long-term changes in loyalty and authority, one significant question is how much change there was in the polity when Brahmins replaced Marathas as the dominant element at the center. In many fundamental ways it did not change the polity. For example, the patronage of Muslim pirs and dargahs continued just as it had under Maratha dominance and earlier under the Deccan sultanates. Differential tax rates in urban markets still favored Muslim traders. Still, there were profound effects, the most obvious of which was widespread, rapid social mobility for Brahmins somehow connected to the polity. They became the administrators of the newly conquered regions as well as in the expanding bureaucracy at the center. Equally important, Brahmins became high military leaders in large numbers. One estimate based on muster lists put the number of Brahmin leaders at almost one-third of such leaders in the Peshwa's army in the 1770s. (The proportion may have been higher towards the end of the eighteenth century.) We have noted that the prominent families which emerged in the second half of the eighteenth century (Raste, Patwardhan) were all Brahmin. Another route of social mobility was the emergence of banking families who loaned money to the government; these were overwhelmingly Brahmin. Outside this circle, there was steady patronage for temple priests, teachers and scholars, and government patronage of festivals such as Diwali and Holi.[5] A second, perhaps less well-known effect of Brahmin control of the center was the direct patronage of temples and pilgrimage sites. From Goa, through the Konkan, up on the Desh, and throughout areas of the Maratha polity, villages and land were given in perpetual religious grants (some of which still exist today as temple trusts). The third effect of this Brahmin dominance was to create another line of cleavage in factional disputes – Brahmin versus Maratha. This was not a major line of cleavage or loyalty, but there was periodic discussion among the big Maratha families of re-establishing Shivaji's line to real power and decreasing the power of the Brahmins.

Let us turn from this discussion of loyalty and authority to our second broad topic, information and revenue collecting. We will begin with the continuities throughout the Maratha period. The entire normative structure of revenue collecting came directly from the Deccan kingdoms. This included the maximum amounts expected of cultivating villages, the methods of assessing land, the categories of land (bagayat, jirayat, etc.), the contractual rights of patils and desh-mukhs, and the expected performance of each office. It is striking that, for example, a document describing how a devastated area was to be redeveloped in 1650 exactly described the process, as it was to be done in the 1760s – including the same terminology of tacavi loans and istawa (stepwise increasing) revenue settlements. On the whole, this is one of the least innovative areas of Maratha rule. If one looks at Nizam Shahi or Adil Shahi grants – deshmukhi, patilki, saranjam, or inam – the structure, rights, and responsibilities are identical to grants of the middle or late eighteenth century.[6]

Especially important is the long-term continuity in the position of the deshmukh. We have seen how these families possessed "nested" rights which included fortified houses, some patil rights in individual villages, and inam villages and land, all in a circumscribed region. Every government, whether Mughal, Nizam Shahi, or Maratha, had to negotiate with them. What should be emphasized here is their crucial role in information and revenue collection, with responsibilities both to the central government and the villages in their jurisdiction.

[5] I have found such support formed 5–8 percent of the expenses of governing in the Peshwa's documents for every area and district I have examined.
[6] The hundreds of Persian loan words found in Marathi today are part of the legacy of these continuities from the Deccan sultanates.

Within these normative and structural continuities were several cycles. The first was the yearly cycle of information gathering and revenue collection throughout the peshwa period in the most settled, directly administered areas. As we have seen (in Chapter 3), the cycle began in the capital, with the peshwa's clerks preparing an estimate of the collection of each collector's area; after the collector accepted the estimate, he raised the advance payment from the Pune banking community. (Incidentally, the variety of names and the variability of the guarantors suggests a relationship more market-style than patron–client.) Well before the monsoon, the collectors left for the field, returning to residences in the largest town of their jurisdiction. From then on, they toured – examining the state of the crops and settling taxes with each village – often trying minor cases along the way. The typical stay in a village was only a day or two, time enough to examine the local land records and note any changes in the actual fields under cultivation. The documents confirming the taxes due were prepared at his residence in the ensuing months, and signed by the village headmen and the deshmukh of the area. Periodically, the village headman sent payments to local Maratha treasuries. At the end of the revenue year, the collector balanced the receipts against the agreed upon revenue and prepared balance sheets for each village. When he once again returned to Pune, he was responsible for the unpaid balance, which he had to collect first in the following year. (If this entire cycle sounds suspiciously like the British District Officer of the nineteenth century, it should. It seems likely that his role was patterned after the Maratha kamavisdar, and it was a pattern and a cycle that met the expectations of village headmen and deshmukhs.) Lest this be construed as some sort of idealized system, recall that there are tens of thousands of working documents of this system in the Pune Daftar, and every researcher who has worked on them has found extraordinary levels of thoroughness, predictability, and detail.

We should also note a common cycle outside the areas of stable control. In areas with armed local lineages, the cycle began with a main-force Maratha army "conquering" the region. This, in fact, meant that the local lineage found it expedient to come to terms rather than fight, or retire to a fort and await siege. Typically, they paid some tribute immediately, and promised some further amount in following years. In these following years, payment either tapered off, or – more commonly – stopped altogether. Note that the Maratha collector dealt only with the court of the local lineage, simply requesting the tribute each year. He received very little information from the surrounding villages, had no relationships with village headmen, measured no fields, collected no revenue. "Revolt" meant that the lineage forced the collector to leave. ("Conquest" by another power functionally meant the same thing, with the opposing power putting their collector in the court of the armed lineage.) It took another main-force Maratha army to "conquer" the lineage and begin tribute again. In some areas, such as Malwa and Khandesh and parts of Gujarat, this sort of cycle was quickly replaced by the regular revenue collection described above. In others – the rest of Gujarat, the Jat and Rohilla areas near Delhi, much of Rajasthan, and all of the Karnatak – the Maratha "conquest" never got beyond this cycle of tribute collection from local armed lineages.

The long-term trends in information gathering and revenue collection represent one of the major accomplishments of the Maratha polity. From the 1720s, there was a steady expansion of area under direct administration, largely at the expense of non-assessed lands under armed, local lineages, but also seized from opposing powers, such as the Nizam. The trend was toward greater quantity, quality, and frequency of information reaching the center. In these records, we can track the trend toward predictability, as areas acquired a reputation for payment or recalcitrance. These judgements were actually quantified by the Pune banking community, and were reflected in the rates of interest charged for money loaned against the receipts of the area. We can track, for example, cropping patterns, cities and trade routes, and the minute details of caste and family conflict. In addition to the revenue records, the peshwa regularly received news from all parts of India, produced by professional newswriters at all the principal courts. In a wider sense, the revenue collectors and newswriters have given us an economic and social record for the eighteenth century unmatched in detail and scope outside of Europe. Generations of historians can utilize this record to answer many of the outstanding questions of pre-colonial India.

A second long-term trend, implied in this sophisticated revenue and information-gathering effort, was that of monetization. Most areas had trade and some money use even in the sixteenth century. Over the period of the Maratha polity, money use moved outwards from cash-crop areas (such as Gujarat, Khandesh, and eastern Malwa) into areas less monetized (such as the Desh, the Konkan, Orissa, and the

Karnatak). The research on this trend is still sketchy, but there was certainly the development of vigorous demand in the new towns of Maharashtra – Satara, Bombay, Kolapur, Pune, Ahmadnagar, Nasik, Junnar – and at the new Maratha capitals – Indore, Gwalior, Nagpur, Baroda. Older towns, associated with the Mughals, generally declined – Surat, Burhanpur, Bijapur, and Shahjapur (in Malwa). There was competition among the various ports on the coast – Bombay, Bassein, Rajapur, Chaul – and traders migrated to the most favorable situation. One marker of increased monetization was commutation of rights formerly collected in kind to amounts collected in cash. There has, as yet, been no large-scale study of this process, but several researchers have found it in the records of even small and remote villages. Commonly, the obligation to cut grass for the Maratha army, or the obligation of a certain number of days of service carrying supplies for the army, was commuted to a cash payment. Even many deshmukhi rights in kind had been commuted to cash quantities by the end of the eighteenth century. The development of large-scale markets, such as vast annual horse fairs and cattle fairs, is yet another marker in this trend.

It should, perhaps, be emphasized that the Maratha polity was not as strongly tied to cities as, for example, the Mughal Empire. Their capitals, for much of the history, were in forts, not cities. In conquest, they took the countryside first, the towns second, and left the cities until much later. (The cities of Surat, Aurangabad, and Burhanpur all fit this pattern.) Cities, also, were not significant producers of revenue, generating less than the agricultural taxes of a small pargana. The administration was based in the pargana towns – where the kamavisdar lived – and did not pass through any nearby city. The Maratha polity produced virtually no monumental urban architecture. In spite of this neglect, cities served important functions. In finance, they were the nodes of a highly sophisticated method of moving money. Hundis (checks, payable at sight or in a specified time in another city) were so commonly used that rates between cities were competitively set and varied slightly with the season and the perceived danger of the connecting route. The cities were also significant sources of manufacturing (such as the specialized cotton cloth of Burhapur) and wholesale markets for stocking the military, to which we now turn.

Unlike other aspects of the Maratha polity, there were virtually no long-term continuities in any aspect of the military – not strategy, tactics, staffing, personnel, provisioning, weapons, even principal opponents. To get a sense of the change, we need only compare Shivaji's Mavali cavalry and lightly armed infantry to Shinde's trained and uniformed infantry and artillery a century later. Recall some of the details of Shivaji's early force. It was composed of mainly of Maratha families of the central Ghat region. They were attracted to Shivaji by his personal charisma and leadership. Commands came quickly; often teenagers gained leadership positions. Warfare outside the mountains was mainly on horseback, which put a premium on dash and strength. Large battles were generally avoided; the winning strategy was to cut off the supplies of the enemy army and raid deep into his territory to draw him off. Battle tactics were simple, consisting mainly of cavalry charges. In the mountains, infantry attacked the enemy in passes or other difficult terrain. Recall how much Shivaji relied on superior knowledge of the local countryside for strategic advantage. Artillery was, for the most part, ignored, and forts could not be taken by mining or sapping. Forts were, however, crucially important as places of refuge, especially in the Ghat area of Maharashtra.[7] When the army was in the field, provisioning was non-existent, and the army was expected to live off the land. The entire Maratha force returned home during the monsoon, much of it to plant crops. Recall that Shivaji himself began the change from this pattern. By the 1670s, Shivaji had 5–10,000 horses of his own and had begun keeping his troops in cantonment through the monsoon. Shivaji, unlike any other Indian monarch (other than Tipu Sultan more than a century later), had made a promising beginning at a navy, to compete in the complex politics of the Konkan coast.

If anything, Maratha warfare reverted to the earliest pattern during the period of pressure by the Mughals (1680–1705), a time characterized by small, mobile bands, individual leadership, and minimal Maratha government control. It was difficult to assemble any force larger than a few thousand troops. We find very few infantry units, other than some garrison troops, in this period. The navy was defeated and burnt.[8]

Change began under the leadership of Bajirao Peshwa (1720–40).

[7] See, for example, Ramchandra Nilkanth's long section on the organization and stocking of forts in the *Ajnapatra* (1700). "The Ajnapatra or royal edict" (trans. S. V. Puntambeker), *Journal of Indian History*, 8, 2 (August 1929), 219–28.

[8] The Angria family, however, built a fleet of small ships which were a factor in the coastal politics until the late 1730s.

CONCLUSIONS

Essentially, the change in this period was from resistance to conquest. Bajirao was able to assemble much larger armies, coalescing them out of the smaller bands. More importantly, he picked a small group of promising young leaders and was able to promote them into large holdings in the newly conquered territories of Malwa and Gujarat. By the mid-1730s, these armies were staying in their areas through the monsoon. After the Battle of Bhopal (which established Maratha control of Malwa), the purpose and function of the armies changed. The significant military events were no longer the large plains battles against a Mughal army. The Marathas, in order to establish control, needed to subdue local armed lineages. Loot was down and tribute and revenue collection were the order of the day. Within a few years, the need for effective artillery was obvious. Both the large leaders (Shinde, Holkar) and the Peshwa knew that siege guns were necessary to take the forts of the local lineages. Cash needs climbed, as leaders and the Peshwa raised artillery units and paid for full-time garrison troops and full-time mercenaries.

From the death of Bajirao (1740) to Panipat (1760), the process of change accelerated. Armies grew to a size that made living off the land clearly impossible. Armies of 30-40,000 were occasionally assembled. These armies no longer looked anything like the lightly equipped, mobile cavalry of a generation earlier. They had become moving cities, complete with thousands of bullock carts, an artillery train, and a complete bazaar. In fact, they resembled Mughal armies in amenities and luxuries. In part, the size and grandeur served the same function that it had under the Mughals, to overawe the local lineages and gain tribute without warfare. What had not changed was actual battle tactics. No matter how large the army, it was simply divided into right, middle, and left wings, which attacked its counterpart in the enemy force. The army was the personal army of the commander; because there was no command structure, in the modern sense, if the commander was killed or retreated, the army, no matter how large, broke and ran.

In the 1750s, there had been several demonstrations of a new structure and organization of the military by the French and English, at war with each other for much of the decade. The forces consisted of trained infantry, using guns superior to anything made in India at the time, supported by relatively quick-firing artillery. Both the guns and the artillery were fruits of the advances in metallurgy in Europe in the first half of the eighteenth century. Across the Indian subcontinent, responses to this new fighting force were mixed. Some leaders, such as the Nizam, eagerly embraced the new forces. Others, like Holkar, were skeptical. In truth, the skeptics were probably correct. Not only had the record of these new forces been mixed (several victories, but some signal defeats), but the evidence from the Nizam was that they were so expensive that they mortgaged state finances to the army. Panipat mainly demonstrated the incompatibility of the various models of warfare – mobile cavalry, trained infantry/artillery, and the huge Mughal-style army. For example, the cavalry was needed to protect the flanks of the infantry, but the cavalry attacked in the hand-to-hand charge (its most effective maneuver). Without a command structure, the Marathas broke and ran when the commander was slain.

After Panipat, the various leader pursued one or the other of the military paradigms. The Bhonsle family, for example, returned to traditional Maratha light cavalry and never raised the new battalions of infantry. Shinde, in contrast, rather quickly began recruiting infantry and cast a large park of artillery. He recruited mainly North Indians (especially Rajputs and Muslims), and within a decade his army was hardly a "Maratha" army at all.[9] Holkar was somewhere between the two. There remained a strong tradition of cavalry and reluctant experiments with trained infantry, but active casting of artillery.[10] In the south, there were mainly changes in personnel. As we have seen, after Panipat, no new Maratha commanders emerged. It is not that there were no opportunities, but those opportunities were given to Brahmins (Raste, the Patwardhan brothers, Hari Pant Phadke), not Marathas. The simplest explanation would be anti-Maratha prejudice among the ruling Brahmin elite at Pune. In the absence of solid research, let us suggest some other factors. There was no Maratha king leading any army, so that personal loyalty and bravery went unnoticed and unrewarded. Perhaps there was a long-term need for close ties to

[9] It has been suggested that Mahadji Shinde, because he was not a legitimate heir, had trouble recruiting Marathas and, therefore, quickly moved to recruiting North Indians, Muslims, and others to his army. On this trend in all the Maratha armies of the second half of the eighteenth century, see S. N. Sen, *The Military System of the Marathas* (Calcutta, reprinted edition, 1979) 62–63.

[10] Right to the end, some Maratha armies resembled the moving cities of the Panipat period. Also, recruitment structure remained largely as it had at Panipat, each man "contracted" for by a leader. Pay was the endless, insoluble problem. See W. H. Tone, *Illustrations of Some Institutions of the Maratha People* (London, 1818), 21–25.

the Pune banking community, because of increased credit needs for a larger army, and they were more likely to back Brahmin commanders. Alternatively, the Brahmin leaders were, perhaps, more flexible in changing from the older mobile cavalry forces to the newer tactics. In any case, the facts are there, awaiting research.

By the 1780s and 1790s, there were two major military changes. The first, as we have noted, was the great increase in the size of the armies of Shinde and Holkar, relative to the troops under the Pune government. In essence, Malwa was a wealthier area than Maharashtra, and both leaders had used their revenues to advantage. Both had also benefitted from tribute levied in Rajastan and the north. The second trend was rapid conversion to the infantry/artillery model of warfare. An arms race was in progress, pitting Shinde against Holkar. It bankrupted both leaders, forcing, for example, Shinde into campaigns against Rajasthan which were only money-raising ventures. It also forced both leaders to use pindaries, which were units of unpaid cavalry (often Afghans) who fought in battle, looted and generally lived off the spoils of war. Wherever they were used, cultivation and revenue collection suffered heavily. By the turn of the century, paying these new armies was the main impetus of government policy. The Pune government raised a regular battalion in the mid-1790s, and planned to raise several more, but simply never had the money.[11] The second change in this period was the declining importance of forts. Artillery had so developed in quality and accuracy that, for example, Shinde was able to take Chittor (one of the largest and strongest forts in Rajasthan) in a matter of weeks. This development was, of course, paralleled by the British, who took Srirangapatan in the same period.

Maharashtrian historians generally conclude a history of the Maratha polity by assigning blame for the conquest by the English. Many factors have been considered from failures of character of individual personalities, to the inability of various families to pull together, to the failure to cast good artillery. These alleged "failures" are always placed within a very narrow Indian regional perspective. It is only in a worldwide context that the conquest of the Maratha polity gains some perspective. We must recall that the Maratha polity fought the most sophisticated military force in the world at the time; it had benefitted by both dramatic breakthroughs in metallurgy, and

---

[11] James Grant Duff, *History of the Marathas* (Jaipur, reprinted edition, 1986), III, 109.

mercenary training developed in the European wars of the mid-eighteenth century. More importantly, for the Indian context, the English already held the most prosperous regions – Bengal and Tamil Nadu. It was these areas which provided the credit and cash for the English to put more than 100,000 trained, uniformed, and equipped troops into the field, and supplied them during two long campaigns. Ultimately, it was superior credit, artillery, and training, and the momentum of victory in the Napoleonic Wars which defeated the Marathas. It is worth recalling that virtually nowhere in the world was this combination successfully resisted at the time.[12]

Finally, let us consider a few of the long-term effects of the Maratha polity. All have been suggested in the text, but let us be explicit. First, there was quite a bit of internal migration within Maharashtra, during much of the period of the Maratha polity. Chitpavan and Karad Brahmins, for example, migrated out of the coastal Konkan and found service at Pune or Satara or with the rural elite. Individual families moved to avoid famine or war. In addition, there was considerable migration out of Maharashtra to areas controlled by the Maratha polity. We find, even today, groups who trace their origin to the Marathas in Gujarat, Malwa, Bangalore, the Kotah-Bundi areas of eastern Rajasthan, the Rajasthan states, and Thanjur. For many of these families, there was long-term social mobility; these Brahmin and Maratha families continued as elites both in Maharashtra and areas of Maratha control, such as the princely states of Gwalior, Indore, Nagpur, and Baroda. The support of these elite families has been a significant factor both in the nineteenth and twentieth century politics of India, but also in the more limited area of patronage of Hindu temples and places of pilgrimage, not only in Maharastara, but throughout India.[13] Second, the heritage of the Maratha polity in tax collection, record keeping, and administration carried on well into the

[12] The few exceptions make for interesting contrasts. China, for example, managed to contain the Europeans to coastal enclaves, though unable to defeat them militarily. Japan remained closed until later in the century. Afghanistan and Thailand remained independent, as buffer states. The defeat of the British expeditions to Afghanistan, in the mid-nineteenth century showed that – as always – a superior military force was vulnerable to severe problems of terrain and supply.

[13] As we have seen, of special importance was Ahilyabai Holkar, who ruled Holkar state in the last four decades of the eighteenth century. She built literally dozens of temples, ghats, wells, tanks, and rest-houses from the Himalayas all the way to the large pilgrimage sites of the south. She supported hundreds of Brahmins and lavish yearly festivals. See the translated documents in V. V. Thakur, *Life and Life's Work of Shree Devi Ahilyabai Holkar* (Indore, n.d.), Chapters 6, 8.

colonial period and beyond. The land-holding patterns and power of the elite families underlay every colonial effort to reform revenue administration or enhance tax collection. Third, we have the Maratha polity to thank for the stirring stories of courage and heroism which form the basis for the self-image of Maharashtra, more than any other period of its history. This "martial" tradition, as it was known in the colonial period, led thousands of Marathas to seek service in the Indian armies of the nineteenth and twentieth centuries. Finally, there is the heritage of two unique cities. Pune, as a Brahmin city, gave Maharashtra a very strong heritage of learning, which continues today in its fine university and many specialized training institutes. Bombay, also, arose in the context of the Maratha polity, from Shivaji's early attacks on Surat which sent refugee business families to Bombay, to the periods of trade, alliance, and strife of the eighteenth century.

INDEX

Abdali, Ahmad Shah, 152–3, 154
Abdul Samad Khan, 114
Ackworth, H. A., 68
Adil Shah government, deshmukh rights under, 27–30, 31
administrative development
in Malawa, 127–8, 139–44
and the Maratha polity, 194–5
Afghanistan, 194
Afzal Khan, 55, 58, 66, 67–8, 70, 84
Agra, Shivaji's visit to, 76, 78
Ahmad Shah Abdali, 138
Ahmadnagar, 18, 37, 41–7, 49, 80, 81, 86
Ajnapatra (Nilkanth), 34–5
Akbar (Mughal Emperor), 41–2, 79, 81
Akbar, Prince, 92
Al Baruni, 14–15
Ala-ud-Din-Khilji, 13
Alam, S. M., 10
Alavi, R. F., 34
Ali I, Sultan of Bijapur, 49
Ali Adil Shah II, Sultan of Bijapur, 29, 66–7, 80
Alivardi Khan, 132–3, 158
Ambarkhan, Husain, 19–20
Amber, Malik, 21, 25, 37, 42–5, 52, 82
Anand Rao Jivaji (Khasgiwala), 174
Anand Rao Raste, 174
Anglo-French war, 135, 150–1
Angre family, 4
Angria family, 105, 123, 190
Angria, Kanoji, 109
Apte, B. K., 68
Apte, D. V., 4
armies, *see also* warfare
and the Maratha polity, 189–94
in the seventeenth century, 37–41
Shivaji's compared with Mughal, 75
Shivaji's military strategies, 81–4, 190
size of Shivaji's, 86
Atre, M. M., 4
Aurangabad, 35, 105, 119, 134
Aurangzeb (Mughal Emperor), 57–8, 63, 106
campaign against Maratha hill forts of, 101–3
death of, 103

and deshmukh rights, 31, 32, 33, 98, 99–100
Jai Singh's letters to, 73, 78
and Prince Akbar, 92
and Rajaram, 96–7
and Sambhaji, 92–3
and Shivaji, 70, 71, 76, 79, 81, 84
authority, and the Maratha polity, 180–6
Awadh, 114

Baglan, 79–80
Bahadur Shah, 104
Bahmani dynasty, 14, 15
Bajaba Purandare, 173
Baji Mudhol, 89
Bajirao II (Peshwa), 171, 172–3
Bajirao, Balaji (Peshwa), 107, 114–31, 137, 184
bakhars, 1
Balapur, Battle of, 117
Ballal, Chimnaji, 121
Banerjee, A. C., 156, 157, 158
Bangalore, 55
Bangash, Ahmad Shah, 152
banking families, 141, 145, 160, 185
in Pune, 159, 188, 193
under Bijarao, 130–1
Bapuji Naik Baramatikar, 173
bargir-giri warfare, 41, 45
bargirs, 15–16
Basavapatan, 56
Bayly, C. A., 146
Bedsa cave, 14
Beg, Nurkhan, 66
Benares, 146
Bendry, V. S., 88
Bengal, 132, 133
Bennett, Charles, 12
Berar, 79–80, 89, 100, 124, 134
Bernstein, Maxine, 8
Bhagwat, A. N., 5
bhakti faith, 18–20
Bhalke, Treaty of (1751), 134
Bhanu, Dharma, 138
Bhatvadi, battle of, 44, 45
Bhavani (goddess), 1
Bhave, V. K., 146

social mobility
  for Brahmins, 185
  in Malwa, 144–6
  and the Maratha polity, 194
  and Shivaji's polity, 80
  under Bijarao, 130
Sri Ranga, 56
Surat, 64, 80, 82, 100, 195
  sack of, 71
Sykes, W. H., 2

Talikota, battle of, 49
Tamaskar, B. G., 24
Tanaji Malusare, 79
Tanjore, 95
Tarabai, queen, 95, 101, 103, 104, 105, 106,
  107, 109, 112, 120, 160
  and Ram Raja, 146–7
taxes, 143–4
  and the deshmukh, 24, 89
  and the Maratha polity, 194, 195
Thailand, 194
Thakur, V. V., 118, 194
Thorat, Mane, 107
Tipu, Sultan, 171–2
Torna fort, 61
trade
  in Bijapur, 50–1
  British, 64
  in Maharashtra, 20–2, 35
Trimbak Rao Mama, 174
Trimbuk, Parashuram, 101
Tulpule, S. B., 8

Untouchables, and Shivaji's reign, 6
uparis (landless labourers), 36

Vaidya, S. G., 6
Vakaskar, V. S., 1
vazirs, 49, 50
Vellore fort, 80, 97
Vijaynagar state, 14
village headman see patil
village records keeper see kulkarni
villages, in Maharashtra, 35–6, 52
Vishalgad fort, 68, 97, 101
Vishwanath, Balaji, 107, 109, 110, 112, 113,
  114, 117
vrittis, 24

Wagle, N. G., 12
Wagle, N. K., 95
Wallace, R., 164, 165
warfare, see also armies
  changes in nature of, 129–30, 149–51
  and the Maratha polity, 189–94
  in the seventeenth century, 37–41
Warna, Treaty of (1731), 112, 123
watan rights (land tenure), 24, 111
Wellesley, Lord, 175, 176
Wink, Andre, 8, 11, 25, 43, 87, 93, 112,
  120, 121, 179
women rulers, 160–2

Yadav, Chandrasen, 105, 106–7, 120
Yadav, Dhanaji, 98, 101, 103, 106, 109
Yadav family, 30–1, 93, 95, 99
Yadava dynasty, 12, 13

zamindars, 127–8, 139–40, 143, 144
Zelliot, Eleanor, 8, 18, 20
Ziegler, Norman, 16
Zulfiqar Khan, 95

THE NEW CAMBRIDGE HISTORY OF INDIA

I The Mughals and their Contemporaries

*JOHN F. RICHARDS, *The Mughal Empire*
*M. N. PEARSON, *The Portuguese in India*
*CATHERINE B. ASHER, *Architecture of Mughal India*
*MILO C. BEACH, *Mughal and Rajput Painting*
BRUCE B. LAWRENCE, *Indian Sufism and the Islamic World*
*BURTON STEIN, *Vijayanagara*
RICHARD M. EATON, *Social History of the Deccan*
GEORGE MICHELL, *Architecture and Art of Southern India*

II Indian States and the Transition to Colonialism

†*C. A. BAYLY, *Indian Society and the Making of the British Empire*
*P. J. MARSHALL, *The British Bridgehead*
*STEWART GORDON, *The Marathas 1600–1818*
OM PRAKASH, *Europeans in the Maritime Trade of India, 1500–1800*
RICHARD B. BARNETT, *Muslim Successor States*
*J. S. GREWAL, *The Sikhs in the Punjab*
DAVID WASHBROOK, *South India, 1750–1850*

III The Indian Empire and the Beginnings of Modern Society

F. CONLON, *Modern Maharashtra*
*SUGATA BOSE, *Peasant Labour and Colonial Capital: Rural Bengal since 1770*
DAVID LUDDEN, *Agriculture in Indian History*
SUSAN BAYLY, *Caste in South Asia*
B. R. TOMLINSON, *The Economy of Modern India, 1860–1970*
THOMAS R. METCALF, *Ideologies of the Raj*
*K. W. JONES, *Socio-religious Reform Movements in British India*
B. N. RAMUSACK, *The Indian Princes and their States*
GORDON JOHNSON, *Government and Politics in India*

IV The Evolution of Contemporary South Asia

†*PAUL R. BRASS, *The Politics of India since Independence*
ANIL SEAL, *The Transfer of Power and the Partition of India*
RAJ CHANDAVARKAR, *The Urban Working Classes in India, 1880–1950*
GERALDINE FORBES, *Indian Women in the Twentieth Century*
FRANCIS ROBINSON, *Islam in South Asia*

* Already published
† Available in paperback

Made in the USA
Lexington, KY
18 January 2010